Oxford, Cambridge and the Changing Idea of the University

SRHE and Open University Press Imprint
General Editor: Heather Eggins

Michael Allen: *The Goals of Universities*
Sir Christopher Ball and Heather Eggins: *Higher Education into the 1990s*
Ronald Barnett: *The Idea of Higher Education*
Tony Becher: *Academic Tribes and Territories*
Robert Berdahl *et al.*: *Quality and Access in Higher Education*
Hazel Bines and David Watson: *Developing Professional Education*
William Birch: *The Challenge to Higher Education*
David Boud *et al.*: *Teaching in Laboratories*
Heather Eggins: *Restructuring Higher Education*
Colin Evans: *Language People*
Gavin J. Fairbairn and Christopher Winch: *Reading, Writing and Reasoning: A Guide for Students*
Oliver Fulton: *Access and Institutional Change*
Derek Gardiner: *The Anatomy of Supervision*
Gunnar Handal and Per Lauvås: *Promoting Reflective Teaching*
Vivien Hodgson *et al.*: *Beyond Distance Teaching, Towards Open Learning*
Jill Johnes and Jim Taylor: *Performance Indicators in Higher Education*
Margaret Kinnell: *The Learning Experiences of Overseas Students*
Peter Linklater: *Education and the World of Work*
Graeme Moodie: *Standards and Criteria in Higher Education*
John Pratt and Suzanne Silverman: *Responding to Constraint*
Kjell Raaheim *et al.*: *Helping Students to Learn*
John Radford and David Rose: *A Liberal Science*
Marjorie Reeves: *The Crisis in Higher Education*
John T.E. Richardson *et al.*: *Student Learning*
Derek Robbins: *The Rise of Independent Study*
Tom Schuller: *The Future of Higher Education*
Geoffrey Squires: *First Degree*
Ted Tapper and Brian Salter: *Oxford, Cambridge and the Changing Idea of the University*
Gordon Taylor *et al.*: *Literacy by Degrees*
Kim Thomas: *Gender and Subject in Higher Education*
Malcolm Tight: *Higher Education: A Part-time Perspective*
Malcolm Tight: *Academic Freedom and Responsibility*
Susan Warner Weil and Ian McGill: *Making Sense of Experiential Learning*
David Watson: *Managing the Modular Course*
Thomas G. Whiston and Roger L. Geiger: *Research and Higher Education*
Gareth Williams: *Changing Patterns of Finance in Higher Education*
Alan Woodley *et al.*: *Choosing to Learn*
Peter W.G. Wright: *Industry and Higher Education*
John Wyatt: *Commitment to Higher Education*

Oxford, Cambridge and the Changing Idea of the University

The Challenge to Donnish
Domination

Ted Tapper and
Brian Salter

The Society for Research into Higher Education
& Open University Press

Published by SRHE and
Open University Press
Celtic Court
22 Ballmoor
Buckingham
MK18 1XW

and
1900 Frost Road, Suite 101
Bristol, PA 19007, USA

First Published 1992

A catalogue record of this book is available from the British Library

Library of Congress Cataloging-in-Publication Data

Tapper, Ted.
    Oxford, Cambridge and the changing idea of the university: the
challenge to donnish domination/Ted Tapper and Brian Salter.
        p.   cm.
    Includes bibliographical references and index.
    ISBN 0–335–15694–0
    1. University of Oxford—History—20th century.   2. University of
Cambridge—History—20th century.   3. University of Oxford-
Administration—History—20th century.   4. University of Cambridge-
Administration—History—20th century.   5. Education, Higher-
Social aspects—Great Britain—History—20th century.
6. Education, Higher—Great Britain—Aims and objectives—
History—20th century.   I. Salter, Brian.   II. Title.
LF522.T37   1992   91–43034
378.425'74—dc20   CIP

Typeset by Graphicraft Typesetters Ltd, Hong Kong
Printed in Great Britain by St Edmundsbury Press Ltd
Bury St Edmunds, Suffolk

Contents

Preface

Rose and Ziman's *Camford Observed* was published in 1964, which makes *Oxford, Cambridge and the Changing Idea of the University* the first in-depth comparative study of the Universities of Oxford and Cambridge for over 25 years. The passage of time alone justifies this book, for even the most conservative of institutions have slowly changing characters and, in our opinion, Oxford and Cambridge are sufficiently important to be reviewed periodically. It is customary to view the Universities of Oxford and Cambridge as exceptional institutions with their own peculiar collegiate model of the university. While we accept this contention, we also believe that higher education in Britain has been influenced strongly by the values that have infused the Oxbridge model of the university. While there are different traditions of higher education in Britain, with perhaps the Scottish universities displaying the most distinctive characteristics, the tradition of university autonomy and donnish domination of the affairs of the university – values associated most closely with Oxford and Cambridge – have permeated British higher education in general.

What has changed radically in the past 25 years is the political environment of higher education. State and society are more sceptical of the demands of the universities, less sympathetic to the virtues of university autonomy, and more insistent that they respond rapidly to the needs of society. How have the Universities of Oxford and Cambridge interacted with this changing environment? Like most ancient institutions, they have been intent on retaining what they consider to be their core values and their essential characters. But their values can be interpreted flexibly and their practices can evolve without seeming to change. It is the analysis of these accommodations to the external pressures that comprises much of the content of this book. We concur with the widely supported contention that increasingly the British universities are offering a more differentiated experience of higher education. Whereas as in the past they may have represented different traditions, there was also a shared value system and a common idea of the university. While Oxbridge will maintain its exceptionalism in the future – indeed, may be encouraged to do so if the intention is to move towards a model of higher education with greater internal diversity – it will not act as a model for the rest of the system. While its exceptionalism may be evident, it will not be for replication.

This book is not simply a descriptive account of some of the important changes that have occurred in the Universities of Oxford and Cambridge. In our opening chapter, we present a detailed overview of our understanding of the process of educational change. This chapter explores the interaction of three crucial change dynamics: the economic, the bureaucratic and the political. On the one hand, there is the attempt to make the universities more accountable for the monies they receive from the Exchequer by tying them into the general educational system and ensuring that they are responsive to the demands of the state. On the other hand, there is pressure to make the universities responsive to the needs of society by making them more directly dependent upon the financial input of those who use their services. In recent years, the differing kinds of pressures have oscillated in their intensity. What is clearly under threat is the model of the university as it was traditionally understood in Britain, and in particular how universities related to state and society.

We lack both the competence and motive to write general histories of the two universities, but the aspects we have chosen to examine have not been randomly selected. Historically, those who wished to reform the universities did so by changing their statutes, while in the twentieth century the universities have been responsive to the administrative and financial pressures of the state. Our chapters, therefore, are built around examples of the internal response to these forms of potential external pressure. This is a book that is directed at the constitutional, administrative, financial and governmental sides of Oxford and Cambridge. However, we recognize that their central purpose continues to be the transmission (teaching) and extension (research and scholarship) of knowledge. We are concerned therefore to show, in general terms, how their commitments in both directions have evolved over time. Again the intention is to understand 'the politics' of the pedagogical process as opposed to its formal educational character.

The research that forms the basis of this book was made possible by a grant from the Economic and Social Research Council. We have also been supported financially by the University of Sussex's School of English and American Studies. We are grateful to both parties for their help. In the text we refer to a few of our many interviews and personal communications which constitute a small proportion of the assistance we have received over the past 5 years. We are deeply conscious of the fact that the informed insider is more likely than ourselves to be subtly in tune with the histories of these ancient institutions. We have had a constructive dialogue with some of those informed insiders and we hope that this is reflected in the final product. We recognize that many of them would not agree with our interpretations, and we know that in offering their views they were making known their personal observations rather than speaking for their universities. Indeed, who can claim to represent the official view of either Oxford or Cambridge is one of the themes of our book!

In particular, we would like to thank the following persons: Dr B. Harrison of Corpus Christi College, Oxford (especially for inviting us to his excellent seminar series on 'The Twentieth Century History of the University of Oxford'); Dr H. Drucker, Director of the Campaign for Oxford; Mr G.P. Allen, Secretary to Cambridge's Council of the School of the Humanities and Social Sciences; Dr M. Horne, Secretary to Cambridge's Interfaculty Committee for Arts and Humanities; Dr D. Franks, Secretary to Cambridge's School of Biological Sciences; Mr J.R. Payne, Secretary to Cambridge's School of Physical Sciences (without whose extensive assistance this book would have been even longer in the making); Dr A. Howatson of Oxford's Department of Engineering Science; Professor A.D. Smith, Head of Oxford's Department of Pharmacology; Professor Sir Brian Pippard, former Head of the Cavendish Laboratory, Cambridge; Dr W. Dorey, the Registrar of the University of Oxford; Dr S. Fleet, the Registry of the University of Cambridge; Lord Bullock, former Master of St Catherine's College, Oxford and former Vice-Chancellor of the University of Oxford; Mr M. McCrum, Master of Corpus Christi College, Cambridge and former Vice-Chancellor of the University of Cambridge; Dr E.B. Smith, Master of St Catherine's College, Oxford and former Vice-Chairman of Oxford's General Board; Dr A.D.I. Nicol, former Secretary General to the Faculties at Cambridge; Mr T. Gardner, former Secretary to Cambridge's Financial Board; Mr B. Shone, former Deputy Secretary to Cambridge's Financial Board and Bursar of Robinson College, Cambridge; Lord Annan, former Provost of King's College, Cambridge; Sir Kenneth Dover, former Master of Corpus Christi, Oxford and Chairman of Oxford's Committee on Undergraduate Admissions; Sir Desmond Lee, former Admissions Tutor to Corpus Christi College, Cambridge; Mrs P.M. Houghton, Secretary to the Cambridge Intercollegiate Applications Office; Mr E.A. Baskerville, former Secretary to the Oxford Colleges Admissions Office; Mr J. Wright, currently Cambridge's Secretary General to the Faculties; Mr D. Taylor, Secretary to the CVCP; Mr J. Farrant of the UFC; Sir Kenneth Berrill, former Chairman of the UGC; Mr R. Butler, former Secretary to the Faculties at Oxford; Dr C. Baron, Admissions Tutor at St Catharine's College, Cambridge; Dr C. Johnson, Bursar of St John's College, Cambridge; Mr B. Campbell, ex-Bursar of Corpus Christi College, Oxford; Dr J. Field, Head of the Laboratory of Physics and Chemistry of Solids, Cambridge; Sir Denys Wilkinson, former Vice-Chancellor of the University of Sussex and Head of the Department of Nuclear Physics, Oxford; Dr N. Tanner, Admissions Tutor, Hertford College, Oxford; Dr Oliver Taplin, former Chairman of the Management Committee of the Oxford Colleges Admissions Office; Dr K. Bowkett, Admissions Tutor, Christ's College, Cambridge; Dr R. Mitchell, former Chairman of the Admissions Forum, Cambridge; Mrs J. Wells, former Chairman of the Tutorial Representatives Committee and the Tutorial Representatives Executive Committee, Cambridge; Mr M. Brock, former Warden of Nuffield College, Oxford; Lord Briggs, Provost of Worcester College, Oxford; Professor A.H. Halsey, Nuffield College, Oxford; Mr M. Stanley, University Officer, University of Oxford; Mr Hardyman, former Secretary to the UGC; Sir Christopher Ball, former Warden of Keble College, Oxford and Chairman of NAB; Lord Franks, former Provost of Worcester College, Oxford; and Mr A.W.F. Edwards, Gonville and Caius College, Cambridge.

Abbreviations and Acronyms

ABRC	Advisory Board to the Research Councils
ACARD	Advisory Committee on Applied Research and Development
ACSIR	Advisory Council for Science and Industrial Research
ACSP	Advisory Council on Scientific Policy
ARC	Agricultural Research Council
AUT	Association of University Teachers
CATS	Colleges of Advanced Technology
CCE	Cambridge Colleges Examination
CIAO	Cambridge Intercollegiate Applications Office
CPS	Centre for Policy Studies
CSP	Council for Scientific Policy
CVCP	Committee of Vice-Chancellors and Principals
DES	Department of Education and Science
DSIR	Department of Scientific and Industrial Research
ESRC	Economic and Social Research Council
GCE	General Certificate of Education
IEA	Institute for Economic Affairs
IT	Information Technology
LEAs	Local Education Authorities
MRC	Medical Research Council
NC	Nature Conservancy
NERC	Natural Environment Research Council
OCAO	Oxford Colleges Admissions Office
PCFC	Polytechnics and Colleges Funding Council
PGCE	Postgraduate Certificate in Education
SCUE	Standing Conference on University Entrance
SERC	Science and Engineering Research Council
SRC	Science Research Council
SSRC	Social Science Research Council
STEP	Sixth Term Examination Papers
THES	*The Times Higher Education Supplement*
UCCA	Universities Central Council for Admissions
UFC	Universities Funding Council
UGC	University Grants Committee

Part I

The Pressures for Change

1

The Universities, the State
and Society

Introduction

'No one', wrote Thomas Arnold, 'ought to meddle with the universities, who
does not know them well and love them well'. Even at the time when Arnold
was writing in the mid-nineteenth century, some would have challenged this
respectful view and insisted that the state has every right to intervene in
university affairs regardless of the nature of its affections. Today, critics of
the universities abound and do not feel in the least inhibited by notions of the
sanctity of academic autonomy. The steady, if gradual, demolition of the
liberal ideal of the university rooted in the Oxbridge tradition is part of
a process of change in higher education which has rapidly gathered pace
over the past decade. Spurred on by social and economic pressures, by the
impetus of its own bureaucracy, and by the attentions of the New Right
radicals, the state has sponsored a series of measures designed to restructure
its relationship with the universities and increase its power over their affairs.

Our analysis of these pressures for change is guided by the theory of
educational change developed in our previous work. In this opening chapter,
we are concerned with how the economic, bureaucratic and political party
dynamics have combined to place ever increasing demands upon the ideology and structure of both the universities in general and Oxford and
Cambridge in particular. The first task is to develop our understanding of
the process of change in higher education and, within this, it will be important to identify theoretically the origins of the unique power and prestige of
Oxbridge.

Power, the state and educational change

In 1852, the Royal Commission on Oxford University stated that:

> ... such an institution [as the University] cannot be regarded as a mere
> aggregate of private interests; it is *eminently national*. It would seem,
> therefore, to be a matter of public policy that such measures should be

taken as may serve to raise its efficiency to the highest point and to diffuse its benefits most widely (Oxford University Commission 1852: Preface, their emphasis).

But it did not explain what it meant by 'eminently national' or why this of itself raised issues of public policy. Why should the state concern itself with the reform of universities, then as now? Why not simply leave them to continue their graceful decline into advanced decay and create alternative institutions? Put simply, the answer to these questions is that universities offer a unique blend of two resources essential for economic and social development: knowledge and status. Furthermore, the history of their control of these resources has placed them in a secure monopoly position so that, from the state's point of view, it makes much more sense to try and change the universities and redirect their resources rather than close them down or create alternative institutions. In this respect, the failure of the polytechnics to live up to the egalitarian and technological values invested in them by the Labour Party, and their subsequent 'academic drift' to become, in the jaundiced view of Pratt and Burgess, little more than 'bowdlerised universities', is a salutary tribute to the power of social forces and the limits these place on the success of state interventions (Pratt and Burgess 1974: 23–30).

Given that they are not the only social institution producing knowledge linked to status – the Church of England being another – how do the universities translate this activity into tangible power? Because they are, and have always been, the institutions at the top of the educational hierarchy, universities make the ultimate decision on how knowledge should be organized and what status should be attached to different knowledge areas. Likewise, any significant change in the content or boundary of a knowledge area has to be sanctioned by the universities if it is to carry lasting weight. Once sanctioned, such changes are then passed down the educational pyramid and the lower levels make the appropriate adjustments. This can be described as the exercise of the universities' educational power.

The further translation of the universities' educational power into different forms of social and political power is a result of the essential part played by education in the process of social change. Through the examination system, education provides a generally accepted and publicly verifiable definition of merit which facilitates movement between, and mobility within, the complex organizations of modern society. By organizing knowledge into status hierarchies, and labelling and allocating this knowledge in a way which is judged to be rational, education not only controls access to the scarce knowledge resources necessary for an individual's occupational and social progress, it also performs an ideological function by persuading people that this process and the resulting inequalities are fair and legitimate. Given this central role in the maintenance of, and change in, the social order, education is subject to ever-increasing demands from the economy for manpower with new types of knowledge, skills, attitudes and values. It is being asked to help introduce at an unprecedented pace changes in the technical and social relations of production.

The state, meanwhile, can be seen as standing between the demands of the economy on the one hand, and the potential response of the education system on the other. In so far as it sees one of its major functions as facilitating the nation's economic development, the state is inevitably going to seek to influence the pace and direction of educational change. In our previous work, we have traced the steady growth in the Department of Education and Science's (DES) control over education and its sponsorship of the economic ideology of education as a system of values appropriate to its ambitions (Tapper and Salter 1978; Salter and Tapper 1981, 1985). Much of the earlier attentions of the DES focused on secondary education, partly because it was an easier target, partly because there was party political support for this option, and partly because the universities had for many years been an ideologically protected species that would be easier to deal with once the rest of education had been subdued. Although the universities could be left to their own devices for a while, ultimately the state had to confront the issue of how it was going to deal with the fact that the universities are the keystone of the whole educational edifice.

To elaborate further on the nature of the universities' power and hence on the reasons why the state is obliged to court, confine or control them, universities act as 'the custodians of the selection process' (Halsey and Trow 1971: 204). Society only accepts that an individual has acquired a particular body of knowledge if the possession of that knowledge has been certified by an appropriate institution and, as the dominant set of education institutions, universities not only award the most prestigious certificates (degrees) they also strongly influence the form and content of certificates awarded by institutions lower down the educational hierarchy. In effect, they define the context within which much individual social mobility takes place. Equally, any occupational group wishing to enhance its social position has to pay due recognition to the universities' monopoly of the access to, and certification of, high-status knowledge. In practice, this means requesting the universities to incorporate an occupation's certification procedure with the result that, historically, no ambitious occupation has been able to achieve full professional status without the universities' seal of approval; for example, the legal and medical professions in the nineteenth century and, more recently, the professions of management and nursing.

It is part of the mystique and inherited right of the universities to define high-status culture, to control access to it and to couple it to the knowledge areas on which particular professions are dependent. Thus in acquiring the mantle of university respectability, an occupation gains access to culture which, judiciously employed, provides the means for self-elevation to professional status. It is, however, a culture which sets its own conditions for entry. Since the ill-fated challenge of the provincial universities to Oxford and Cambridge in the late nineteenth century, British universities have been dominated by a culture with its roots in the idea of a liberal education centred on the arts and humanities (Shils 1955). In gaining entry to the universities, new professions therefore have to accept that they do so on the condition that their curricula are adapted to the assumptions of a liberal education. Since this gives their members access to the social and cultural capital they require to join the ranks of the professionals, they are unlikely to object too strongly to the condition.

Universities therefore perform key social functions by controlling both individual and social mobility and change in the status of professions. In addition, their monopoly in education of the union of high-status knowledge and culture endows them with a third kind of power: the unique authority to make authoritative statements about values. That is, it gives them ideological power. Since social and economic change has to be accompanied, if not preceded, by a corresponding shift in the ideology which legitimates the status quo, universities are inevitably called upon to use their ideological power to resist or to facilitate such change. Given education's central position in contemporary society, the conflict centres increasingly on the role that education in general, and universities in particular, should play in social and economic change. Of late, universities have therefore found themselves in the interesting position of having to use their ideological power to protect themselves.

All universities may have the power derived from their special control of knowledge and status, but some have more power than others. From within and without the university system, the universities are seen as a hierarchy of institutions led by Oxford and Cambridge and dominated by their ideas of how the traditions of higher learning are to be maintained (Halsey 1979: 416). Halsey's work shows that the Oxbridge dominance continues to be manifested in academics' perceptions of the best departments, preferred posts and job satisfaction, and this is confirmed by the annual *Times Higher Education Supplement* peer review ranking of research and teaching, which regularly shows the ancient universities maintaining their pre-eminence. The academic profession recognizes, and by this recognition helps to make real, the dominance of Oxford and Cambridge in the three arenas of university power.

Despite the various pressures since the nineteenth century Russell Commission, the ancient universities have never lost their hypnotic sway over the university hierarchy. Their primary and inalienable resource has always been that they are the finest embodiment of the liberal idea of education and its associated culture. While this is valued so are they. Others may emulate them but none can replace them, since the resource is historically embedded in the collegiate character of the two universities. Eventually, and however reluctantly, the provincial business classes of the late nineteenth century accepted that the universities they wanted to establish would be dominated by the culture of Oxbridge and not by their own indigenous bourgeois culture (Halsey 1961a). Since then, all fresh additions to the university system have followed the same path and made the same concessions.

The status dominance of Oxford and Cambridge within the university system is paralleled and reinforced by their unique power and reputation among the upper echelons of the class structure. 'The "magic" of Oxford and Cambridge', as Halsey and Trow put it, 'is an essential part of the status symbolism of British elites' (1971: 206–207). It enhances their appeal to both established and aspirant professions, sets them apart from other universities, and allows their graduates favoured access to the centres of political power, the Church, the courts and the major industries. At the same time, it provides the academics of Oxford and Cambridge with a highly valuable and marketable commodity which gives them a distinct edge in their competition with other universities for funding from government, industry and charities. As the two most powerful institutions in the university system, Oxford and Cambridge thus exercise an unrivalled influence over the way in which universities carry out their functions and their response to pressures for change assumes unusual significance.

Historically, the state has used a number of methods in its attempts to persuade the universities to conduct their affairs in a manner which it deems appropriate. As the method of intervention has changed, so the universities have been obliged to relate to a different part of the state. Writing in 1852, Sir William Hamilton, an energetic critic of the universities, remarked that:

> A university is a trust confided by the state to certain hands for the common interest of the nation; nor has it ever heretofore been denied that a university may, and ought, by the state to be from time to time corrected, reformed, or recast, in conformity to accidental changes of relation, and looking towards an improved accomplishment of its essential ends (Hamilton 1852: 583).

According to this view, periodic legal intervention was sufficient to achieve the desired objectives, and during this time the universities' relationship with the state was limited to intermittent contact with Parliament and its temporary arm, the Royal Commission and the Statutory Commissioners. However, with the steady growth in public funding for the universities in the twentieth century, the situation became more complex. Administrative mechanisms were required to determine and allocate the flow of monies and were placed on a regular footing, beginning with the setting up of the University Grants Committee (UGC) in 1919 and the various research councils soon thereafter. In effect, these bodies replaced the Royal Commission and Statutory Commissioners as the arm of the state. The differences arising from this metamorphosis were several. First, the relationship between universities and state was now permanent and continuous rather than temporary and *ad hoc*. Secondly, the nature of the state's power *vis-à-vis* the universities was no longer simply that of legal fiat; indeed, quite the reverse, since the UGC never had any statutory basis, but was embedded instead in an administrative and financial relationship where the exercise of power was unclear and dominated by ideological considerations which we will deal with shortly. Thirdly, the universities now related to institutions deliberately positioned on the periphery of the state as a device for maximizing university autonomy.

In 1964, the UGC and the research councils became the responsibility of the newly formed Department of Education and Science (DES). Up to that point, the UGC had received its money directly from the Treasury and for much of that period had, with the able assistance of the Treasury, resisted the doctrine of accountability in general and Parliamentary scrutiny in particular. In addition, the picture of the state side of the relationship seen from the universities' viewpoint had been further fragmented by the funding of the research councils by different government departments. With the 1964 reforms the universities' view of the state became comparatively clear and focused as the DES assumed formal responsibility for their destiny. Although the UGC and research councils were still there as institutional 'buffers' between universities and state, their accountability to the single department responsible for formulating policy on higher education meant that their ability to fragment the pressures from the state and so protect the universities were much reduced. Later of course, Parliament was once more to form part of the relationship as it became one of the vehicles for the New Right's drive to take the universities into the marketplace.

The objective of state pressure on the universities is to achieve change in the way they order the knowledge-status hierarchy, transmit knowledge through their teaching and produce new knowledge through their research. Educational change is therefore defined as change in the way in which the universities undertake their key functions, that is those very functions which constitute the basis of their power. Obviously, this change is manifested in institutional reorganization, but the important conceptual point is that the production of new organizational forms is the result of demands for change in the manner in which universities carry out their sociopolitical functions: that is why the state is interested in them. But the situation is further complicated by the fact that any change in the internal structure of universities, or in their relationship with the state, has to be preceded by an ideological shift capable of legitimizing the proposed change in the exercise of university power. It is at this point that life becomes difficult for the state. How is it to achieve ideological supremacy over institutions which have ideology-creation as one of their inherited social functions? Even its administrative and financial lines of control over the universities were, historically speaking, designed so as to be acceptable to traditional university values and could not overtly be used as a lever. It is to the unravelling of this conundrum which we now turn through, in the first instance, an analysis of the ideological conflict generated by the insistent pressures from the economic dynamic.

The economic dynamic and the traditional university ideal

There is pressure from the economy for the education system to produce both manpower and knowledge relevant to the economy's needs. However, the translation of such pressure into the ideological and political vehicles for educational change has faced its stiffest test in the case of the universities whose traditional values are unequivocally opposed to any such relationship. For many years, a major stumbling block for the economic dynamic was that the higher echelons of British society and state automatically shared and espoused the universities' values. Indeed, it used to be regarded as axiomatic that the British élite was a unified, homogeneous group with a common value system and cultural identity. Since the leading members of both universities and state were happily included in this definition, the idea of an internecine conflict between the two, such as we have witnessed over the past decade, was never taken seriously. Now that it is regarded as axiomatic that universi ties and state exist in a situation of perpetual ideological tension, it is as well to remind ourselves how far we have travelled in the past two decades. Writing in 1969, A.H. Halsey noted the 'historical continuity . . . of de facto control of elitist instructions [the universities] by likeminded members of the elite' (Halsey 1969: 137). This, he observed, in turn demonstrated 'the extraordinary stability of the British system of elite recruitment to positions of political, industrial or bureaucratic power' (ibid.).

His view was not remarkable. Ever since the foundation of the UGC in 1919, it had been assumed that university life was part and parcel of the élite at cultural play. University and state were joined by a seamless web of shared understandings and values within which the UGC nestled comfortably and harmoniously. Hence, as one observer commented, 'the success of the UGC rests fundamentally upon unwritten conventions and the personal and social relations of a homogeneous community of university men, in and out of government, who share common tastes and a common outlook' (Dodds 1952: 73). Many of the members of the UGC and the Treasury officials belonged to the Athenaeum Club and conducted a good deal of business in its convivial surroundings (ibid.). In this situation, it was difficult to envisage any disagreements between the representatives of university and state which could not be resolved through gentlemanly discussion. Hence when in 1946 the Committee of Vice-Chancellors and Principals (CVCP) specifically requested that the universities should have 'a greater measure of guidance from the Government than until quite recent days they have been accustomed to receive' on how they should 'devise and execute policies calculated to serve the national interest', it did so within well understood parameters (Niblett 1952: 168). As Niblett points out, 'unless there had been fundamental trust that any British government would have a close understanding of what university ideals were, no such request for guidance could or would have been made' (ibid.). Part of that trust was that government would never challenge the central value of university independence and that the universities would decide for themselves how best they should fulfil national needs.

The assumption that a shared ideology existed in itself formed part of the universities' value position and meant that they were totally unprepared for any aggressive action by the state. Reflecting on the possibilities of state intervention in 1959, having examined the universities' relationship with the state in some detail, Berdahl wrote: 'It is inconceivable that . . . these people [of the Treasury] should ever initiate any state action hostile to the universities' (Berdahl 1959: 168). Of its nature, the hegemony of the university ideal was such that it refused to acknowledge that such a possibility could exist. We will shortly trace the way in which this complacency was rudely shattered by the emergence of an ideology hostile to the universities and useful to the state. The immediate question, however, is the nature of the shared value position which so unified the universities and the state for so long. What are its main components, what are the reasons for its longstanding dominance, and wherein lie the seeds of its decay?

The formulation of the Oxbridge ideal as we know it today took place in the second half of the nineteenth century when the ancient universities were obliged by external pressure from the state and internal pressure from the professional demands of a new breed of dons to justify their place in society (Rothblatt 1968; Engel 1983). In so doing, they drew selectively on two main traditions: the Christian-Hellenic, as Sir Walter Moberly described it, and the more recent liberal tradition. For Newman and Jowett, 'the chief duty of the university is to produce good citizens. It should train an elite who are to be the future leaders in affairs and in the learned profession' (Moberly 1949: 31). In order so to do, the university must ensure that teachers and learners live together as a family. It must be, in Cardinal Newman's words, 'an Alma Mater, knowing her children one by one, not a foundry, or a mint, or a treadmill' (as cited in ibid: 33). Out of this experience will be forged a continuity of élite identity founded upon a common experience and shared values. Until the nineteenth century Royal Commissions on Oxford and Cambridge, it was assumed that this experience would be not only fundamentally Christian but thoroughly Anglican. With the reforms that followed the Commissions' reports, the Anglican stranglehold was broken and a broader, more liberal, and more secular education came into being.

None the less, although the educational experience had changed, its social purpose remained that of ensuring the maintenance of an élite identity. At the same time, the closely knit college community acted as a very effective vehicle for the 'conservation of the most highly prized beliefs and skills in the cultural heritage', and thus performed a vital cultural, as well as social, function (Halsey 1961b). With the convenient, and efficient, integration of the social and cultural functions came the flowering of the liberal view of education as concerned with considerably more than simply the transmission of knowledge. Within the liberal educational experience, high-status culture was also transmitted as a natural and unavoidable part of college life: 'character' education was easily combined with the cultivation of social style and appropriate leadership qualities. To be successful as a means for preserving élite identity, liberal education also has to be exclusive. It has to foster a suspicion of non-élite forms of education and in particular of vocational education. Whereas liberal education applauds the importance of learning for learning's sake and 'the enthusiastic study of subjects for the love of them and without any ulterior motive' (Moberly 1949: 37), in its purest form it finds any kind of specific occupational training distasteful. It can generally be said that pure knowledge is acceptable to the liberal ideal and applied – or vocational – knowledge is not. Hence when Oxford and Cambridge eventually began to allow the sciences into their hallowed halls it was the pure sciences which were admitted many years before the applied sciences. Moreover, it can be said that directly vocational disciplines, such as law and medicine, were only incorporated into the idea of a liberal university education because of the burgeoning social and economic power of the legal and medical professions.

For the liberal ideal of education, in contrast to its predecessor the Christian-Hellenic tradition, the pursuit of knowledge for its own sake included the advancement of knowledge as well as its transmission. Interestingly, the ideological weight attached to the research function of universities has increased in proportion to the resources available. By the 1940s, a then well-known advocate of university values writing under the nomme de plume of Bruce Truscot in *Redbrick University*, adamantly maintained that the search after knowledge for the sake of its intrinsic value is paramount and all else was subordinate to this objective. 'A university without research', he argued, 'would be nothing but a super secondary school' (Truscot 1943: 49). It is also the characteristic of a university education which, at times, has been used to set them apart from the polytechnics and to justify a higher unit of resource.

That the liberal ideal as we have described it here was intentionally élitist there can be no doubt and is a faithful reflection of the time in which it was born. The view was, as T.S. Eliot puts it, that 'it is an essential condition of the preservation of the quality of the culture of the minority, that it should continue to be a minority culture' (Bantock 1965: 113). None the less, as times changed it maintained its vitality and its ability to legitimate the diversion of public resources to support the socialization of a small élite. This needs explaining. Its initial advantage was that it heavily emphasized its educational and cultural functions with the effect that its political function, the preservation of élite power, was disguised. It also sought to develop for itself an absolute status which would insulate both itself and the universities from the normal political round and from the indignity of having to reply to any ideological challenge. University autonomy was thus presented as an essential precondition for the disinterested search for knowledge and for the preservation of those values on which a civilized society depends. As the aristocrats of the education system, naturally – some would say divinely – ordained with the right of sustaining the cultural heritage over time, the universities also had duties. Theirs was the responsibility of maintaining a critical distance from society and of 'focusing the community's intellectual conscience', as Sir Walter Moberly (1949: 161) put it. To question this autonomy was therefore to question the basis of society's civilized existence.

The continuing ideological power of the liberal ideal is demonstrated by its ability to influence the direction of policy during a period when its objective relevance was decidedly questionable. From the 1950s onwards, many of the ideas guiding the move towards a *mass* higher education system were derived from an ideology of *élite* university education. In 1956, the UGC calculated that student demand would double from the then current figure of 85 000 places to 168 000 by 1968 – a massive expansion by the standards of the day (UGC 1964: 70). Yet the Niblett Report of 1957 on halls of residence, an example of the initial response to this expansion, is a pristine restatement of what were by then seen as the traditional university values. The ideas of 'community', 'character training' and 'cultural transmission' were held as central. The fact that the raw university material was increasingly coming from a non-university background meant that the means for inculcating élite values had to be even more assiduously applied. Such students would be required to accept that 'university standards should influence their whole personality, their range of interests and their social being' and that they should undergo 'a revolution of mind and attitude' (UGC 1957: 9).

More significantly, 6 years later in 1963, when the 1968 estimate of this 'minority culture' had risen to 200 000, the Robbins Report on higher education was published and, in the words of the UGC, established 'publicly and authoritatively, the principles which should govern the scale and pattern of higher education in this country' (UGC 1968a: 49). Viewing Robbins from several decades distance, it is important not to underestimate the ideological significance attached to the Report at the time: so much so that Sir Robert Aitken, former chairman of the CVCP, could write with an exaggerated flourish that 'Robbins, like the Flood, is a watershed in history' (Aitken 1969: 185). In the context of a rapidly changing situation, upholders of the traditional university values saw it as essential that a definitive statement of ideological intent should be made as a guide to the future. Of the four aims of higher education laid down by Robbins, only one, 'instruction in skills', departs from the path of the liberal ideal. The others are the education of 'not mere specialists but rather cultivated men and women', the advancement of learning and 'the transmission of a common culture and common standards of citizenship' (Committee on Higher Education 1963: 6–7). Robbins saw these as the sole responsibility of the universities for which special provision should be made: for example, the ratio of teachers to students in the universities should be more favourable than in other institutions of higher education that do not have 'in the same measure the duty to preserve and advance knowledge' (ibid.: 170).

As an ideological statement, the Robbins Report is also significant because it recognizes the need for an explicit defence of academic freedom and devotes a separate chapter to the subject. In the halcyon days when the liberal ideal reigned supreme and unquestioned, no such defence would have been considered necessary. Within this set of values, given the function of the university as the preserve of élite values and producer of élite people, conflict between one part of the élite, the state, and another, the universities, was unthinkable: élite homogeneity assumed élite consensus. However, once a split occurred between the universities and another section of the élite, then the idea of university autonomy became an essential part of their ideological defence and the frequency of its use a measure of their insecurity. Thus Robbins feels obliged to state categorically that:

> We are convinced also that such freedom is a necessary condition of the highest efficiency and the proper progress of academic institutions, and that encroachments upon their liberty, in the supposed interests of greater efficiency, would in fact diminish their efficiency and stultify their development (ibid.: 228).

In so doing, he signalled the beginning of the fragmentation of the élite and division between the universities and the state.

The power of an ideology can, to an extent, be measured in terms of its ability to ignore, or selectively interpret, reality. By 1963, the move towards a mass higher education system was well under way and was justified by the commitment of the Robbins Report to the principle of 'social demand', which asserts that higher education should be available to all those qualified to receive it (ibid.: 7–8). Yet at the same time, the Report insisted that the unlimited expansion to which this principal gives rise should be guided by a high-quality and expensive form of élite education. The fact that the reality and the ideology are fundamentally irreconcilable made no difference to the attempt to legitimate the former with the latter. The need to justify ideologically a policy juggernaut which no-one knew how to control had to be fulfilled and this need coincided with the universities' desire to maintain their hegemony of the higher education sphere. In the longer term, however, the relevance of the traditional values to a mass higher education system was bound to be questioned, particularly since an ideological challenge to the liberal ideal was already beginning to emerge.

The roots of the challenge lay in the belief that education is fundamentally an economic resource which should be employed so as to maximize its contribution to Britain's industrial development. From this premise all else flows. The consequent 'economic ideology of education', as we termed it in 1978, is opposed to the traditional university values in all respects (Tapper and Salter 1978: Ch. 7). The idea that education should serve the needs of the economy has a long history but, until the 1980s, was not a value which the universities took seriously, at least partly because they did not have to. Although the economic ideology of education began to make inroads into the state bureaucracy immediately after the Second World War, it was not into that part of the state to which the universities related, namely the Treasury and UGC, but into the Ministry of Education and the further education sector. The entry point is logical: the technical colleges in further education had traditionally been characterized by vocational training and links with local industry, and in the economic stringencies of the post-war situation were naturally the first to respond to the demands for the manpower to support Britain's international competitiveness. Numerous reports beginning with the Percy Report of 1945 and the Barlow Report of 1946 had highlighted the need for Britain to produce more scientists and technologists, but by the 1950s the Ministry of Education was convinced that whereas the technical colleges understood and responded to this need the universities did not.

This conviction is clearly expressed in the Ministry's 1956 White Paper on Technical Education which begins with a warning of the dangers of Britain being outpaced in the production of qualified manpower by the USA, Western Europe and the Soviet Union and then spells out the implications for education: it must take on a 'national responsibility', be responsive to 'social need' and ensure that what it does is 'socially relevant'. There can be no shirking of education's economic duty:

> The management of full employment, with its much greater need for a responsible attitude to work and its challenge to greater output per man as the only way further to raise living standards, has brought a sense of dependence on education as the key to advance (Ministry of Education 1956: 37).

Once it is assumed that education's primary goal is to serve the economy, all else has to be subordinated to that goal. As an educational principle, disinterested pursuit of knowledge is devalued. Knowledge no longer has an absolute status but one contingent upon the yardstick of social relevance so that applied knowledge is highly valued and pure knowledge regarded with suspicion. Education, or training, for occupations which will enhance economic performance is laudable and, conversely, education for purposes such as individual development is peripheral.

It might be assumed that once one part of the state began to sponsor an ideology which explicitly linked education to the needs of production, that other parts of the state apparatus would rapidly follow suit. In fact, although the process was under way, bureaucratic and ideological inertia saw to it that progress was slow; the traditional liberal ideal was so firmly ensconced that one can concur with Halsey's (1961b: 461) observation that 'the British case is instructive as one in which the medieval and aristocratic traditions of the universities have hitherto acted as a powerful brake against movement towards the technological society'. The result was that two irreconcilable ideologies confronted one another across intra-state boundaries.

There was no logical reason why the economic ideology of education should concern itself purely with the type of manpower produced by the technical colleges and pressure developed for the Ministry of Education to control the production of highly qualified, degree level manpower. Since the universities were reluctant to bow to demands for a greatly expanded flow of scientists, engineers and technologists, and since the ministry had no influence over them, the obvious solution was for it to create a new type of institution, cast in the appropriate mould. Hence the Colleges of Advanced Technology (CATs) were invented: a tangible tribute to the ideological divide within the state apparatus. Indeed, the ministry's annual report *Education in 1958* quite happily acknowledges the divide when it said of the CATs:

The main justification for their existence, however, will lie not in their ability to copy the universities but in their success in marking out a distinctive place in the educational system. For this purpose, their principal instrument is their intimate link with industry ... the more strictly academic approach of most universities and the close association with industry that characterises the colleges of advanced technology can form a stimulating complement to each other to the national advantage (Ministry of Education 1958: 57)

The report then makes it perfectly clear what it means by 'the national advantage' when it comments: 'One thing is certain: neither the colleges not the universities (unless they were to be dominated numerically by their technological faculties) could alone produce the number of technologists which this country so urgently requires' (ibid.: 38). Since the universities' traditional values rendered them inherently hostile to any suggestion that they should gear their activities to the production of economically relevant manpower, the ministry considered the apartheid of 'separate but equal development' a necessary policy option.

As the idea of education as the servant of the economy gained ground in the ministry, so the prestige accorded to the technical colleges increased. At the same time, the ministry's reports of the late 1950s and the early 1960s contain an important addition to the developing ideology; namely, that if education is to serve the economy, then the state must ensure that it does so efficiently. Manpower planning had entered the ideological arena. Its entry coincided with a growing political dynamic within the Labour Party which drew together egalitarian and technological values and which, in the period of Labour government between 1964 and 1970, reinforced the position of the economic ideology of education within the state apparatus. In practical policy terms, this overlap of values found expression in Labour's inauguration of degree-awarding polytechnics announced by Mr Crosland, then Secretary of State for Education, on 27 April 1965. His speech was a clear and unequivocal statement of the new educational ideology. It recognized that 'there is an ever-increasing need and demand for vocational, professional and industrially-based courses in higher education', that a 'public' sector of higher education, separate from the universities, is required to promote such courses, and 'that a substantial part of the higher education system should be under social control, and directly responsive to social needs' (THES 1975: 15). The important political step had thus been taken to legitimize state intervention in higher education.

A major problem faced by the economic ideology of education was how to make convincing its claim that education should be linked to economic need. In the early 1960s, manpower forecasting was still in its infancy and the precise identification of the requirements of economic growth impossible. Faced with this situation the DES, which succeeded the Ministry of Education in 1964, engaged in the general and largely undiscriminating encouragement of science and technology. To this end, the Committee on Manpower Resources for Science and Technology chaired by Sir Willis Jackson produced a series of reports in the late 1960s (e.g. the Dainton, Jones and Swann Reports) which championed the idea that one of the major weaknesses of the British educational system was its failure to train and keep the quantities of scientists and technologists necessary for an expanding economy.

With the onset of the economic recession in the early 1970s, and a growing preoccupation with the efficient use of resources, it became clear that the indiscriminate production of scientists and technologists was no longer a tenable goal and that further refinement was required. Given limited resources, the DES argued, choices would have to be made according to known and rational procedures. Thus we see the department's sponsorship of output budgeting and human capital planning emerging as an integral part of a more developed version of the new ideology. It found its first formal expression in 1970 in *Educational Planning Paper No. 1* and *Educational Planning Paper No. 2* (DES 1970a, b).

Whereas the legimating power of the traditional liberal ideal relied heavily on ideas with an 'absolute' status – such as the preservation of civilized values – that of the new ideology rested on its claim to incorporate 'objectively necessary' goals – such as economic growth – which could be both identified and achieved using 'scientific methods'. In seeking to promote economic growth, it after all aimed at what was best for everyone. This 'inevitable' quality of the ideology was reinforced by its use of the 'impartial' sciences of economics and statistics in the construction of educational policy. In this way, it legitimized itself by claiming to be value-free and non-ideological.

It can be no coincidence that the department's sponsorship of the economic ideology of education provided it with an essential tool for the expansion of its bureaucratic power. In the same way that the traditional liberal ideal was used by the universities as ideological protection, the application of economic values to education was used by the department as a form of ideological attack. If the sociopolitical power of the universities was to be harnessed and directed within an overall policy framework for higher education, state intervention had to be justified before it could be properly implemented. However, given the department's inexperience in the business of generating educational values, it was inevitable that the DES would make slow progress. So it was not until the early 1970s that it began to address the specific changes required in the roles of institutions, staff and students if the universities were to be sensitive to the needs of the economy. When it did so it was immediately obvious that all the proposed changes were completely at variance with the traditional university system. The DES spelt out the message in the 1972 White Paper *Education: A Framework for Expansion* when it stated:

> ... at the same time they [the government] value its [higher education's] continued expansion as an investment in the nation's human

talent in a time of rapid social change and technological development. If these economic, personal and social aims are to be realised, within the limits of available resources and competing priorities, both the purposes and the nature of higher education ... must be critically and realistically examined. The continuously changing relationship between higher education and the subsequent employment should be reflected both in the institutions and in individual choices. The Government hope that those who contemplate entering higher education, and those advising them, will the more carefully examine their motives and their require ments; and be sure that they form their judgement on a realistic assessment of its usefulness to their interests and career intentions (DES 1972: 34).

According to the new economic values, students should base their decisions about their higher education on how it will contribute to their future employment and not, for example, on whether they will find it intrinsically interesting. This will enable them to become part of the 'efficient' distribution of human capital and so facilitate the linkage between economic demand and human supply. Equally, institutions should assist the process through the selection of appropriate students, by the manipulation of entrance requirements for particular courses and by internal restructuring. What they should not do is to resist the demands of the economy by seeking refuge in the traditional principle of academic autonomy.

Unfortunately for the DES, as it found to its cost, formulating a new ideology is merely the first step and getting other structures to accept it is rather more difficult. Although by the early 1970s the economic ideology of education was firmly established in the department, within higher education itself it had made few inroads; in fact, quite the reverse. Its vanguard and embodiment of the new values, the polytechnics and colleges of advanced technology, had all too readily been seduced and subverted by university values. In its 1976 report, the Select Committee on Science and Technology lamented:

> ... the transformation of the CATs into universities, and the present tendency of the polytechnics to seek 'parity' with the universities, reflect the distressing British habit of attempting to bestow status and prestige on institutions and individuals by changing their names rather than encouraging them to do well the things for which they are best suited (THES 1976: 17).

The Committee saw the incorporation of the CATs by the university system as an attempt 'to eliminate a potential threat to its traditional freedom and independence by turning that threat into an asset to be deployed in defence of the freedom of the universities from direct state control'. Such is the power of the traditional university values that they succeeded, in the Committee's view, in rebuilding CATs in 'the image of the institutions [the universities] which were regarded as having failed to provide the manpower which the nation required' (ibid.). So by the mid-1970s, after two decades of state sponsorship, the economic ideology of education had signally failed to make any inroads in the university sector. The traditional values were as firmly ensconced in the universities as ever, and the prospect for educational change in this sector seemed remote.

The bureaucratic dynamic: Colonizing the middle ground

Although up to the mid-1970s the universities themselves remained largely immune to the combined blandishments of the economic ideology of educa-tion and bureaucratic dynamic of the DES, the middle ground between the universities and the state, that is the UGC and the research councils, faired rather differently. As the administrative means whereby the state allocated resources to the universities, these organizations were the first to feel the effect of the gradual sea-change in the state's attitude towards the univer-sities. As the arguments between the state's growing demand for university accountability, and the universities' implacable assertion of their right to autonomy, moved back and forth over several decades, the UGC and the research councils inevitably formed the major battleground. Effectively they constituted the universities' first and only line of defence and the eventual erosion of their ability to protect the universities opened the way for the attack on the universities themselves.

While the economic ideology of education provided the justification for the state's attempts to colonize the middle ground of UGC and research coun-cils, the bureaucratic dynamic provided the impetus and the means. In this section, we trace the history of those attempts, the trenchant resistance of the traditional liberal ideal and the ambiguities and confusions which resulted.

The UGC

The UGC was established on 14 July 1919 by a Treasury minute. It had no statutory basis or powers, no bank account, no income-generating capacity, and no grant was made to it. And so it was to remain for the next 70 years. As an advisory committee, a common enough device, its terms of reference were: 'to enquire into the financial needs of University Education in the United Kingdom, and to advise the government as to the application of any grants that may be made towards meeting them'. Of itself this was nothing new. Several other advisory committees on university grants had preceded it beginning in 1889 with the *ad hoc* Committee on Grants to University Colleges in Great Britain, also created by a Treasury minute. As an ex-Secretary of the UGC, John Carswell observes: 'the UGC was invented as a device in recognition of the autonomy of the universities, which was then financial as well as constitutional' (Carswell 1985: 12).

Although to begin with some universities were sceptical of the state's intentions and of their ability to control the way in which the university–state relationship should develop, this scepticism soon faded. Throughout the first two decades of the UGC's existence, it came to be considered axiomatic that the universities themselves should enunciate the guiding framework of values since they were, demonstrably, independent institutions. The UGC, after all, supplied only one-third of the universities' total income, the remaining two-thirds coming equally from endowments and local authorities, and it was thought essential by all concerned that this balance should be maintained. Statements about university self-determination during this period were seen as simply reflecting the reality of financial autonomy. Thus in 1921, the UGC urges universities to regard endowment funds as their central source of revenue: 'it was indisputable that only by a consolidation of a stable and substantial income from independent sources could the autonomy and progressive development of a university be assured' (UGC 1921: para. 18).

There was never any doubt in the collective mind of the UGC between the wars about the kind of university education they should be encouraging and their uncomplicated enthusiasm for the task before them illuminates the reports of that period. Much of their zeal centres on the quality of the experiences available to the student. Clearly, they argue, 'he' [*sic*] should be concerned with much more than just vocational training:

> Has he also received that stimulation and enrichment of the whole mind which will enable him to lead a fuller and more interesting human life and to play more adequately his part as a member or leader of the community? (UGC 1936: 11).

How can arrangements be made to ensure that the student lives in an atmosphere of intellectual argument, daring and adventure so as to evoke in him 'an energy of the soul in the pursuit of excellence', asks the Committee rhetorically. Quotations from Bacon and Newman are used to support their reply that opportunities for fellowship are the best means available (ibid.: 13). From a statement of principle the Committee then moves to a detailed and practical discussion of how student unions, sports facilities, a health service and halls of residence ('a great humanising force') can contribute to the realization of that principle (ibid.: 14–18).

In the inter-war years, the UGC acted as the vehicle of the Oxbridge definition of academic orthodoxy and dispensed state monies to the universities with very few strings attached. However, with the Second World War all changed: the middle ground became state territory and the universities themselves were effectively colonized. The total and willing subjugation of the universities to the war effort created the habits, procedures and legitimations of massive state intervention in their day-to-day lives. The movement and co-ordination of departments, the requisitioning of buildings, the whole-scale evacuation of universities, including London University, from vulnerable areas, the stimulation and control of university activities and in particular scientific research 'directly related to the various and developing needs of the war machine', took place on a much larger scale than in the First World War (UGC 1948: 6). When the war ended, such an administrative and ideological impetus had been built up that it took some years before the old academic orthodoxy was able to re-establish itself. By the 1950s, it had done so, but so many aspects of the universities–state relationship had altered in the meantime that significant amendments had to be made to the old orthodoxy to enable it to cope with the new situation.

In 1938–39, the proportion of university income received from the UGC was 36 per cent. By 1951–52, this proportion had more than doubled to 65 per cent and, in addition, the state had taken on the fresh function of funding capital development projects in universities (Armytage 1955: 274). As the UGC observed, this dramatic change of scale was 'rightly interpreted by the universities as initiating a new era in their financial relations with the state (UGC 1948: 11). The pre-war idea that the state should be a minority shareholder supplying one-third of the universities' income was abruptly and, it would seem, permanently destroyed. But if private money was no longer the final guarantor of university independence, what was?

The answer, which swiftly and conveniently assumed the status of ideological myth and duly became part of an adapted version of the liberal ideal, had three parts. First, pre-war scepticism about the intentions of the state was replaced by the belief that, so far as the universities were concerned, the state was benign. Secondly, the view developed that the state needed the universities in order to produce qualified manpower and scientific research, as much as the universities needed the state. An equal 'partnership' based on mutual respect was therefore seen as emerging quite naturally. Thirdly, just in case, the UGC itself took on the newly vacant role of guarantor of university autonomy and was henceforth presented as the 'buffer' between universities and state. As the trusted servant of university interests, the Committee became a necessary part of the new academic orthodoxy and thus completed the remarkable journey between 1919 and the early 1950s from administrative device to ideological symbol.

By the end of the 1947–52 quinquennium, the adapted traditional liberal ideal was fully ensconced in the UGC. The universities had compromised but were once again in control of the middle ground following the peacetime retreat of the state from their hallowed territory. But in the ensuing years, a number of pressures were to combine to shatter this new consensus between universities and state and bring an end both to this privileged treatment and, eventually, to the UGC itself. As we have seen, the state developed an educational ideology which was, and is, fundamentally incompatible with the traditional liberal ideal and helped to illuminate the inherent contradiction between the élitism of the Oxbridge ideal as a guiding set of principles and the realities of mass higher education. In the course of attempting to manage the resulting tensions, the UGC evolved into an administrative entity with an identity, logic and preferences of its own which never resolved, and frequently simply focused, the underlying contradiction of its position.

Initially, the flexibility of the administrative web linking universities and state enabled the UGC to cope with the immediate pressures of expansion in the late 1950s and early 1960s. When a fresh administrative need was identified, an extra part was bolted on to the existing structure. By 1963, there were ten sub-committees and panels (e.g. medicine, new universities, building procedures), six independent *ad hoc* committees (e.g. methods of university expenditure, halls of residence, teaching methods) and several joint committees (e.g. libraries, superannuation). In the short term, the generous and uncritical flow of funds from the Treasury protected the UGC from having to make many hard choices. But with the transfer of the UGC to the DES in 1964 came exposure to the economic ideology of education with its emphasis on responsiveness to national needs, an increased supply of scientists and technologists, and the positive management of the education system.

The report for the 1962–67 quinquennium saw the UGC responding to DES pressure, albeit with many a show of reluctance. In science and technology, the Committee relied on blanket exhortation of the universities to gear a larger part of their 'output' to the economic and industrial needs of the nation, arguing that 'few things could be more vital to the national economy at the present time than the proper deployment of highly qualified scientific manpower and the application of research to the solution of current technological and economic problems' (UGC 1968a: 107). Internally, its move towards quasi-management of the universities is reflected in the doubling of its staff numbers from 50 in 1962 to 112 in 1968, the introduction of more sophisticated information and financial systems, and its continuing attempts to promote greater cost-consciousness among the universities.

As its own bureaucratic dynamic responded to the management ethos of the DES, so the duality in the Committee's thinking became more and more obvious. In the case of the block grant principle, the Committee stated its view in its 1962–67 report that this principle 'has long been regarded as necessary to ensure a reasonable measure of academic freedom and to avoid the "management" of the universities by the Government or by the Committee. We regard the maintenance of this principle as one of our cardinal duties' (UGC 1968a: 137). In fact, by 1967, the block grant principle had become no more than a useful political myth. In order to receive a block grant, universities were obliged to submit detailed development plans and the UGC made it perfectly clear that once the grant had been allocated 'no major departures from the lines of development that have been discussed should be made without reference to the Committee' (ibid.: 138).

For the 1967–72 quinquennium, the UGC took the logic of this position a step further and, in addition to sending a private letter to each vice-chancellor, issued a public Memorandum of General Guidance, which covered in detail the UGC's judgements about the general policies and particular problems common to most of the universities for the quinquennium. In the private letter, each university was informed of an individual target of student numbers, divided into four categories by postgraduate and undergraduate and by science and art-based subjects. By this stage, the UGC was starting to act on what at least part of its personna had previously accepted that 'we are now inescapably involved in making positive judgements, *an activity which goes far beyond the capacity of a buffer or shock-absorber'* (UGC 1968a: 179, our emphasis).

When the inflation rate reached 20 per cent in 1975, the government abruptly ended the quinquennial planning system and the universities' building programme. As we have shown in *Education, Politics and the State* (Salter and Tapper 1981), the DES saw the economic crisis as an opportunity to argue that educational power should be more centralized to ensure the efficient use of education as an economic resource. But during the 1970s, it concentrated its efforts and its ambitions on the secondary sector of education and left the UGC and the universities on ice, crisis planning and wondering what was going to happen next.

In July 1981, the attack on the universities began with the announcement of cuts in the recurrent grant which were to amount to 17 per cent over the next 3 years. As a catalyst for jolting the UGC into a more active management stance, the cuts produced considerable effect as the Committee suddenly found itself in the business of the allocation of even scarcer resources. There was no time for the considered discussion of the ideological soundness of the task before it. Selection criteria had to be rapidly developed and judgements made using an information base which had not been designed for the task because intervention on such a scale, with the exception of the Second World War, had historically been regarded as unnecessary and decidedly undesirable. Precisely what these criteria were is unknown, but they produced reductions in the recurrent grants of universities ranging from 44 to 6 per cent.

As the bureaucratic dynamic of the DES and the economic ideology of education combined to shove aside the UGC's remaining attachments to the principles of the liberal ideal and university autonomy, a short, sharp ideological battle ensued with predictable results once the state had shown it was prepared to use its financial muscle. In 1963, Robbins had noted that:

> ... there is no absolute safeguard against interference with the distribution of grants to universities. It is a convention that Government abstains. But it cannot bind its successors, nor is its agreement likely to imply abstention in the face of major difficulties (Committee on Higher Education 1963: 164, 237).

As the system of values of which that convention formed a part withered, so did the convention.

There is little indication in relevant public documents of the 1980s that the liberal ideal was able to offer much resistance. The amount of movement towards acceptance of the state's management of the universities varies, with the UGC's *A Strategy for Higher Education into the 1990s* (1984) accepting it with reservations and the CVCP's Jarratt Report (1985) on efficiency in universities embracing it wholeheartedly. The debate culminated in the publication in 1985 by the DES of *The Development of Higher Education into the 1990s*, which is a clear statement of the economic ideology of education as it applies to higher education, with the dimension of the state's management of educational change very much in evidence. Not surprisingly, it constantly echoes the Ministry of Education's reports of the 1950s with their emphasis on education and economic performance, international competition, and the need for qualified manpower, particularly scientists, engineers and technologists.

The research councils

Running parallel to the saga of the state and the UGC has been the changing relationship between the state and the other major funding mechanism of the universities, the research councils. Although similar battles have been fought with a common end result, the timing and nature of these conflicts has varied, at least partly because until 1965 when the research councils became the responsibility of the DES, their relationship with the state had taken a number of different forms.

The principles on which the research councils have traditionally based their operation derive from the *Report of the Machinery of Government Committee* (Ministry of Reconstruction, 1918. The Haldane Report), which recommended that the funding of external government scientific research should follow the model of the Department of Scientific and Industrial Research (DSIR) established in 1916. As the idea of the semi-autonomous research council, this model was characterized by independence over scientific decisions, a council membership consisting of independent individuals (both scientific and laymen), full-time scientifically qualified secretaries and direct negotiation of funding from the Treasury. What is rarely mentioned is that Haldane saw this model as a temporary device which would have to be superseded by a different structure, possibly a Department of Intelligence and Research, once government research expanded further (ibid.: 35). In the event, the 'Haldane principle', as it became known, provided the model for the establishment of the Medical Research Council (MRC) in 1920, the Agricultural Research Council (ARC) in 1931 and the Nature Conservancy (NC) in 1949.

The transition of the research council model from, as Haldane saw it, an administrative compromise with a limited life-expectancy, to an ideological symbol of the necessary autonomy of research to be protected as a sacrosanct principle in a civilized society, was accomplished with remarkable ease in the same way as the UGC had gained its own mossy respectability. One of the reasons for this and the state's lack of concern was the small amount of public money involved: in 1939, expenditure on the research councils amounted to £1 328 000 (ACSP 1964).

In 1947, the research councils became part of the newly formed Advisory Council on Scientific Policy's (ACSP) general responsibility for civil science. The ACSP advised the Lord President to the Privy Council who was responsible to Parliament for the research councils and their establishments.

However, the research councils continued to report directly to him through four Privy Councils, one each for the MRC, ARC, NC and Advisory Council for Science and Industrial Research (ACSIR), which oversaw the work of the DSIR. However, although in formal constitutional terms a line of accountability to Parliament was thus established, it left the Lord President in the position of responsibility with no executive power. The accountability relationship between the research councils and Parliament was further weakened by the way in which they were funded. Only the DSIR received its finance through a separate Parliamentary Vote which MPs could debate and challenge, the other three being supported by grants-in-aid which do not allow any opportunity for Parliamentary discussion.

Under the new structure, the Haldane principle was used to legitimate the idea that, so far as the research councils were concerned, scientists should manage their own affairs. The councils were allowed to determine for themselves what funding they thought they should have, using their own internal criteria. Annual submissions for funding were simply channelled from the research councils to the Treasury via the ACSP and the Lord President of the Council.

Throughout the ACSP's 17-year life until its demise in 1964, its constant preoccupation was with how science could be employed to produce the maximum impact on economic productivity. It was a natural proponent of the economic ideology of education in the field of research. Reviews were held of how state-funded scientific organizations could better perform their task of serving the economy. In its reports, the targeting and allocation of resources to achieve this goal were accepted without question. But until the late 1950s, the research councils and universities were excluded from its strictures on the grounds that they carried out 'pure' rather than 'applied' research.

The dawning realization that the state could not afford to give the university scientific community a blank cheque indefinitely came with the massive expansion of expenditure in the late 1950s and early 1960s. Between 1955–56 and 1959–60, the total government research and development budget rose by 40 per cent in constant value terms: between 1955–56 and 1961–62 it had risen from 1.7 to 2.7 per cent of GNP. By far the largest part of this increase was taken by spending on nuclear science, a field dominated by university scientists, which in 1961–62 amounted to half of the total civil science budget (ACSP 1962: app. F). With equipment costs soaring and internal projects such as the CERN accelerator creating open-ended commitments to unknown future expenditure, the ACSP was a man astride a juggernaut over which he has no control.

In common with the reports from the Committee on the Management and Control of Research and Development (Zuckerman Report) and the Committee of Enquiry into Civil Science (Trend Report), the ACSP came to the conclusion that the state funding of scientific research required positive management and central co-ordination if resources were to be used efficiently, and it was forced to accept that the research councils could no longer be excluded from that process. The universities and research councils stoutly resisted such heretical ideas and were rewarded by the abolition of the ACSP in 1964.

In 1965, the Science and Technology Act redefined the nature of the middle ground between universities and state occupied by the research councils. The Act created three new research councils: the Science Research Council (SRC), the Natural Environment Research Council (NERC) and the Social Science Research Council (SSRC). The first two of these followed the recommendations of the Trend Report and the SSRC owed its existence to the Heyworth Committee. The DSIR was disbanded and its work split between the SRC, which took on the pure research, and the Ministry of Technology, which assumed responsibility for the research establishments oriented primarily towards technology and its application to industry. All five research councils (ARC, MRC, NERC, SRC and SSRC) were brought under the Secretary of State for Education and Science whose own post had been created in 1964 by the merger of the Ministry of Education and the office of the Minister for Science. At the same time as assuming responsibility for the research councils, the DES also gained control of their finances. Annual budgets to the research councils were henceforth to be allocated by the DES through the Science Vote rather than primarily through grants-in-aid from the Treasury. Financial accountability to Parliament and political responsibility were therefore integrated for the first time. Since in the previous year the UGC, the other arm of the dual funding system, had also become the political and financial responsibility of the DES, the initial impression is that the state is finally bringing together the disparate lines of accountability and gaining effective control over the middle ground and university research. Such an impression is illusory.

From 1965, the forum for the annual arbitration of research council budgets was a newly created body called the Council for Scientific Policy (CSP). Although similar in title to the ACSP, the CSP's brief was much narrower, since it carried responsibility solely for the research councils rather than for the whole of civil science as the ACSP had done. With its membership dominated by academic scientists, the CSP soon made plain its views about the values which should dominate the research councils' deliberations. In its first report it stated:

> We believe that Research Councils must be free to determine, in relation to scientific priorities, their own programmes within their own terms of reference. If this principle is damaged the system, which has stood the test of time since its enunciation in the Haldane Report, is certain to decay (CSP 1966: 10).

However, the CSP also had to face the fact that in 1965 the research councils' budget was expanding at a rate of 13 per cent per year, which meant that it would double every 6 years. In the following year's report it noted:

> Inevitably these trends will impose an increasing need for careful selection in planning research programmes and if resources of the right magnitude are to be deployed there will have to be further progress towards specialisation at selected centres together with concentration of resources in some fields of science (CSP 1967: 16).

From early on in its life, the Council therefore began to display the same qualities of schizophrenia as we have already diagnosed in the UGC. Caught between, on the one hand, the demands of a role which, in the absence of infinite governmental largesse, inevitably entailed the selective allocation of finite resources and, on the other, the claims of traditional university values which rejected any attempts at the central direction of research, the CSP entered a perpetual circle of equivocation.

In 1971, its musings on this ambiguity were rudely interrupted by a fierce ideological attack from the Rothschild Report, *A Framework for Government Research and Development.* Rothschild insisted that applied research and development should be governed by what he called the 'customer–contractor principle' where 'The customer says what he wants, the contractor does it (if he can) and the customer pays' (Rothschild, Lord 1971: 3). Although Rothschild explicitly excluded basic, fundamental or pure research from the application of this principle, he also maintained that an appreciable part of the work of the ARC, MRC and NERC was applied and therefore subject to the customer–contractor principle. In passing, Rothschild made short work of the Haldane principle and concluded: 'The concepts of scientific independence used in the Haldane Report are not relevant to contemporary discussion of government research!' (ibid.: 10).

In its reply, the CSP simply reasserted the orthodox university position that 'It is a characteristic of basic and strategic science that neither the devising of programmes of work nor the assignment of relative scientific priorities to each programme can be carried out by non-scientists' (CSP 1971: 13). Although the CSP was replaced by the Advisory Board for the Research Councils (ABRC) in 1973, rather more important as an indicator of the state's attitude were the cuts of the same year. The effect of the cuts was to reduce the 1974–75 science budget of the research councils by £6.5 million, 2.1 per cent less than the previous year and 4 per cent less than the expected total (ABRC 1976: 13). For the first time in the post-war era, university science had received a reduction in its budget. The effect was as much psychological as economic: no longer could the universities assume they were a privileged sector of state expenditure. They were as vulnerable as the rest.

However, for the remainder of the 1970s, the DES was too preoccupied with the secondary sector of education to exploit this advantage. There is certainly nothing in the ABRC's reports of this period to indicate that it felt obliged to assume a more directive stance towards science in the universities. Its *Second Report* describes the strengthening of that 'long standing feature of science planning', the 'Forward Look' method of estimating future research council expenditure – a method responsive to the scientific community's definition of research priorities (ibid.). Admittedly, mention is made of selectivity and the research council committees are 'invited' to use a suggested list of ABRC criteria, but the rhetoric is unconvincing.

When the 'phony war' ended with the university cuts of 1981, the state was aided in its bid for greater control over university science by the sudden realization by the ABRC and UGC that the historic dual funding system was already on the point of collapse. Reporting in 1982, the Joint ABRC/UGC Working Party on the Support of Scientific Research, chaired by Sir Alec Merrison, conducted the first statistically based analysis of the dual funding system and showed that the whole infrastructure of university science had been eroded over the previous decade. With the certainty of further reductions in UGC spending, it was obvious that choices were going to have to be made and scientific resources selectively allocated. But assuming it accepted the truth of this proposition, how was the ABRC to develop its role?

The debate was carried forward initially by a joint report from the ABRC and the Advisory Committee on Applied Research and Development (ACARD), *Improving Research Links between Higher Education and Industry* (ABRC/ACARD 1983), followed by ACARD's *Exploitable Areas of Science* (1986), which explored the methodology and management necessary for the deliberate exploitation of science. The latter report took the economic view that 'the support of exploitable areas of science can properly be viewed as an investment decision, in which current outlays are incurred in anticipation of future returns' (ibid.: 25). Meanwhile, the other arm of the dual funding system, the UGC, responding to pressure from the DES, announced in 1984 in *Higher Education into the 1990s: The UGC's Advice*, that 'to ensure that resources for research are allocated and managed to their best advantage' certain principles should apply. These included the selective allocation of research support among universities (UGC 1984: 17).

The gradual acceptance by the research councils that the demand-led funding of university science through a self-regulating scientific community was no longer acceptable to the state, meant the retreat of the liberal university ideal from the middle ground between universities and state. In its place has come the new language of the managerial component of the economic ideology of education. Hence the ABRC's *A Strategy for the Science Base* (1987) presents strategic advice on the development of the science base and deals with its organization and management, strategic priorities and exploitation, and the adequacy of the funding of the science base. It also suggests a future pattern of higher education provision where institutions would be categorized into three types according to the amount and type of research conducted. Although the specific recommendations of this report were not implemented, its ideological impact was to press home the point that the state would no longer allow universities the autonomy to define the nature of the system they inhabit.

The political party dynamic

Until recently, both of the two major political parties were reluctant to place pressure on the universities to change their ways. This reticence cannot be due simply to an absence of policy but has to be seen as further evidence of the universities' ability to out-manoeuvre their opponents ideologically, at least for a time, by asserting the sanctity of university autonomy.

Although the Labour Party had been inhibited during the 1950s by an exaggerated respect for university status, its growing belief in science and technology as an essential ingredient of economic growth coupled with its analysis of universities in general, and Oxford and Cambridge in particular, as élitist and socially divisive institutions, created an impetus within the party for the reform of higher education (Labour Party 1961, 1963). Then Crosland effectively diverted this impetus away from the universities with the creation of the polytechnics in 1965. In the following decade, despite the recommendation of the party's 1973 Study Group Report, *Higher and Further Education*, that all institutions of higher education be unified under a single Adult Education Commission, no threat to the universities emerged from the Labour Party during their 1974–79 period of office (Labour Party 1973). It remains to be seen whether Labour's renewed commitment in the 1980s to lifelong education has any practical effect on the organization of higher education if and when they are returned to office.

The case of the Conservative Party is rather different and constitutes the major political party dynamic for change in the universities. However, it was not until the late 1960s that some Conservative intellectuals began to question seriously what was happening in education. Part of this concern was undoubtedly stimulated by student rebellion in the universities, but for the most part the focus was on secondary education. The goal of the New Right in education was, and is, to create a social market where consumer choice can operate unfettered by state controls or professional resistance by teachers. Such a market, it is argued, will force up standards because the educational producers (schools, colleges, etc.) will have to compete for the business of the consumers (parents, students). Their first tangible effect on Conservative Party policy came with the inclusion of *A Charter of Parent's Rights* in the election manifesto of October 1974. The Charter had five components: the state and local authorities should take account of the wishes of parents; there should be a local appeal system for parents dissatisfied with their allotment of schools; parents should be represented on school boards; headteachers should be obliged to form a parent–teacher association; and schools would be encouraged to publish prospectuses about their record, existing character, specialities and objectives to allow parents to make a sensible choice. And in the 1979 manifesto, parental choice was linked to standards: 'Extending parents' rights and responsibilities, including their right of choice, will also help raise standards by giving them greater influence over education' (Conservative Party 1979: 25). However, in neither manifesto were market principles applied to higher education.

Although the major part of the New Right's energy has, until fairly recently, been concentrated on the secondary education sector, some work was carried out in the 1960s and 1970s on how their principles could be applied to university education. Much of this work was sponsored, not surprisingly, by that well-known broker for free market values, the Institute of Economic Affairs (IEA). In two articles published by the Institute, Peacock and Wiseman (1964) and Prest (1966) examined in some detail how student loan schemes could be employed to finance university education and, in a third article, Ferns (1969) discussed the market principles which could be used to organize universities. Ferns's contribution is particularly interesting because it was commissioned by the IEA for a conference about the practicalities of setting up an independent university which, in turn, led to the creation of the University of Buckingham. Ferns's starting point is that the interposition of the UGC and the state between the universities and their customers has created a situation in which the universities can neither respond to the demand for their services nor tap directly into the resources required to meet it. Instead, they are trapped within 'an elephantine system of centralised control' which 'is bound to engulf more and more university activity in the cobwebs of committee decisions primarily concerned with the system itself and only secondarily with the problems of education and research' (ibid.: 17). Because the universities are not directly accountable to the community through a market mechanism, he argued, there is no objective way of judging the quality of the education provided.

In a later paper commissioned by the IEA, Maynard (1975) examined the feasibility of using student loans as the principal mechanism for funding universities. To the alleged economic advantages conferred by a loans system – market responsiveness, lack of dependence upon the state, and the ability of consumers (the students) to penalize inefficient producers (universities) by withdrawing their custom – Maynard adds the advantage of social equity:

> The main argument for the repayment by the student of part or all of the cost of higher education is distributional equity. It is regarded as contradictory to redistributive objectives that the potentially affluent student should receive subsidies from a society the majority of whose members have lower incomes than the beneficiaries of higher education (Maynard 1975: 51).

Although this argument went largely unnoticed at the time, it was to surface with renewed vigour a decade later as the New Right switched its attention from secondary education, where the tide was turning, to higher education, where for them the battle was just beginning.

The first signs that the universities were soon to feel the heat came in a publication by the Conservative Political Centre in 1985. In the appropriately titled *No Turning Back*, the main policy areas were reviewed in terms of what should be done next to carry the new Conservative radicalism forward. Under education the opinion is expressed that:

The same problem which afflicts our schooling, that of producer cap-
ture, is to be found in our tertiary education. Students have a nominal
choice between universities and colleges, if they can secure acceptance.
But the method of funding denies them any kind of input as consumers,
and prevents their choices from having any serious impact on the system
(Conservative Political Centre 1985: 14).

The document is not reticent about what should be done. As with the
schools, funds should be re-routed to ensure the operation of a consumer
market in higher education in order to turn 'what are now the decisions of
the bureaucrat into opportunities for choice by the consumer' (ibid.: 17).
Student loans are the preferred mechanism because they introduce economic
and commercial calculations into the operation of student choice.

The competition between the New Right think-tanks for influence over
Conservative Party policy making is well illustrated by the rush of recent
publications on how higher education can best be led into the marketplace.
Forthright advice has come from the Adam Smith Institute, the Centre for
Policy Studies and the Institute of Economic Affairs. In *University Challenge*,
Mason (1986) uses the concept of real student choice to link the demand for
higher education, the supply of courses and the needs of the economy. If
higher education is free and involves no cost to the student, then demand is
only limited by the available supply. If, on the other hand, there is a cost
to students when they choose to enter higher education, for example they
receive a loan not a grant, then apparently they will choose courses which
will provide them with economic benefit when they graduate. As a result,
the demand for higher education will be shaped by a student's cost-benefit
assessment of taking a particular course. If, in addition, higher education
institutions receive the majority of their income from student fees, then they
will be obliged to tailor their supply of courses to student demand and
student purchasing power.

By waving its magic wand, the market mechanism will, Mason maintains,
remove the need both for those increasingly complex projections of student
numbers used by bodies like the DES, UGC and CVCP and for the largely
futile attempts to push student demand in one direction or another in order
to satisfy the needs of the economy. Both will be rendered redundant by the
operation of consumer choice. Then, of course, there is the moral case. 'It
is clearly unfair', Mason argues, 'to subsidise one form of investment in a
person's future when no other is so supported' (ibid.: 39). It is even more
unfair that those who leave school at 16 should subsidize through their taxes
those who go on to higher education (ibid.: 42).

Similar arguments appear in the CPS's *Diamonds into Glass* (Kedourie
1988) and the IEA Education Unit's *Higher Education: Freedom and Finance*
(Letwin *et al.* 1988). Both emphasize the importance of shifting power away
from the bureaucrats and into the hands of the consumers through the
exercise of competition in the marketplace. At the same time, both recognize
that this will not be easy. Officialdom, in the words of Kedourie (1988: 20,

22), has through successive investigations acquired 'an obsessive momentum' in 'its restless quest for new and better methods of controlling universities and their activities' and will not willingly loosen its grip. Part of the task of the New Right intellectuals is therefore to help develop the details of the policies required to liberate the universities from the chains of the state and the IEA's contribution contains an in-depth examination by Stuart Sexton of how and why a student loans system could be made to work.

The success of the New Right in asserting and then implementing its ideology in secondary education reached its fruition in the 1988 Education Reform Act and has given it a confidence that a parallel victory can be achieved in higher education. With the social networks well established between the New Right intellectuals and the formal elements of Conservative Party policy making, it is difficult to resist the conclusion that this confidence is well-founded. After 15 years of ideological conflict, they have seen themselves move from the margins to the mainstream to the extent that Ferns's (1969: 13) plea that vice-chancellors should be 'inventing ways of selling their products to an ever-widening body of consumers' has changed its status from the muttering of an eccentric to a statement of the obvious.

Conclusions

Our theory of educational change is clear that in order to direct the socio-political power of the universities in the way which its considered fit and appropriate, the state had first to develop its own ideology, and hence its own self-belief in its right to influence university affairs, and then use this ideology to dominate the traditional liberal ideal in the public arena. By the mid-1970s, the battle had been joined, but the state was not yet in a position to launch a sustained onslaught on the Robbins principle that educational investment cannot be 'measured adequately by the same yardstick as investment in coal or electricity' (Committee on Higher Education 1963: 205). At that point, it had not resolved the riddle of how to out-manoeuvre an opponent with the kind of historic resources enjoyed by the universities.

It is also clear from our analysis that the pressures upon the state to control the universities' use of their considerable power are overwhelming and inescapable. Modern economies require an ever-changing blend of new knowledge and educated manpower if they are to function effectively and no state can afford to leave its higher education system to its own devices. Such action would amount to an abdication of responsibility which no present-day bureaucracy could tolerate either in terms of its internal organizational dynamic or in terms of the external demands upon it. This is not to say that the state will be able to translate the pressures upon itself into policies which produce the desired results. Indeed, it may fail dismally. But it is inevitable that it will make the attempt.

In its bid to orchestrate the process of educational change in universities, the state will be influenced by a number of factors. First, although the economic ideology of education as we have described it above is what one might call its 'natural' ideology, in the sense that it legitimates the state's managerial role in the rational language of all bureaucracies, it has not been the only attack on the traditional values of the universities. The rise of the New Right's view of education as a marketplace where educational products should be bought and sold and where supply and demand should be left to resolve distributive problems, directly challenged the universities' belief in their inherent right to state largesse. But it also challenged the DES claim to manage change in the universities in the light of the needs of the economy. A decade of Conservative government prepared to promote the market ideology has left the DES with no alternative but to try and affect some kind of compromise between the two value positions so that a common front can be held against the universities.

Secondly, the state has to be aware of the fact that the ability of individual universities to combine knowledge and status into a form of sociopolitical power varies considerably. Oxford and Cambridge have far greater status to lend to a knowledge area than does the average university. In addition, the social and cultural advantages of having attended one of the ancient universities reinforces these other differences and results in a university system which is highly differentiated in terms of the amount of sociopolitical power possessed by individual institutions. Any attempt by the state to impose ideological, financial or administrative pressure upon the universities is therefore likely to produce a different response from different institutions.

The combined impact of the economic, bureaucratic and, very recently, the political party dynamics has been greatest in the middle ground between the universities and the state: the UGC and the research councils. Although the resilience of the traditional liberal ideal of the university is considerable, and it is undoubtedly alive and well and living in universities, particularly Oxbridge, it is now equally certain that the struggle for the middle ground is over and the state has won. Given the strength of the economic ideology of education, there is no possibility that values of academe will again dominate the universities–state relationship.

The shift in the balance of power between universities and state since 1919 has not been a steady and predictable process of educational change. Between the wars, the universities' initial suspicion of routinized state contributions to their resources was soon replaced by a confidence in their own ability to determine the form that relationship should take. Despite massive state intervention in their affairs and the subordination of the universities to the war effort during the Second World War, this confidence was soon renewed, though in the context of an amended set of values. Whereas previously it had been the universities' ultimate financial independence which had been seen as the guarantor of their autonomy, now the UGC was accorded that honour and duty. Within this revised system of values, the Committee was the 'buffer' between universities and state and the relationship was characterized as a 'partnership' based on mutual dependence.

In science, the 'Haldane principle' was used to legitimize the right of the research councils to regulate their own activities, funding and priorities. It was a useful ideological device, married readily with the insistence of the liberal ideal on academic autonomy, and maintained its political relevance well into the 1970s despite periodic onslaughts from the ACSP and the Rothschild Report.

In the 1960s, the demands of the economic ideology of education that the universities be responsive to industry's needs for scientific knowledge and manpower coupled with the massive expansion in student numbers produced evidence of a split personality in both the UGC and the research councils. The objective need for more management, or at least more co-ordination, of state investment in the universities, periodically pricked by the bureaucratic dynamic of the DES, conflicted sharply with the principle of non-interference in academic affairs and produced what the UGC (1968a: 180) whimsically characterized as a 'Janus-like posture'.

With the economic crisis of 1974–75 and the effective end of the quinquennial system, the UGC was placed in a position of limbo from which it was rescued only by the 1981 cuts. Prior to this, the DES had concentrated its efforts to expand its ideological and managerial power on the primary and secondary sectors of education and had largely left the universities alone. But with the cuts the pace of change quickened as the UGC, in company with the ABRC and the research councils, was forced to devise new methods of allocating resources which were too scarce even to be spread thinly. As a result, the mid-1980s saw the publication of a plethora of reports from the UGC, DES, ABRC and CVCP where the final decline and fall of the liberal ideal of a university and the rise of the new managerialism was duly recorded.

In the short term, the three dynamics produced a triple alliance of forces which have colonized the middle ground between universities and state. But it is, at best, an uneasy alliance. Although there is common agreement that the universities should be accountable to the needs of the economy, the political dynamic of the New Right intellectuals differs sharply from the bureaucratic dynamic of the DES over the preferred means to achieve that end. For the former, the market is the natural mechanism whereas, for the latter, some form of central management is seen as inevitable. The fresh set of pressures for change which will emerge from this tension are as yet unknown.

Part 2

The Underpinnings of Autonomy:
Government, Administration and Finance

2

Constitutional Authority: Understanding the Formal Machinery of University Government

What are the statutes?

It is not the intention of this chapter to present a detailed overview of how the Universities of Oxford and Cambridge are formally governed. Such a diet would be very plain fare indeed and not very rewarding given that both universities regularly publish updated editions of their statutes and ordinances (the University of Cambridge) or their statutes, decrees and regulations (the University of Oxford). Constitutions express, either through explicit statements of purpose or implicitly in the formal procedures, the values that guide institutions in the conduct of their affairs. By examining the statutes of the two universities we intend to explore the values upon which their governments are founded. Although sufficient of the formal procedures will be presented in order to illustrate our interpretation of the value system, such description will be kept to the minimum felt necessary to make the point.

It is well-known that throughout their respective histories, the Universities of Oxford and Cambridge have felt it necessary from time to time to bypass their statutes in order to ensure effective government. For example, in his history of early Victorian Cambridge, Winstanley has argued that not only were the University statutes outmoded but also they were literally unenforceable (Winstanley 1940: 156). The Franks Commission of Inquiry into the University of Oxford illustrated the continuing gap between the statutes and contemporary practice:

> But if Council exercises this general interest and initiative and takes decisions or moves to get them taken by the relevant bodies, a question arises about the evolution of practice in the relations of Council to Congregation. According to the Statutes, Council does not decide: it makes proposals on which Congregation legislates. However, since the time of the last Royal Commission, Council has in fact begun to decide and act on a number of matters of great importance to the University without going to Congregation at all (University of Oxford 1966a: 200).

The then university Registrar (Sir Douglas Veale) listed for the Franks Commission as many as seven important powers that Council exercised without 'the direct and formal sanction of Congregation'.

None of this is particularly surprising. The early Victorian universities were not reformed, and perhaps could not have been reformed, without parliamentary intervention. Moreover, even if opposition to statutory change should be limited, institutions invariably will find it easier to modify their practices informally. Clearly, the process of accommodation to changing circumstances has its limits and an articulate and increasingly potent Victorian bourgeoisie demanded that the statutory obstacles to change be tackled head on. To some extent, Oxford's Franks Commission was a response to the criticism that the university was an institution bound by obscure statutes that prevented necessary reform. The university had reached a point at which it was felt necessary to reconcile the statutes with current procedures.

A key question is whether modifications to the machinery of government also alter the values which are embedded in the governmental process. It is unusual for reformers to challenge the established value system; invariably they argue that the intention is to enable the institution to function more efficiently while continuing to maintain its core values. A perfect illustration of this point is to be found in the recent Report of Cambridge's Wass Syndicate which was established 'To Consider the Government of the University'. In the synopsis of the report, we find the following words:

> The University of Cambridge must conduct its business efficiently, and it must be prompt and decisive in its dealings with outside bodies. *It must also remain, as it is now, a self-governing community of scholars.* Our recommendations, which are to be seen as an integrated whole, are designed to satisfy these two fundamental requirements (University of Cambridge 1989a: 616, our emphasis).

Similar sentiments were expressed by Oxford's earlier Franks Commission of Inquiry. What we have to assess is whether these two fundamental requirements can indeed be easily reconciled. Is it not possible that in order to increase the effectiveness of its machinery of government, Cambridge may have to become less of a self-governing community of scholars, or at least interpret the meaning of that idea in a very different manner? We already know how the Franks Commission proposed to reform Oxford's statutes, which of its proposals were adopted – and perhaps more significantly which were not adopted – and the impact of the changes upon the university's machinery of government. Was Oxford changed fundamentally?

As collegiate universities, it is impossible to understand how Oxford and Cambridge function without considering the interaction of the universities and their respective colleges. However, as institutions with their own charters and statutes, the colleges have separate legal identities. What we wish to analyse in this chapter is the government of the two universities. But the statutes do prescribe the financial relationship between the universities and

their colleges and it would be reasonable to interpret parliamentary intervention in the late nineteenth and early twentieth centuries as directed primarily
at changing the balance of power between both the resident and non-resident
members of the universities, and between the colleges and the universities.
The means of achieving the latter goal was to redirect resources from
the colleges to the universities, the terms of exchange were laid down in the
statutes. These are matters that will be taken up in our discussion of the
recurrent incomes of the universities and colleges. None the less, there are a
number of statutes of both universities which link in various ways university
institutions to the colleges. The most notable example is the office of vice-
Chancellor, which until very recently was restricted to college heads at
Cambridge and was so restricted at Oxford until the implementation of the
Franks reforms (the office is now confined to members of Congregation).
Although there are institutional ties between the universities and their colleges, and a few of these are defined by statute, the major ties are inevitably
informal. The universities and their colleges form an integrated social network and the holders of key posts in the colleges are, or have been or will be,
those who hold offices of responsibility in the universities. The Oxbridge don,
therefore, wears a college as well as a university hat, and this transcends any
formal ties laid down in the statutes.

Since 1926, with the implementation of the recommendations of the
Asquith Commission, the resident members of the Universities of Oxford and
Cambridge (i.e. those listed as members of Congregation and the Regent
House respectively) have had – subject only to the ultimate sanction of
Parliament – the authority to amend their statutes. In this sense, the univer-
sities have been more in control of their own affairs and it is interesting to
note that the very substantial changes to the University of Oxford's statutes
recommended by the Franks Commission were not discussed by Parliament,
neither in the Commons nor the Lords. Neither have the current reforms to
Cambridge's machinery stimulated much interest outside of the university.
At the time of writing, no outsider has looked through the evidence to the
Wass Syndicate other than ourselves. On the one hand, the universities may
feel more comfortable that their statutes are not a matter for wider debate
but, on the other hand, such silence is a reflection of their decline as an
important national institution, or perhaps that they have become a different
kind of national institution.

The core statutes of the Universities of Oxford and Cambridge, known as
Queen-in-Council statutes, still require the approval of the Privy Council
before they can be changed. In this sense, there remains state control of the
process of statutory change. But it is not a particularly effective instrument
with which to beat the universities, as the initiative for such change invariably comes from within the universities themselves. It is possible, as in the
past, to create a royal commission and appoint statutory commissioners to
act on its proposals. But this is to suggest a degree of malaise that no longer
exists and, moreover, it is not a route that can be pursued too frequently.
The state requires fine-tuning mechanisms to regulate its relations to the

universities, whereas statutory change that flows from the recommendations of a royal commission is blunter intervention – necessary at times but to be used very sparingly. However, the fact that important internally promoted changes require parliamentary sanction means that the potential for action is there. Furthermore, the creation by the 1988 Education Reform Act of statutory commissioners who have the responsibility for rewriting those university statutes that protect academic tenure, demonstrates the state's ability to act rather than wait upon events. But the central purpose of this chapter is not to explore how the state has used its ultimate control of statutory change to reshape the characters of Oxford and Cambridge, but rather to explore the values upon which their processes of government have been constructed while recognizing the external pressures that both universities have experienced when reshaping the ways in which they have chosen to govern themselves.

Interpreting the systems of government

In an historical note that serves as an introduction to its statutes, the University of Cambridge proclaims that:

> The University is a common law corporation, being a corporation by prescription consisting of a Chancellor, Masters, and Scholars who from time out of mind have had the government of their members and enjoyed the privileges of such a corporation (University of Cambridge 1988d: xv).

The most persistent and powerful part of the Oxbridge belief system is that the two universities are self-governing communities of scholars. The institutional base for donnish domination is the Regent House at Cambridge and Congregation at Oxford. However, it is only since the implementation of the recommendations of the Asquith Commission that self-government has meant that sovereignty rests with the resident members of the universities. Prior to the statutory changes of 1926, the sovereign bodies were the Senate at Cambridge and Convocation at Oxford, both dominated by the non-resident members of the universities. The belief system may have persisted from 'time out of mind', but this has not prevented radical shifts in the relative influence upon the government of the universities of their various categories of members.

But in what sense are the Regent House and Congregation sovereign bodies? The statutes of the University of Oxford state unequivocally that 'Congregation shall be the legislative body of the University' (University of Oxford 1989a: Title 11, Sect. 1.1). But the statutes proceed to prescribe very tightly the way in which that legislative function can be exercised and Congregation cannot be said to possess an exclusive right to speak on behalf of the university. In an observation on his Inquiry's Report, Lord Franks noted that 'there was a large field in which the decisions of Council were not put to Congregation, and another large field where they *were* put, in order that they might be legalised' (Franks 1986: 3–4). It was possible for the Hebdomadal Council to speak on behalf of the University of Oxford without the prior approval of Congregation and even when Congregation's approval was sought it could be simply for the sake of appearances.

Circumstances are more equivocal at Cambridge as its statutes do not define the Regent House as the university's legislature in explicit terms. However, the statutes do state that:

> Whenever it is provided that an act or thing shall or may be done or determined by the University, it shall be done or determined by Grace of the Regent House (subject to the provisions hereinafter contained) unless it is expressly stated that it is to be done or determined otherwise (University of Cambridge 1988d: Statute A, Ch. 111.9).

Interpreted literally, unless there is statutory blessing to the contrary, nothing can be done officially in the name of the University of Cambridge unless it is 'determined by Grace of the Regent House', which has led some to claim that the Regent House has both legislative *and* executive powers (Edwards 1981: 4). Be this as it may, the key legislative function of both Congregation and the Regent House is their control of statutory change and it is this particular authority which persuades us that they are sovereign bodies. In each case the point is made in terse, direct language:

> The functions, powers and duties of Congregation shall be: (a) to decide upon proposals submitted to it by Council for amending, repealing, or adding to the statutes (University of Oxford 1989a: Title 11, Sect. 1.2(a)).

and:

> Any power of making, altering or repealing Statutes which is assigned to the University ... shall be exercised by the Regent House by Grace subject to the provisions hereinafter contained (University of Cambridge 1988d: Statute A, Ch. 111.7).

Put simply, the Regent House and Congregation are the guardians of the constitutions of their universities. Other university institutions may have been required, and may still be required, to act contrary to both the spirit and letter of the statutes if the university is to function effectively, but they lack the authority to legitimate that behaviour. It may be deemed necessary to act in such a fashion, but strictly speaking it is unconstitutional, and if it is necessary to change university statutes, then the Regent House or Congregation have to be persuaded. Thus the Report of the Franks Commission was *not* implemented in full at Oxford and the same fate may well befall parts of the Report of the Wass Syndicate at Cambridge.

Although Congregation and the Regent House are sovereign bodies in the

sense that they have to approve of statutory change, the control of that process is not their sole prerogative as the initiative for innovation originates
elsewhere. At Oxford it is the Hebdomadal Council that submits proposals to
Congregation 'for amending, repealing or adding to the statutes', while at
Cambridge the same responsibility rests with the Council of Senate: 'No
Grace shall be submitted to the Regent House unless its submission has been
sanctioned by the Council' (University of Cambridge 1988d: Statute A, Ch.
111.14). Incidentally, it is this absolute inability of the Regent House to
control its own agenda that makes it quite inappropriate to describe it as an
executive body. There is a historical mystery here as some evidence to the
Asquith Commission (A Memorandum by the Committee of Younger Cambridge Graduates) recommended that a reconstituted Senate (remember that
at that time this was the sovereign body) should have the right to propose
statutory amendments (Royal Commission on Oxford and Cambridge Universities 1922b: App. 1). Significantly, this was supported in the Report of
the Commission (Royal Commission on Oxford and Cambridge Universities
1922a: 64–5), but not implemented by the statutory commissioners.
Obviously, there was a powerful body of opinion within Cambridge that was
opposed to it and which succeeded in swaying the commissioners.

The procedures of Oxford's Congregation require that proposed statutory
change be handled in a very precise fashion. The overall process is marked
by the need to inform the registrar of intentions, to work within set time
periods, to gain minimal levels of support from members of Congregation,
and to publish notices in the University's *Gazette*. Even the actual passage
occurs in stages: votes on a preamble to the statute which deals with principles and then the consideration of amendments. Although careful procedure
may always be advisable, the present detail suggests a keen desire to avoid
the unexpected, to rule out the influence of mavericks, and above all to ensure
that the will of the Hebdomadal Council eventually prevails. If Council does
not get its way in Congregation, then it actually has the right to call for a
postal vote (University of Oxford 1989a: Title 11, Sect. X.1(a)).

No matter how severely the sovereignty of Congregation may be prescribed, it is none the less an ongoing institution that has a central part to
play within Oxford's system of government. The same cannot be said of
Cambridge's Regent House. The members of the Regent House are sovereign
in the sense in which we have used that term, but they exercise that power as
individuals rather than within an institutional context known as the Regent
House. Should the Regent House meet to consider a Grace (which would be
known as a Congregation of the Regent House), then similar procedures that
govern the conduct of business in Oxford's Congregation would come into
play. However, not only does the Council of Senate control the submission of
Graces to the Regent House, but it can also determine 'that a vote shall be
taken upon it by ballot' (University of Cambridge 1988d: Ordinances,
Ch. 1.3(b)). And this is precisely what happens. Except for the essentially
ceremonial function of awarding degrees, the Regent House as such never
meets and is thus defunct as a serious instrument of university government.

Such developments persuaded some Cambridge dons that Cambridge's democratic heritage was in terminal decline.

This is not to say that the members of the Regent House cannot meet to discuss university business. The ordinances on the Conduct of Business state that:

> The Council have agreed to continue the arrangement whereby if the Registrary receives a request that a topic of concern to the University should be brought forward he will, provided that the request is supported by not less than three members of the Regent House, ask the Council to include it among matters for consideration at an early Discussion' (University of Cambridge 1988d: Ordinances, Ch. 1: Discussions, Fly-Sheets and Ballots, Notice 1).

In other words, it is Council that formally initiates discussions and it should be remembered that when a meeting for a discussion takes place it is not a gathering of the Regent House as such and certainly motions are not put to the vote. Moreover, to describe such occasions as 'discussions' is misleading, for the participants recite set speeches rather than engage in debate.

Curiously, although the Wass Syndicate recognized that one of the reasons for its own creation was the feeling within the University of Cambridge that 'the democratic rights of members of the Regent House had been eroded over the years by encroachment of the central bodies and that this process ought to be reversed' (University of Cambridge 1989a: 619), there is no consideration in its report as to whether the Regent House needs to assume an institutional form. The Syndicate's report argues that the power to make and amend statutes should remain with the Regent House while its other powers – to enact ordinances, to issue orders and to take executive action – should be shared with the central bodies (ibid.: 621). In effect, the Wass Syndicate would represent another stage in the erosion of the authority of the Regent House should its recommendations be adopted. In return for its loss of authority, it is proposed that the Regent House be given the opportunity to discuss and vote on an annual report made by Council on behalf of the central bodies. Supposedly, the Regent House would thus act as 'the final arbiter of University policy' (ibid.: 622). Inevitably, the Regent House would be deciding on policies formulated elsewhere and invariably passing judgement only after the implementation stage was well advanced, or even completed. The Regent House would relinquish specified authority for the dubious right to make *post facto* judgements. Perhaps this is the route the university has to travel but, other than reaffirming the Regent House's responsibility for statutory change, the proposals scarcely represent the reaffirmation of donnish domination, although – as we will discuss – they have been amended in a manner that requires more equivocal evaluation.

Seizing on the rightful claim of Oxford's Congregation to be regarded as the university's sovereign body, the eminent Oxford sociologist A.H. Halsey has written:

> ... the key to understanding internal power in Oxford is to recognize that this pluralistic assembly of scholars is organized essentially along syndicalist lines. In simple constitutional terms, Congregation rules. The Hebdomadal Council or the General Board may propose, but the demos of the assembled dons disposes. It can, and does, say *non placet* to the wishes of those it has elected to the formal heights of university authority. The central university bodies may thus justly if satirically be described as 'the executive committee of the collegiate class'. The public life of Oxford is quietly led and controlled by the private life of its colleges (Halsey 1984: 14).

But this is to confuse sovereignty and power. As we have shown, the constitutional terms that govern Congregation are far from simple and, moreover, as the Franks Commission clearly demonstrated, it is vital to be aware of the almost inevitable gap between statutory edicts and current political realities. Furthermore, neither Congregation nor the Regent House control completely the election of those who occupy 'the formal heights of university authority'. Indeed, not all the key personnel are elected! It is important to stress, however, that although self-government in the pristine form that he understands it may be purely a figment of Halsey's fertile imagination, both the Universities of Oxford and Cambridge may claim, and justly so, that they remain in control of their own governmental machinery. Congregation and the Regent House both retain considerable power however much it has been eroded in recent decades, and it is true that they can on occasions vote *non placet*, although it is equally true that this is the exception rather than the rule. What constrains the real controllers of executive authority is the *potential* power of Congregation and the Regent House. It is wise to tread warily to avoid unleashing a storm. Finally, the fact that sovereignty rather than control of the day-to-day decision-making process is the prerogative of Congregation and the Regent House may signify no more than a redefinition of the idea of self-government. One, so the realists would argue, more in tune with contemporary realities. Thus change apparently protects the core values of the past.

For 'the demos of the assembled dons' to dispose it is necessary for them to ensure that their rivals for power are kept at bay. Central to the value system on which Oxbridge's machinery of government is based is the exclusion of lay persons, university officials and students from the decision-making process. While lay persons and students in this model occupy marginal positions within the machinery of government, university officials do no more than proffer the advice upon which others (i.e. the dons) make the decisions. We have excluded students from our discussion of the rivals to donnish domination because their challenge has been historically specific and appears to have been resolved, if not to the satisfaction of all parties, then in a fashion that has led to a long period of student quiescence on these issues. In essence, students have been accorded a measure of representation on many committees at all British universities, but they have been excluded from the real centres of power. The questions of lay representation and the functions of university officers are not only recurring twentieth-century themes, but they also have considerable contemporary relevance.

The exclusion of lay persons from the machinery of government is well-established and appears, at least within the two universities, not to be a matter for discussion. Although the Asquith Commission had been advised that non-university representatives should sit on the universities' governing bodies, this advice was rejected:

> Our conclusion is that it would be inadvisable to adopt the proposal, and that the presence of such representatives would hamper the Council [the Commission's Report is referring specifically to Oxford's Hebdomadal Council] in its work without securing as a rule any compensating advantages (Royal Commission on Oxford and Cambridge Universities 1922a: 73).

And that appears to be the end of the matter. Lord Robbins very pointedly brought the question of lay representation to the attention of the Franks Inquiry (University of Oxford 1965: Pt 11) but the report itself makes scant comment. The report of the Wass Syndicate, while recognizing the important contribution that lay opinion makes to decision making in the civic universities, rejected its inclusion in Cambridge's main executive authority the Council of Senate and significantly did so in terms of the need to preserve the established ideology: 'We believe that it is important to preserve the traditional character of Cambridge as a self-governing community of scholars; self-government demands self-discipline, and this is an ideal we do not wish to undermine' (University of Cambridge 1989a: 626). However, the report does recommend the creation of an advisory body, to be called the Consultative Committee, on which there would be lay representation. It comes across as a talking shop for distinguished persons and it is difficult to conceive that it will have a serious input into the decision-making process. Whether Oxford and Cambridge can continue to resist lay representation in the government of their universities remains to be seen, but to date they have been spectacularly successful.

If there is one issue that unites Oxbridge dons it is the assertion that is they who should make policy while the function of university officials is to act as their obedient servants. In its evidence to the Franks Commission, Merton College made the point succinctly: 'Education in general and university education par excellence are worlds in which the administrator should be kept in his place' (University of Oxford 1965: Pt 13). Although the sentiment may still be widely shared by the dons of both universities, there is undoubtedly also a widespread fear that they may be losing their grip on policy making as the officials slowly usurp their authority. Traditionally, both Oxford and Cambridge have been parsimonious in their use of officials and there is also a tradition that some of the key administrative posts are always held by former academics. At Cambridge, for example, the secretary general of the faculties is by custom a former academic, which may in part account for the post's much greater authority than Oxford's equivalent, that is the secretary of the faculties. The key university officers are as follows:

Oxford	Cambridge
The registrar, secretary of Congregation and of the Hebdomadal Council	The registrary, secretary of the Council of Senate
Secretary of the Chest, secretary of the Curators of the University	The treasurer, secretary of the Financial Board
Secretary of the faculties, secretary of the General Board of the Faculties	The secretary general of the faculties, secretary of the General Board of the Faculties

Besides being secretaries of the central university bodies, these key university officers are also secretaries of the most important committees they spawn. Stated simply, the post of secretary means that its holder is not a member of the committee and has no voting rights. It is not unknown for this formal position to be subverted, but clearly the statutes are designed to make the distinction between those who belong to the committees and those who service them. Officials will offer their advice if requested and some would offer it in any case if they felt the need to intervene. Naturally, the weight their advice carries will depend on the strength of the personalities involved and their experience.

The relationship between the offices of vice-chancellor and the registrar(y) is probably the most interesting example of the interaction between 'administrative' and 'policy-making' institutions. The statutes of the University of Oxford relate the two offices as follows:

> The Registrar shall, under the Vice-Chancellor, be the head of the central administrative services of the University, and shall have such functions and powers as are or shall be assigned to him by the statutes or by the Vice-Chancellor.... Under the direction of the Vice-Chancellor he shall be responsible for communications which express the general policy of the University, and shall conduct correspondence with public bodies (University of Oxford 1989a: Title 1X, Sect. V11.1).

Cambridge's statutes do not spell out the relationship, although it is likely to be understood in similar terms since, as at Oxford, the registrary is secretary to the Council of Senate and the vice-chancellor its chairman. As the vice-chancellor holds office for only a short period of time (currently 4 years at Oxford and until recently only 2 at Cambridge), both universities are more reliant upon their officials for policy continuity than if the vice-chancellor were a permanent appointment. However, vice-chancellors do not spring from nowhere, but are drawn from those who have been long-serving members of the policy-making circles within the two universities.

Just as it is difficult to be categorical about the relationship between ministers and civil servants, so it is impossible to say with any degree of certainty that university officials are encroaching upon the territory that belongs to the formal policy makers. Various internal committees of enquiry have argued for more and better administrative support within the two universities, but few have spelt out the potential consequences. The Franks Commission (University of Oxford 1966a: 241) did not envisage any significant dangers in such developments and saw the risks as more than compensated for by the enhanced effectiveness of the University of Oxford. In a personal reminiscence, Lord Bullock, a former Oxford vice chancellor, confirmed the close rapport between the offices of vice-chancellor and registrar. While the university business for which they were both responsible generated a great deal of personal contact, he had seen the two roles as clearly differentiated and was happy to testify that this was understood by the officials. Interestingly, he had found it difficult to perceive them as university officers, preferring to see them as friends who were part of a team that helped the university to remain a self-governing institution (Bullock 1986: 9–10).

But it would be unwise for the dons to be too blasé. Besides the rotation of the vice-chancellor's office, it has to be remembered that his officials are the registrar(y)'s officials. Recent developments have forced the universities to operate with declining recurrent incomes and to produce detailed academic plans that incorporate the concomitant financial forecasts. The decision-making process is ever more dependent upon the generation of information, the construction of alternative scenarios, and forward planning. These are the functions of officialdom and only those few dons, either in policy-making positions or motivated mavericks, are likely to have their noses sufficiently close to the ground to be able to follow the scent.

It is likely that a protracted period of working together has brought about a measure of trust between senior officials and that cadre of dons who occupy the key roles and fill the most influential committees. The parties may know, à la Bullock, what their respective positions are, but this is so deeply ingrained in the nature of things that they rarely need to think about it. In other words, it is an issue that bothers them considerably less than outsiders. Even if this is true now, that it was not always so is evident from the fascinating evidence that the Revd H.E.D. Blakiston, a former vice-chancellor of Oxford, gave to the Asquith Commission. Blakiston revealed his suspicion that permanent officials could usurp the authority of the vice-chancellor, raised objections to giving the vice-chancellor an office that would be closely linked to the registrar, and implied that the vice-chancellor needed only clerical help for filing and indexes purposes (Royal Commission on Oxford and Cambridge Universities 1922b: App. 1). Fortunately for the University of Oxford, present-day vice-chancellors appear to work harmoniously with their staffs but whether Blakiston's deep-seated fear has been realized or not is another matter.

If university government is to be controlled by the dons, then how are they to exercise their authority? There are four traditional principles: that university business is best managed by committees; that committees should represent all the interested parties; that co-ordination of committee activity can be achieved by overlapping membership; and that there should be a steady turnover of office holders. The purpose of these methods of government is to build consensus out of the range of inputs into the policy-making process. It is not surprising that the Universities of Oxford and Cambridge generate committees, for this is a characteristic of all large institutions and there are particular pressures within universities – that is, all universities – which have reinforced that expectation. Government by committees means orderly procedures, carefully weighted judgements, broad consultation and slow-moving machinery. These are decision-making qualities that are consistent with an academic culture that emphasizes involvement and rationality; a tradition reinforced by the fact that until comparatively recently the universities had experienced a stable and generally supportive external environment. In effect, the universities have been able to afford government by committee.

Whereas it is almost axiomatic that Oxford and Cambridge will function through committees, this has not prevented considerable discussion of how broadly representative those committees should be. Most of the debate at each of the two universities has centred upon the organization of teaching and research in the various faculties and departments, culminating in the General Board of Faculties. We will return to the issue again when we consider how the universities have organized their academic activities, but the point of contention is straightforward enough. If the academic bodies represent all their various interested parties, what chance is there of decisions that do little more than divide the spoils? Evidence to the Asquith Commission suggested that this was the established *modus operandi* of both universities' general boards from the very start. Of Oxford's General Board, the Revd Blakiston observed that, 'Its members were often inclined to abstain from voting. It was too large a body to deal with finance, and its administration of the Faculty Fund of £7,100 annually was haphazard and unsatisfactory' (Royal Commission on Oxford and Cambridge Universities 1922b: App.1). His Cambridge equivalent, Dr P. Giles, was marginally more flattering: whereas he felt that his university's general board had become more effective over the past 20 years, none the less it remained 'too large and unwieldy a body and was incapable of exercising a really effective control of the teaching and educational policy' (ibid.).

The key issue has always been the size and composition of the General Boards. At Cambridge, of the 13 members of the General Board, 8 are elected by the faculties, i.e. 2 members for each of the four groups of faculties. Of Oxford's 21 members, 16 are elected from the members of two groups of faculties, 8 representing 'humanities and social studies' and 8 'science and mathematics'. However, the potential brake on effective action, suggested by the very size of Oxford's General Board, did not prevent the Board itself from offering a positive interpretation of its functions in its evidence to the Franks Commission:

> More specifically, the board considers that it does not require any extension of the *powers* it now has ... and believes that its *composition* as

now revised is satisfactorily arranged to enable it to play a proper part in the formulation and in the execution of policy. It is true that in present circumstances it may on occasion find itself ... immersed in details at the expense of more general questions. But this is not necessarily a bad thing: the making of policy is a function which is perhaps better discharged by a body intimately in touch with the things and persons whom policy affects (and hence involved in details) than by one which operates *de haut en bas* in isolation from the trivial particularities of the daily task (University of Oxford 1965: Pt 12).

The Franks Inquiry was less enamoured of the General Board's evident satisfaction with its own performance. It clearly expected it to take a more positive role and to this end proposed that the General Board should be a smaller body of 14 members of whom 10 would be elected by five new large faculty groupings (University of Oxford 1966a: 248). In fact, this was one of the inquiry's recommendations that was not adopted by the university, although the General Board is now undoubtedly a more effective body thanks to the innovation of a full-time vice-chairman (who since 1989 has had the title of chairman), one of the commission's proposed changes that was implemented. Of course, the new financial context which has necessitated a greater measure of academic planning has also changed the situation dramatically.

Cambridge's approach to the alleged ineffectiveness of its General Board has been somewhat different from Oxford's. It has opted for the less politically sensitive strategy of delegating responsibility from the General Board to the faculties, as opposed to tackling the question of faculty representation on the General Board. Of course, these are not mutually exclusive approaches, but rather the question is where the emphasis is to be placed. As long ago as 1967, in a report on 'The Administrative Organization of the University', we read:

> We believe that one of the most likely ways in which to bring about an improvement will be by greater use of delegated powers. The volume of business with which the General Board now deals must be reduced, whether by delegation to Faculty Boards or other University bodies, or by delegation to Committees of the General Board itself, with authority to take decisions within specified fields (University of Cambridge 1967b: 345).

The report followed this up by suggesting that the General Board's administrative staff should service the bodies to which authority was delegated and that the chairmen of the Councils of the Schools (the various academic units are divided into four schools, although not all four share this label) should serve on the General Board. The intention was to create a more integrated administrative structure and an overlapping political one. Like so many of the Cambridge attempts to reform itself, the Grave Report, as it is known, produced few tangible results. However, the notion of delegated authority is central to the recommendations of the Wass Report which are under current consideration. Time alone will decide its fate.

If power is to be shared among a range of committees that are broadly representative of each university's interested parties, then the next question is how committee activity is to be co-ordinated. At what point does the diffusion of authority give way to chaos? The traditional explanation is that the overlapping members of the key decision-making bodies act as the channels of communication. They provide the glue that cements the fragmented model. As the Franks Commission recognized, without a formal institutional hierarchy, personal contacts were integral to the process of Oxford's government (University of Oxford 1966a: 203–4). The statutes of both universities continue to encourage the building of alliances across committees through their overlapping members. Thus at Cambridge at least, three members of Council (that is including the vice-chancellor) have to be members of the General Board and of the Financial Board (University of Cambridge 1988d: Statute C, Ch. 1V.8(c) and Statute F, Ch. 1.1(d)). But the statutes tell only part of the story. If the overlapping members are to perform their role effectively, then they have to be trusted members of the machinery of government, which means they are almost certainly persons of high repute who have been accustomed to exercising authority. The delicate task of co-ordination cannot be left either to the inexperienced or those with questionable reputations. Moreover, it is exceedingly helpful if all those who belong to the communication network possess common sociocultural reference points. For example, the inclusion of lay members within the machinery of government – unless well-impregnated with the Oxbridge cultural style – would slow down communication. Similarly, if a separate administrative identity were to develop, in conjunction with an increased reliance upon administrative expertise for effective decision making, then again committee co-ordination would need something more than the overlappers. Undoubtedly in such circumstances, the officials would be the real co-ordinators.

Except for the officials, all the important holders of policy-making positions within the Universities of Oxford and Cambridge – and remember officials are not supposed to be policy makers – occupy their posts for limited periods of time. There is powerful support within the statutes for the rotation of offices, as if the business of government was best left to the gifted amateur. Undoubtedly, the best example of this is the vice-chancellor's office, a post which at other British universities is invariably a permanent appointment. Prior to the Wass Report, the post at Cambridge was held for 2 years. As a former Cambridge registrary remarked in his evidence to the Franks Commission: 'Since 1923 the Council have made their nominations in such a way as to enable the same head (that is head of college) to be elected as Vice-Chancellor for two consecutive years but for no longer' (University of Oxford 1965: Pt 11). At Oxford a committee 'shall propose a name for Congregation for appointment as Vice-Chancellor' and 'unless it is rejected with at least seventy-five members voting in favour of rejection' this person serves for 4 years (University of Oxford 1989a: Title 1X, Sect. 111.7(a) and (c)). All the central bodies incorporate the same principle with members in office for varying lengths of time, usually ineligible for immediate re-election, and with a percentage of them standing down at fixed intervals.

In a collegiate university it may make sense to restrict the vice-chancellor's office to college heads – although the current Oxford vice-chancellor is not a college head! – and to ensure that the post is rotated. Likewise, there is nothing surprising about rotating the membership of the central decision-making bodies. Indeed, this is common practice in many British universities. If the intention is to spread participation in the decision-making process, and to prevent the concentration of authority in the same few hands, then the circulation of offices is an obvious procedural device to employ. But it is a device which implies that a wide range of dons are both interested in, and capable of, participating constructively in the governmental process. Thus the purpose appears to be to give further substance to the idea of the Universities of Oxford and Cambridge as self-governing institutions.

It would be instructive to follow the career lines of the most prominent university decision makers. Although there is a statutory imposed rotation of offices, we have the clear impression that the top posts are passed around a comparatively small number of persons, that is small in relation to the actual size of the pool of eligible candidates. Some persons exclude themselves from university government, despite the expectation of involvement, while others have to demonstrate their suitability before they can join the inner circle. In terms of the vice-chancellor's office the inner circle used to be confined to the college heads which gave it a very precise boundary. Generally speaking, the boundaries are defined more informally: length of service on particular committees, an established reputation for past performance, and knowing those who also count. Again such behaviour is to be expected in large and complex institutions. Few of us are prepared to give authority to unknown persons and once a 'celebrity' status has been established it has a momentum which opens up further possibilities either in university or college government, or indeed both. The career of the recently deceased T.C. Nicholas is instructive. Described in *The Times* obituary as a 'geologist and servant of Cambridge', in his long career Nicholas administered the Sedgwick Museum, was Senior Bursar at Trinity College for 27 years, was Assistant Secretary to the Statutory Commissioners who drafted the 1926 Statutes, was chairman for over a decade of the Faculty Board of Geography and Geology, served for some years on the Council of the Senate, and was a long-term member of the Financial Board (*The Times*, 16 November 1989).

If we are correct about the presence at both universities of an inner cadre of almost perpetual office holders, then this would suggest a significant challenge to the popular insider's view, strongly reiterated by Halsey, of grass-roots donnish control of policy making. We may still think of the universities as self-governing institutions, but it would become more difficult to think of them as under the sway of popular sovereignty. This possible concentration of authority may help to explain the generally relaxed attitude of contemporary Oxford towards its officials in comparison to the evident suspicion of the former vice-chancellor, the Revd Blakiston. Blakiston clearly had had little experience of officialdom, and university administration was in its infancy when he was vice-chancellor. Nowadays the key university policy makers have been at the centre of power for long periods of time, continuously interacting with the officials. They are indeed, to use Bullock's phrase, 'old friends'. It is more likely to be the mavericks and/or those excluded from the charmed circle who manifest the greatest suspicions of the bureaucracy.

Regardless of what the contemporary realities as to the distribution of authority may be, it is our contention that the traditional value system – manifested in the procedures it sanctions – aims to maximize consensus building within the two universities. This is especially so should proposed policies require new statutes, that is the universities are changing formally their established structures or procedures. It is more accurate, therefore, to argue that rather than maximizing democracy, the primary purpose of the machinery of government is to maximize consensus. Lord Annan, one-time Provost of Cambridge's King's College, was so disenchanted with the extent to which both Oxford and Cambridge took the consensus building process, that he was moved to remark in his evidence to the Franks Commission that they proceeded at the pace of their most recalcitrant members (University of Oxford 1965: Pt 11). Annan, in order to make his point forcefully, is probably allowing the trials and tribulations he experienced as a would-be Cambridge reformer to run away with him. None the less, it is still possible for very small minorities, especially if they are well-organized, to thwart the reformers.

No matter how far the established procedures enhance consensus building, invariably there will always be a number of individuals who are opposed to a proposed course of action and they do have the means of forcing a vote of the Regent House at Cambridge or taking the matter to Congregation at Oxford. Once this happens, then the outcome is far from a foregone conclusion, for there is no party discipline in the universities. However, if the consensus building process has worked effectively, then initiatives proposed by the central bodies should carry the day, albeit perhaps later than they would have liked. The ability of Oxford to undertake a substantial revision of its statutes following on from the Franks Commission poses the problem of why the reformers did not also carry the day at Cambridge. Certainly, Oxford's Franks Commission engaged in a more substantial review of the university's character than anything Cambridge has attempted, including the recent Wass Syndicate. However, it does appear that as the University of Cambridge acts on the recommendations of the Wass Report, so the government and administration of the two universities is again converging. Another way of looking at the matter is to say that they are simply different universities, and although – as we have argued – they have similar values, these are expressed through their own systems of government. It is also possible that past Cambridge reformers failed because of both the quality of their reports and the tactics they adopted to win over majority opinion within the university. In other words, did Annan take the easy option in his evidence to the Franks Commission by blaming recalcitrant elements within the demos?

A revamped machinery but the same principles?

There have been three main challenges to the consensual model of government that has prevailed at Oxford and Cambridge since 1926. The first challenge has stressed the need for stronger personal leadership and inevitably the office of vice-chancellor has been the focus of attention. The second has argued for a more coherent relationship of the central university bodies. The University of Oxford moved in both directions in the wake of the Franks Commission. The third challenge, which has achieved limited success at both universities (Cambridge more so than Oxford), has urged the devolution of the decision-making process so that within prescribed boundaries decisions of the grass-roots units of government are either binding or need only the formal ratification of the appropriate central body to become university policy. Within this model, the central bodies set the parameters and then act essentially as rubber stamps.

Formally, the functions of the vice-chancellors of Oxford and Cambridge are remarkably similar. They are *ex-officio* chairmen of all the committees and bodies of which they are members. They have the right to delegate their chairmanships although the statutes of the University of Cambridge expect that 'the Vice-Chancellor shall in general himself take the chair at the meetings of the Council, the General Board and the Financial Board' (University of Cambridge 1988d: Statute D, Ch. 111.6(b)). Despite the similarities in their official duties, there are two key differences between the offices: Oxford's is a 4-year appointment while until the present incumbent, Cambridge's served for only 2 years, and continued to fulfil important college duties. The Report of the Wass Syndicate strongly recommended that Cambridge should enhance the vice-chancellor's office:

> These considerations lead us to the firm conclusion that the Vice-Chancellorship should in future be a full-time post and that the holder should not combine the office with any other University or College duties. They also lead us to the view that the Vice-Chancellor should spend considerably more than two years in the post; our considered opinion is that he or she should be appointed for five years with the possibility of extension for a further two years (University of Cambridge 1989a: 635).

The intention was to move the Cambridge model closer to that adopted by Oxford some 20 years ago. The Wass Syndicate made it very clear why it felt that this was necessary. Arguing in almost identical terms to the Franks Commission, the Syndicate saw the vice-chancellor as providing the university with a strong sense of purpose, keeping a finger on the pulse of university government, and representing the interests of the university in influential circles (ibid.). The vice-chancellor's office should be the flagship of the university, and its central figure – so the Wass Syndicate maintained – needed to have very special qualities: 'proven administrative ability, experience of management, diplomatic and political skills ... and a substantial academic record' (ibid.). The Regent House acted on the Syndicate's recommendation by approving a 5-year period of tenure, renewable for a further 2 years (University of Cambridge 1991a: 285). It is an open question whether persons possessing such imposing qualities really exist, and even more problematic whether they can be persuaded to become the university's vice-chancellor.

The leadership of the vice-chancellor should not be seen as solely dependent upon his personal action. Long before the Franks Commission, Oxford's vice-chancellors had started to think of ways of co-ordinating more effectively the university's administrative structure within the vice-chancellor's office. In his very revealing evidence to the Commission, Sir Douglas Veale claimed that, prior to the 1930s, there was no strategy guiding appointments:

> The Vice-Chancellor normally presided in person in Council, the General Board, the Chest, the Visitorial Board and the Bodleian. Of most other bodies it could be said that the chairman of each was some member who happened to be interested in the subject matter and was willing to take it on (University of Oxford 1965: Pt 13).

But this haphazard approach was to change:

> It was not until 1931 that the Vice-Chancellor began to be selective in his choice of chairmen, and all such bodies were made to send their agenda and circulated papers to the Registrar, as laid down by Statute. This was the first real attempt to secure direct communication between those bodies and the central administration (ibid.).

One can only guess at the extent of Veale's pivotal role in rationalizing this administrative structure, but it was evidently substantial.

Besides recommending the extension of the vice-chancellor's term of office, the Franks Commission wanted to formalize the office's central role in the administrative hierarchy and the policy-making process. On the recommendation of the commission, the university established a General Purposes Committee to '... advise the Vice-Chancellor and Council on such matters as shall be referred to it by the Vice-Chancellor or by Council' (University of Oxford 1989a: Decrees and Regulations, Ch. 11, Sect. 1.1). The Franks Commission had seen the General Purposes Committee as a small think-thank, composed of very senior members of the university whose function was to chart the general, long-term policy direction of Oxford (University of Oxford 1966a: 226). In parallel fashion, Cambridge has established the Vice-Chancellor's Advisory Group. While the Wass Syndicate has proposed that this group should be retained, it has also argued that 'this body should not be seen as an executive body' but rather as one 'in which the Vice-

Chancellor can share some of the burdens of the office with an informal group of senior members of the University' (University of Cambridge 1989a: 636). The Wass Syndicate sees the Council of Senate as the university's indisputable executive body and that this should not be muddied by the presence of other potential contenders.

Although the stress on quality leadership can be seen most clearly in relation to the vice-chancellor's role, the Franks Commission sought to upgrade the performance of Oxford's General Board by providing it with a fulltime vice-chairman. Although rejecting the commission's proposals for the reorganization of the faculties, the General Board now has its chairman who serves full-time for 2 years. There is widespread agreement within Oxford that this has helped to increase the effectiveness of the General Board. Indeed, some would argue that at both universities the General Boards are more important than the Hebdomadal Council (Oxford) or the Council of Senate (Cambridge), which in statutory terms may be more potent bodies. It is true that many of the vice-chancellor's duties are either ceremonial or arise out of rather trivial historical obligations, while the General Boards have overall responsibility for the universities' central function, that is the organization of teaching and research. However, the vice-chancellors are the key link between their two universities and the outside world. Given the greater external financial and administrative pressures, the profile of the vice-chancellors and their respective Councils has increased. They are responsible for spelling out the universities' policy positions while their officials in the registrar(y)'s office reply to the never-ending demands for more university forward planning.

The external pressures have made the central bodies, along with their leading figures, more prominent in the government of both Oxford and Cambridge. Whereas vice-chancellors have to deal with a more intrusive environment, so much of the academic planning – in the recent past more often than not a euphemism for the management of cuts in recurrent income – falls to the General Boards. As the bodies responsible for the largest slice of expenditure this was to be expected. In such circumstances, it is inevitable that Oxford's General Board would come into its own. The pressures have acted upon both universities in similar fashion, but because Oxford has developed more fully than Cambridge the notion of strong personal leadership, the responses to the changed environment have inevitably been different. Cambridge's vice-chancellor was not in a position to act like his Oxford counterpart and most certainly could give the lead to the General Board, that has been taken by Oxford's full-time chairman.

An equally critical difference between the Universities of Oxford and Cambridge is the extent to which they have reshaped the statutory relationships between their central bodies since 1926. Regardless of equivocations in the statutes, the Hebdomadal Council's own evidence to the Franks Commission reveals that it saw itself as Oxford's chief executive authority. It had come to act for the university in many matters 'not specifically reserved by statute' to the other bodies and, although it was sensitive to the constraints of Congregation, these had not 'inhibited the ability of the Vice-Chancellor and Council to speak and act for the University' (University of Oxford 1965: Pt 12). The task of the Franks Commission was to persuade the university that it needed statutes that reflected this changed reality.

The current statutes of the University of Oxford affirm the Hebdomadal Council's dominant executive position in unequivocal terms:

> Subject to the provision of the statutes, Council shall be responsible for the administration of the University and for the management of its finances and property, and shall have all the powers necessary for it to discharge these responsibilities (University of Oxford 1989a: Title 1V, Sect. 1.1).

In addition, Council has the authority to submit proposals to Congregation for amending, repealing or adding to the statutes, and can change decrees autonomously and order others to change regulations as long as the changes are not inconsistent with the statutes (ibid.: Title 1V, Sect. 1.3). Finally, in order to establish the Hebdomadal Council's ultimate control over the university's administrative structure, the Franks Commission had to end the formal independence of the Chest by making it a committee of Council. In reality, the Chest had become a committee of Council before the recommendations of the Franks Commission were implemented, although this was not reflected in the statutes.

In very interesting evidence to the Franks Commission, the then Secretary to the University Chest, H.H. Keen, argued vehemently that financial authority should be located in an independent body which had the right to exercise at least a quasi-veto over policy decisions which involved spending university income. He maintained that:

> It is absolutely basic, therefore, that the financial authority should be independent and should have an ultimate veto or quasi-veto. Situations can arise where financial considerations should be overridden by other considerations, but this should be only after delay for rediscussion and renewed weighing up of the financial risks and the alleged consequences so that these are accepted with eyes wide open. . . . It is vital in my view that the Chest should occupy this absolutely independent position and should be in a position to veto anything that it considers impossible or gravely imprudent. It could not occupy such a position as a committee of Council (University of Oxford 1965: Pt 14).

The power of the Chest had already been eroded by the creation of the Hebdomadal Council's Financial Questions Committee which had been established on the prodding of Sir Douglas Veale (Bullock 1986: *op.cit.* 21). Keen was to lose this further battle, for the Chest is now a committee of Council and the vice-chancellor is its chairman. All Keen gained was the token concession of the right of the secretary of the Chest to make his views known directly to the vice-chancellor and to Council on 'financial, professional and technical matters'.

The integration of Oxford's administrative machinery is complete in the sense that the secretaries to the Chest and to the General Board are both subordinate to the authority of the registrar, indeed are a part of his office. However, although the Chest no longer has an independent policy-making position, this does not apply to the General Board of the Faculties. The General Board remains a separate body from Council with whom it shares a number of committees, and while it has to work through Council for any approaches it needs to make to Congregation, it retains control of academic policy. What we have at Oxford, therefore, is an integrated administration and two interrelated policy-making processes, one looking inward at the direction of the university's academic goals with the other looking outward at Oxford's relations to state and society.

As far as the statutes were a meaningful guide, Cambridge – prior to the Wass Report – had more diffused administrative and policy-making structures than Oxford. Although the statutes placed both the registrary and the secretary general of the faculties 'under the direction of the Council' (*Statute* D, Chapter VII,1) there was no suggestion that the registrary was the superior official. The Council of the Senate had 'general responsibility for the administration of the University, and for the planning and management of its work' (*Statute* A, Chapter IV, 1) but the other central bodies were not formally under its auspices. It could oversee their activities but this gave Council little formal control over them. Significantly Cambridge's Financial Board retained the degree of independence that Keen had fought for on behalf of Oxford's Chest. It is reasonable to argue that pre-Wass the Cambridge statutes placed the university's executive authority ultimately in the hands of the Council of Senate but inevitably that authority was circumscribed as long as neither the Financial Board nor the General Board were formally subordinate bodies and there was no co-ordinated administrative structure. The steady implementation of the proposals of the Wass Report have pushed Cambridge's administrative and policy-making structures towards the model of government that emerged at Oxford after the Franks Inquiry.

At Oxford, the formal administrative structure is hierarchical and the links between the central bodies and their various committees are established by the registrar's staff located in Wellington Square. Oxford has been less afraid of its officials than Cambridge, which is not to say that there are fewer of them or that they are necessarily any more deferential. If the Oxford officials are organized hierarchically, at Cambridge the three central bodies formed an administrative plateau. In policy-making terms, the distinctions have been less sharp, although again Oxford's Hebdomadal Council has been a more potent body than Cambridge's Council of Senate. The Hebdomadal Council has absorbed the Chest, is under the chairmanship of a vice-chancellor who serves a 4-year term, and has stronger statutory support for its claim to be the university's executive. On all three points, it has the advantage – perhaps only temporarily – over Cambridge's Council of Senate.

Periodically, various parties within Cambridge have attempted to move the university in the same political and administrative direction as Oxford.

The 1967 Report on the Administrative Organization of the University recommended that:

> ... under the Regent House, the Council should become the principal policy-making and policy-deciding body of the University, and that the Financial Board and the General Board should have the status of Committees of the Council ... [and that] ... it would be an advantage, and would be logical, if the separate offices of the three central bodies were amalgamated into one office, under the Registrary as the chief permanent administrative officer of the University (University of Cambridge 1967b: 341).

Nothing could be clearer. But the advocacy was not persuasive and the model, both politically and administratively, took longer to change.

In recent years, the pressures to change the Cambridge model have intensified. On the one hand, some dons have claimed that the university's democratic traditions have been eroded over time and want changes that would restore them, while others have become convinced that the cumbersome administrative machinery has made it difficult for the university to respond swiftly and positively to the new external environment. Both pressures found expression in a Memorial that was issued on 5 November 1987 (University of Cambridge 1987: 158). As a direct consequence of that Memorial, the Wass Syndicate was appointed 'To Consider the Government of the University'. But, as the Wass Syndicate itself reveals, there is another pressure at work which makes the contemporary situation very different from that of the past. The universities were required by the UGC to review their administrative practices in the light of the Jarratt Report and Cambridge gave an essentially self-satisfied response which was rejected by the UGC. The Wass Report quotes the harsh UGC reaction to what it obviously viewed as Cambridge complacency:

> Cambridge has not yet adequately faced these issues [the Wass Report refers to the questions of leadership, co-ordination and strategic planning] and Cambridge's central bodies may not have the capacity to produce the strategic, academic, and financial plans that are essential in the current climate (University of Cambridge 1989a: 619).

Thus the UGC added its voice to the chorus favouring a review of the university's machinery of government.

There were a number of recommendations in the Wass Report on how Cambridge could better co-ordinate its administrative structure and allegedly improve the efficiency of its policy-making process which, have moved Cambridge closer to the Oxford model of government. The intention was to place the executive powers of the Regent House in the hands of the Council of Senate and to make it clear that Council is 'the principal policy-making body of the University'. The General Board and the Financial Board would be subordinate to Council, with the latter being little more than a committee of Council, as at Oxford (ibid.: 625). The registrary would be 'designated the principal administrative officer of the University' and he would be responsible for 'a single cadre of administrators' (ibid.: 633). Both the tone of the report, and its specific recommendations, demonstrate conclusively the particular pressures to which it was most responsive. Those within Cambridge, concerned to see the Regent House restored to its allegedly rightful place at the centre of the policy-making process, could be rueing their Memorial. However, they can take comfort in the fact that in December 1990 the Regent House, in the process of approving graces designed to implement the recommendations of the Wass Report, has approved the amendment: 'That the Regent House be entitled to put down motions and amendments along the lines of Oxford's Congregation, this being a power appropriate to it as a governing body' (University of Cambridge 1990: 284). Given the need to secure as broad support as possible for the new system of government, it was important that those fearful of the demise of Cambridge's democratic traditions should secure this concession.

The devolution of the decision-making process attacks the traditional model of consensus government at a more fundamental level than either the search for more effective academic leadership or the drive for better structures of policy-making and administration. To devolve the decision-making process is to suggest that there is no need for processes that will encourage consensus building across the full spectrum of university opinion. The universities are perceived as agglomerations of differing interests and the local parties are assumed to be best equipped to resolve those issues that affect their particular interests. University policy becomes the accumulation of local decisions. If an overarching view remains, it is consequent upon either the centre establishing parameters within which the regional units of government have to act, or the sharing of responsibility between the levels of governments with the centre presumably retaining control of those decisions which entail long-term financial commitments such as the creation of new permanent posts. Each of these possibilities suggests a machinery of government organized on federal lines in which authority is devolved rather than a unitary system of government.

The operation of the federal model can be seen most clearly in relation to the academic organization of the two universities and, as this is a matter to which a separate chapter is devoted, only the broad outlines need be presented here. Traditionally, academic decisions were made within the departments and faculties but invariably subject to ratification by the General Board. Should strong feelings have been aroused, there was always the possibility that the interested parties would call upon either Congregation or the Regent House to act as an ultimate court of appeal. In other words, there was widespread local democracy but always open to the possible interference of a higher body – perhaps the least desirable decision-making model! An interesting distinction between the two universities is Cambridge's development of a middle tier of government between the General Board and its faculties and departments known as the Councils of the Schools. This is a development that the Wass Report encouraged with further responsibilities being delegated to the Councils of the Schools (University of Cambridge 1989a: 630). The justifications for delegating authority are two-fold: it is appropriate that many decisions should be made at the local level because that is where the expertise is concentrated; and if the central bodies shed their less important responsibilities, then they have more time to spend on what should be their central function – the formation of long-term policy options. Contrast this with the evidence, noted above, of Oxford's General Board to the Franks Commission in which it argued that it should be both enmeshed in detail and that it was not its purpose to impose anything on the departments and faculties. Evidently, the times have changed and with them the understanding of how Oxford and Cambridge should govern themselves.

Our analysis of the two systems of university government has clarified two points: that the Universities of Oxford and Cambridge evolved different systems of government and that there has been considerable tension within both universities on how to reconcile their governmental machinery with their traditional understanding of how a university should be governed. To out-siders, the differences between the two universities may seem less significant than the similarities, but to insiders – as a reading of the evidence to the Franks Commission would verify – the peculiarities of the systems can command considerable loyalty. Undoubtedly, Keen did not feel that he was quibbling over a minor point when he sought to persuade the Franks Com-mission that the Chest should not become a committee of the Hebdomadal Council. Inevitably, there are going to be conflicts between what university statutes sanction and what universities actually do. At both Oxford and Cambridge there is the further point, and one which they undoubtedly share with other universities, of the statutes containing different ideas of govern-ment. It is inevitable that such institutions will reflect their complex his-tories. The reforms of the latter half of the nineteenth century, as well as those instigated by the Asquith Commission, both reconstituted and added to what was already in place. Most certainly they did not build anew.

It is our contention that the model of government established within both universities as a result of the Asquith Commission was one in which author-ity was widely diffused. Not only did statutory change depend upon majority support in either Congregation or the Regent House, but it was also danger-ous to say categorically that something was official university policy unless it had been approved by one of these two bodies. The Regent House and Congregation were executive bodies in the sense that, although they did not formulate university policy, they had to sanction what was to count as university policy. Moreover, at neither Oxford nor Cambridge, was the formulation of university policy – in either a political or administrative sense – especially well co-ordinated. The political and administrative structures were fragmented, relying upon devices such as core membership of the key committees to achieve a measure of common purpose. It can be argued that the Asquith Commission ushered in an age of donnish domination, that henceforth neither Oxford nor Cambridge would move unless the ranks of the assembled dons first signified their approval. In our opinion, the truth is somewhat less dramatic. Those who wished to govern had to practise the art of consensus building and hope that should the issue reach the assembled ranks of the dons, either that their own support was strong enough to carry the day or sufficient time had elapsed to see the opposition dissipated. Alternatively, things could slip through quietly which presumably, if the Report of the Franks Commission is to be believed, seems to have happened frequently at Oxford. The Hebdomadal Council apparently spoke on behalf of the university without feeling constrained to seek the approval of Congregation.

The University of Oxford has moved towards a somewhat different model of government. The statutes have been changed to enhance the leadership of the vice-chancellor and the authority of the key officials, to clarify the Hebdomadal Council's claim to be the university's executive body, and to establish the registrar's office as the hub of the university's administration. The unity of the administrative services is probably as much a consequence of their concentration on a purpose-built site in Wellington Square as of statutory change, an observation made by the present registrar (Dorey 1986: 16–17). This is not to say that the Franks Commission rejected out of hand the old style of government. To some extent, it strengthened the importance of consensus building through its advocacy of joint committees, but the Commission felt that it was essential that there should be a definite administrative and executive structure. If all else failed it would be clear where authority resided. For reasons that are not easy to discern, the University of Cambridge has been slower to change its model of government. It has clarified somewhat the executive authority of the Council of Senate, and its academic organization has moved towards a more devolved form of government. However, once the recommendations of the Wass Report are fully implemented, then enhanced devolution will be accompanied by stronger leadership from the vice-chancellor and an administration integrated under the auspices of the registrary. The two models of government will then be formally almost as close to each other as they were following the enactment of the proposals that flowed from the Asquith Commission.

Conclusions

Just as it would have been foolish to see the reforms of the late nineteenth century and those of the Asquith Commissioners as constituting a revolution, so it is equally important not to be carried away by the statutory changes since 1926. The statutes are meant to sanction systems of government that enable the two universities to perpetuate themselves as self-governing communities of scholars. This is what the Franks Commission saw itself as trying to achieve and to what the Wass Syndicate has attested. In the resistance to lay membership in their governing counsels (note there is token lay representation on Oxford's Chest and Cambridge's Financial Board with the

obvious intention of bringing in outside expertise to aid investment decisions), and the firm reiteration of the principle that administrators are policy
advisers and not policy makers, the tradition of donnish self-government has
been upheld, at least in theory. What is more debatable is whether the dons
at large at either university have much control over the formulation of
university policy. Inasmuch as the 1926 statutes required a complex process
of consensus building before policy could be said to exist, let alone be
implemented, this was the guarantor of donnish domination. While Halsey
has analysed this with a hint of nostalgia, Annan has been appalled by its
tortuous nature, and Edwards is forever convinced that it exists more in
theory than in practice. But over time, and this is as true of Cambridge as of
Oxford – although not necessarily to the same degree – the central bodies
have taken it upon themselves both to formulate and implement university
policy and then seek ratification. It would be absurd to see this as the normal
state of affairs or to assert that when it does occur that no grass-roots
consultation whatsoever takes place. However that it does occur, and on
critical issues, would be equally absurd to deny. We have the testimony of
the Wass Report as supportive evidence and, rather than showing alarm at
such a development, the report accepts it as 'inevitable' (University of
Cambridge 1989a: 620–1). Allegedly, the issues to which the University of
Cambridge had to respond were so complex and pressing that the statutes
needed to be circumvented. Apparently, the external world cannot be changed
and therefore Cambridge will have to go the way of Oxford and ensure that
its central bodies, more particularly the Council of Senate, have the executive
authority to determine what university policy should be.

One consequence of the above developments may be universities that
arrive at their decisions more swiftly (not the same as saying that they are
inevitably more efficient or effective), but it also means that there will be *less*
consensus building and that the amount of influence exercised by some of the
dons will increase. This may be the inevitable price that has to be paid for
the retention of self-government, but it is a different form of self-government.
Oxford's branches of government have been more unified than those of
Cambridge with Council the dominant partner. Oxford has moved from
government dependent upon consensus building, and subject to the ultimate
approval of the general assembly, to government by representative bodies that
are more co-ordinated institutionally and more confident of their own authority
but which still function better if the traditions of encouraging consensus and
showing sensitivity to the demos are not forgotten. However, we could go
further and raise the question of whether the notion of self-government has
very much meaning when the very machinery of government has to adapt to
a particular mould in order to cope with the external context. In fact, the
situation is even more dire than this for, as the Report of the Wass Syndicate
makes clear, the UGC was quite prepared to tell Cambridge that the
machinery the university believed was appropriate for dealing with the world
was in fact inadequate. It is not simply enough to respond to new demands,
for you also need to change in a manner that those who are making the new

demands judge to be appropriate. And the fact that Oxford changed earlier than Cambridge, and therefore has appeared more in control of the situation, does not isolate it from the same pressures. In his farewell oration to the University of Oxford, the Vice-Chancellor, Sir Patrick Neill, reflected:

> Again, I find worrying the emphasis which is placed on the document known as the U.F.C.'s Aims. A bidding university will apparently score points if their future plans contribute to those Aims. In my view, if a university is really autonomous it will have its own aims and will be pursuing these without any reference to any externally-dictated norm (University of Oxford, 1989b: 298).

Perhaps the time has come to abandon the notion that universities, including Oxford and Cambridge, are 'really autonomous' institutions. Oxford and Cambridge may continue to perceive themselves as communities of self-governing scholars, but the terms on which they are governed, although not imposed, are not of their own making. At both universities, the consequence has been repeated attacks on the 1926 statutory settlement of which the recent struggles at Cambridge are but the latest example.

3

Eroding the Preconditions of Autonomy: The Changing Financial Relationship between the State and the Universities

Why be fearful of the state's largesse?

The primary goal of this chapter is to compare the annual incomes of the Universities of Oxford and Cambridge with British universities in general. The intention is straightforward: to see whether or not the sources of Oxford's and Cambridge's incomes since 1920 differ from those of other British universities. While naturally the size of their recurrent grants from the Exchequer have been of interest to the universities, the terms on which they were to be received have been of equal, if not greater, importance.

Inevitably, the provision of annual recurrent grants by the state to the universities would raise the spectre of state control. It is part of conventional wisdom that whoever pays the piper will call the tune. If the recurrent grant at its inception in 1919 had been administered by the Board of Education, the possibility of state direction of the universities would have loomed large. To calm the fears of the universities, the creation of the UGC was perhaps inevitable and, furthermore, it has to be remembered that the remit of the Board of Education covered only England and Wales. However, this did not prevent the board from making its bid for administrative control, and in his reassurances to the Asquith Commission its president, H.A.L. Fisher, stressed the need to preserve 'the liberty and autonomy of the Universities within the general lines laid down under their constitution' and went on to state that, although the universities were in receipt of state grants, it did not follow there would be 'state inference in matters for which they are themselves properly responsible' (Royal Commission on Oxford and Cambridge Universities 1922b: App. 4). But the Board of Education was not to carry the day. While the universities may have been happier with the UGC, its goodwill had to be proven before its benevolence could be guaranteed.

It should not be assumed that as the Universities of Oxford and Cambridge were in such dire financial straits at the end of the First World War, that they turned in desperation to the government for assistance. The correspondence between the President of the Board of Education (that is Fisher) and the vice-chancellors of the Universities of Oxford and Cambridge (ibid.)

demonstrates that the initial approach to the government came from the universities already in receipt of a Treasury grant and that Oxford and Cambridge were drawn into the negotiations only after the initiative was widened to include the Scottish and Irish universities. Opinion within the two universities, especially Oxford, as to the wisdom of the approach was divided. It was the scientists who were most prepared to press the case for the infusion of state resources. Not only could such an approach be expected to result in tangible financial gains for them, but also the state would support a shift towards an enhanced place for scientific research within the universities. If it were true that current university resources made it difficult for both Oxford and Cambridge to maintain, let alone extend, their pre-1914 scientific work, then there was little alternative but to welcome recurrent state grants, for there appeared to be no other parties who were both capable of and willing to meet the need.

While the two universities – and in particular their fledgling science departments – would benefit financially from the state's input, the dominant political forces of the day had to be persuaded that it was a good investment to make. There was a clear expectation that Oxford and Cambridge would respond positively to the social and academic pressures of the post-war era. The Asquith Commission urged the universities to increase educational opportunities for women and poorer students and to extend their provision of extra-mural work. The willingness to underwrite at least part of the cost of the expanding scientific effort was in the belief that it would be in the national interest to do so. The Asquith Commission painted a picture of rather seedy institutions; they had seen better days and urgently needed to refurbish and expand their libraries, museums and laboratories if they were to meet the new expectations. At this stage in the history of the relationship between government and state on the one hand and universities on the other, there was little consideration of whether the universities could be relied upon to deliver the goods and certainly few were prepared to compel them to do so.

Integral to the image of the Universities of Oxford and Cambridge is that they are wealthier institutions than other British universities. Did they need the annual recurrent grant that the other universities were in receipt of from 1919? It was part of the purpose of the Asquith Commission to investigate this question. Historically what wealth the Universities of Oxford and Cambridge possessed was to be found in their colleges. For example, in 1919, the General Fund of the University of Oxford totalled £58 878, whereas the net revenue, on which college contributions to the Common University Fund were assessed, amounted to £326 490. In 1918, Magdalen College alone had a net revenue of over £50 000 and Christ Church College of over £30 000. The picture was substantially the same at Cambridge. During the war years, the income of Cambridge's University Chest had averaged only £25 155, while in 1918 the taxable income of the colleges, which created a fund to be used for university purposes, was £233 964, to which Trinity College contributed close to £60 000 and St John's College over £30 000 (ibid.: App. 16).

The Asquith Commission came to the conclusion that what resources the colleges possessed were no more than sufficient to meet their own needs. In other words, they were not so well endowed that they could refurbish their universities. Having been satisfied on this point, the initial emergency grants of Oxford and Cambridge were placed on the same footing as the annual recurrent grants of the other British universities. It would be unwise to conclude that all the financial problems of British universities, including those of Oxford and Cambridge, had been resolved at one fell swoop. The Asquith Commission argued that both Oxford and Cambridge each required an annual contribution from the Exchequer of £100 000 if they were to meet their reasonable goals. In fact it was some 10 years before the figure of £100 000 was reached! Like other needy institutions, the universities experienced the consequences of the draconian restrictions upon state expenditure in the aftermath of war.

It became part of the established folklore on university-state relations that the autonomy of the universities was guaranteed by the character of its financial partnership with the state. Just as the UGC had a special relationship to the Treasury, and thus was a quasi-autonomous part of the state apparatus, so the universities were bound financially to the UGC by particular procedures. It has been assumed that university autonomy was aided by the decision to restrict the state's input to that of a minority shareholder. The apparent intention was to confine the UGC's annual recurrent grant to approximately one-third of the universities' total income with endowments, fees, local authority grants and research contracts supplementing this. One tangible expression of the erosion of university autonomy was the increasing interest in the post-1945 period of the Public Accounts Committee in university expenditure. According to John Carswell, the universities received some protection from 'the ministrations of the Comptroller and Auditor General', while they received less than half of their income from the Exchequer and 'only when this fraction was exceeded did any special defence from parliamentary audit have to be mounted' (Carswell 1985: 11). Clearly, the 'one-third' formula was no more than a crude rule-of-thumb guideline, and it is difficult not to believe that the actual *size* of the Exchequer's input was also a consideration for the Public Accounts Committee. In 1920, the total incomes of the Universities of Oxford and Cambridge, excluding the emergency grants, were £195 360 and £223 015 respectively. The Asquith Commission proposed an annual UGC grant of £100 000 for each university, which is just about consistent with the 'one-third' formula but there is no indication within the Commission's report that their recommendation was guided by this consideration. Even so, if the recommendation of the Asquith Commission had been implemented in full, the state, in the form of the UGC, would have moved from being a marginal financial contributor to the major shareholder overnight. One has the impression that the Asquith Commission arrived at the nearest convenient round figure that would meet the needs of the universities – that is as the commissioners saw them – and that principles were of secondary consideration.

There is some evidence from within the two universities that the key issue for them was not the size of the grant but the conditions attached to its award. In one of his letters to the President of the Board of Education, the acting vice-chancellor of the University of Cambridge (Thomas C. Fitzpatrick) made the point concisely:

> On all these grounds, therefore, it seems not unreasonable in my opinion that the University should receive a *substantial* grant from National sources provided that *the conditions under which it is given* do not interfere with the autonomy to which throughout the long history of the University the Senate has always attached the utmost importance (Royal Commission on Oxford and Cambridge Universities 1922b: App. 4, our emphasis).

The word 'substantial' is open to varying interpretations, but there was no suggestion in the letter that the state must avoid over-generosity in order to preserve the university's autonomy. The implication is that the university was prepared to accept all that was given as long as it was made available on terms of which it approved. There may be a general expectation that whoever pays the piper will call the tune, but government spokesmen were assuring the universities that they were immune from such considerations, and it could be argued that universities were esconced in a world that made them the exception to general expectations!

In fact, the dire economic circumstances of the day meant that successive governments had no intention of being over-generous, so the threat to autonomy from the mere size of the UGC's input was not to become an issue until after the Second World War. Closely related to the notion of the state as a minority shareholder was the provision of the UGC's grant on the basis of what has been termed 'the deficiency principle'. According to Carswell (1985: 11), a 'needs test' was applied 'to each institution on the grant list in terms of money' and the difference between this figure and 'each university's income that came from other sources . . . was taken as each university's basic need'. The intention, therefore, was to act parsimoniously, to meet only those costs that the universities could not meet from their other sources of income. The problem was how to define the essential requirements of a university. If these were to expand, while non-UGC sources of university income remained stagnant, then the deficiency principle would do little either to protect the Exchequer from increasing demands upon its purse or the universities from the potential consequences of an ever larger financial input from the state. Only if the university system were static, or the universities increased their non-Exchequer revenue as they expanded, could the deficiency principle operate meaningfully.

The most potent guarantor of university autonomy has been the concept of the block grant. In theory, the universities have received their recurrent income from the UGC in the form of a block grant which each individual university then spends as it sees fit. It is ironic that the former Vice-Chancellor of Oxford, the Revd H.E.D. Blakiston, in his evidence to the

Asquith Commission, objected to this form of grant because it 'would involve the University as a whole in a struggle with all or most of its Departments' and he much preferred 'special subventions' to named departments (Royal Commission on Oxford and Cambridge Universities 1922b: App. 1). Blakiston appeared to have overlooked the influence that 'special subventions' would give to those who made them. But it must also be remembered that much of the UGC's financial input that flowed into Oxford and Cambridge after the Asquith Commission had in fact been earmarked for expenditure approved by the Commission's report. The universities have never been given a blank cheque. In the steady-state model, current commitments consumed resources in a predictable fashion, and once there was growth plans had to be submitted to indicate where it was expected to occur and how much it would cost. And even before 1939, the UGC was not above indicating where it felt that expansion should actually take place.

The principle of the block grant was reinforced by the quinquennial cycle of financial planning. Taken together, they reinforce the impression that the state distanced itself from the day-to-day affairs of the universities. A 5-year financial cycle suggests that universities were not to be subjected to the rigours of an annual scrutiny but could undertake a considerable measure of forward planning confident in the knowledge that the UGC's recurrent grant would be available at the end of the day. An alternative way of looking at the UGC's financial relationship to the universities is that the state has at the very least supervised the pattern of university development. The extent to which it also actually directed the course of that development requires an analysis of the interaction between individual universities and the UGC with respect to their quinquennial applications. It is possible at this stage, however, to argue that universities tailored their development to fit into expectations of what the UGC would find acceptable. Moreover, as later events were to demonstrate, although the universities and indeed the UGC may have believed in the sanctity of the quinquennial system, there was nothing to prevent hard-pressed governments from thinking otherwise.

While it is possible to argue that the UGC awarded its recurrent grant on the basis of principles which protected university autonomy, as far as the Asquith Commission is any guide, it is evident that the contemporary debate was as much about the immediate financial needs of Oxford and Cambridge as the long-term threat to their autonomy. Once the state, however reluctantly, had been permitted to underwrite the costs of what Carswell has termed the universities' basic needs, then – with the wisdom of hindsight – it is hard to see how it could avoid becoming the dominant financial partner. The alternative scenarios were the perpetuation of a static model of the university or the emergence of new financial partners. In the long run, the pressures for expansion – broadening the social character of the students, expanding new and existing knowledge areas, and gearing the universities to national needs – were irresistible. Other possible financial benefactors either lacked the resources or were unwilling to underwrite the universities, and there were no overwhelming reasons why these circumstances should change. If the financial dominance of the state were to increase, then the embrace of government and state could be expected to become more intense, if not more endearing. But in the context of 1919, these were remote considerations. The universities were soon reconciled to the way that the UGC made its recurrent grants, it formed an acceptable bridge between themselves, governments and the state apparatus. And if they were not to remain the rather seedy institutions portrayed in the Asquith Report, then it was a question of Hobson's choice.

Phase 1, 1919–39: The state as minority shareholder

It is not until the academic year 1925–26 that the UGC returns allow direct comparisons to be made between the sources of income for all institutions in receipt of a recurrent grant. Table 3.1 compares income sources for the years 1925–26 and 1939–40, and any significant changes between the conclusion of the Great War and 1925–26 are discussed in the text. Does the relative importance of the various income sources change over time?

The most striking feature of Table 3.1 is the comparative stability of the distribution of the income figures over time. The only notable change was the sharp decline in income from 'other government grants' which was to be expected, as these were mainly special subventions which were increasingly replaced by the UGC's recurrent grant. The fact that endowment income held up so remarkably well is perhaps surprising in view of the protracted economic crises of the inter-war years. The different income patterns of Oxford and Cambridge, although not especially distinctive, are none the less interesting. Oxford had a consistently higher endowment income, whereas Cambridge received a higher percentage of its income from fees, reflecting the fact that the stronger scientific presence at Cambridge made teaching more the responsibility of the university as opposed to the colleges, as was true of Oxford.

Table 3.1 does not reveal the extent to which the colleges contributed to the incomes of the Universities of Oxford and Cambridge which, in 1919–20, according to evidence submitted to the Asquith Commission, amounted to approximately 10 per cent of the income of both universities (compare the data in Royal Commission on Oxford and Cambridge Universities 1922b: App. 16 with that in Table 3.1 for 1925–26). This was an income source that was simply unavailable to other British universities. In much the same way, the local authority input was unavailable to Oxford and Cambridge. The civic universities were invariably the product of local pride of which one tangible continuing expression was the local authorities' inputs into their coffers. The Universities of Oxford and Cambridge have evolved from different roots; historically, their benefactors were the Crown, the Church and the landed classes and, consequently, they have always been national, even international, rather than local institutions. The other point worth noting is the distinctive differences in endowment incomes. Consistently the relative

Table 3.1   Sources of university income: 1925–26 and 1939–40

	Oxford		Cambridge		All universities	
	1925–26 (%)	1939–40 (%)	1925–26 (%)	1939–40 (%)	1925–26 (%)	1939–40 (%)
Endowments	29.4	39.1	18.7	26.4	13.1	15.2
Local authority grants	–	–	0.2	–	10.7	9.2
UGC grant	20.3	20.6	20.6	17.7	31.6	33.1
Other government grants	12.3	5.2	11.4	7.9	6.6	4.7
Fees	27.2	23.0	35.0	31.6	29.7	26.2
All other sources	10.8	12.1	14.1	16.4	8.3	11.6
Total income (£000s)	420	530	453	689	4816	6488

Sources: UGC (1925–26, table 9; 1939–40, table 5).

endowment input into Oxford's total income was more than double that of all British universities and, although the differences for Cambridge were not as great, they were none the less notable. Inevitably, neither Oxford nor Cambridge were as dependent upon the UGC's recurrent grant as other British universities, a natural enough state of affairs in view of their very different historical origins.

The above picture of relative stability reflects both the fact that the university system was evolving only very slowly in the inter-war years, and the particular years that the UGC's presentation of its statistics has forced us to compare. While between 1919–20 and 1925–26 the relative importance of the differing sources of income for the overall university system scarcely shifted, during those same years the UGC's recurrent grant almost doubled in importance at both Oxford and Cambridge, that is from constituting approximately 10 per cent of income to just over 20 per cent. Thus for Oxford and Cambridge, the immediate post-war years were marked by considerable uncertainty – in a very short space of time, both became more financially dependent upon the state and Cambridge actually saw a decline in the relative importance of its endowment income. By 1925–26, the situation had stabilized and the pattern we have just discussed emerged. The preconditions for the maintenance of the established financial relationship between the state and the universities existed, therefore, throughout the inter-war years. In due course, the expansion of the university system was to test the basis of that financial relationship to the limit.

Phase 2, 1939–74: The dominant state in good times

The intensification of the financial dependence of British universities upon the Exchequer was completed in a comparatively short space of time. By

1939, the UGC grant made up close to one-third of their total annual incomes, and any increase would threaten the established principle of the central state as a minority shareholder. In fact, by 1951–52, the UGC grant was contributing approximately two-thirds of the universities' annual incomes, which represented a significant erosion of the principles that had governed the financial relationship between the state and the universities. Did this fundamental change between the state and the universities also embrace Oxford and Cambridge with their much larger endowment incomes and a traditionally less pronounced reliance upon the UGC's grant?

The UGC's presentation of its statistics does not make for easy comparisons over time and, therefore, we have extracted key pieces of information to illustrate the main trends (UGC 1950–51: 35; 1970: 86–7). In the inter-war years, endowment income, local authority grants and college contributions made up the most distinctive differences between the incomes of Oxford and Cambridge and other British universities. Between 1950–51 and 1970–71, the endowment income of all British universities declined from 7.4 to 2 per cent – the actual figures for Oxford were from 21.2 to 6 per cent and for Cambridge from 14 to 6 per cent. The decline in the importance of grants from local authorities was even more dramatic. By 1970–71, they comprised less than 1 per cent of total university income and no more than 6 per cent of any one university's income. Academic fees was the other major contributor to university income to suffer a sharp tailing off in its relative importance, from between 15 and 20 per cent for each university in 1950–51 to 6 per cent or less by 1970–71. The fees had little relationship to the real cost of a course and in any case came to be met mainly by the Exchequer, so establishing another channel through which the state made resources available to the universities.

The steep erosion of the relative importance of these three established inputs into university incomes meant that either new sources of income were being found or that the contribution of the remaining major partner, that is the UGC, was increasing sharply. In fact, both developments were taking place. In 1950, the UGC's grant formed approximately half the annual income of the Universities of Oxford and Cambridge, while the figure for all institutions on the grant list was over 60 per cent; by 1970, the same figures were over 60 per cent for both Oxford and Cambridge and over 70 per cent nationally. The rise in the UGC's input can only be described as remorseless. Another critical development was the growth in the income from research grants and contracts. As early as 1950, Cambridge had an income of almost £400 000 (18.4 per cent of its total income) that fell substantially into this category, whereas at Oxford the figure was much lower, nearly £119 000 or 7.1 per cent of its total income. The 1970–71 UGC statistics record figures of 22 per cent for Oxford and 20 per cent for Cambridge compared to a national total of 14 per cent. During this time period, the University of Oxford entered the big science research league. Evidently, both the Universities of Oxford and Cambridge were in the vanguard of a movement that saw research income assuming a larger and sharper profile within university budgets.

Although in relation to total income figures both endowment income and local authority grants were in relative decline, it would be unwise to write them off too quickly. Of course, the national trend was repeated at all the individual institutions, but none the less the 6 per cent contribution that endowment income made to Oxford's and Cambridge's total income for 1970–71 was still a sizeable figure, amounting to some £900 000 at both universities. Also, endowment income actually continued to increase after 1945: between 1950 and 1970, it doubled at Cambridge and almost tripled at Oxford. By comparison, between 1920 and 1939, it had almost quadrupled at Oxford and more than tripled at Cambridge. Although the post-1945 increases in endowment incomes were not as significant as those for the inter-war years, the main reason for the erosion of their relative importance in the budgets of Oxford and Cambridge was the massive increases in the overall size of their incomes between 1939 and 1970 in comparison to the increases between 1919 and 1939. It is the sheer scale of the expansion in university budgets that changed their income profiles.

Table 3.2 is self-explanatory: the initial post-1918 expansion – inevitable in view of the stagnation of the war years – tails off sharply after a few years, whereas the post-1945 boom is still going strong two decades later. The continuing increases in endowment income are simply insufficient to keep pace with the massive inputs from the Exchequer. Local authorities were not in a position to contemplate commitments on this scale and private bene-factors lacked the motivation if not the resources.

The most striking overall conclusion that can be drawn from the post-1945 income patterns is that both the Universities of Oxford and Cambridge are being driven along the same path as the rest of the British university system. After the Second World War, the British universities loosen their remaining local ties while resources generated by themselves in the form of endowments increasingly are marginalized. The UGC's annual recurrent grant becomes the financial input which underwrites the complete range of university activ-ities, and neither Oxford nor Cambridge are exceptions to this generaliza-tion. While the growing importance of research income is not peculiar to Oxford and Cambridge, in the company of a few other universities they lead the field. By 1970, the Universities of Birmingham, London, Manchester, Southampton, Sussex and York, besides Oxford and Cambridge, were all receiving at least 15 per cent of their total incomes from research grants and contracts (UGC 1970: 87). The incomes profiles of the British universities converged over time so that by 1970 there emerged a British university system in which the individual institutions were all substantially dependent upon one benefactor – the Exchequer. The overall financial profile, therefore, was the aggregation of like parts rather than the product of the integration of differing components.

The whole basis, therefore, of the established financial relationship be-tween the state and the universities was destroyed in a comparatively short time. Most obviously, the notion that the UGC's grant should be restricted to one-third of a university's income was no longer tenable, which made it

Table 3.2 Expansion of university income: 1920–70

	Oxford		Cambridge	
	£000s	*% increase*[a]	*£000s*	*% increase*[a]
1919–20	225		253	
1929–30	411	83	579	129
1939–40	530	29	689	19
1949–50	1 567	195	2 004	191
1959–60	3 955	152	4 485	124
1969–70	11 712	196	12 322	175

[a] The percentages represent increases in income over the previous figure.
Sources: UGC (1929–30, 1939–40, 1949–50, 1959–60, 1970); Royal Commission on Oxford and Cambridge Universities (1922b: App. 16).

increasingly difficult for the universities and the UGC to resist the intrusion of the Public Accounts Committee. Furthermore, once the state's input into the universities became so dominant, it was absurd to persist with the understanding that money was granted on the basis of 'the deficiency principle'. The Exchequer was no longer meeting just the basic needs but almost *all* the needs of the universities. The taxpayer was not only footing the bill for the UGC's recurrent grants but also paying more of the tuition fees (plus student maintenance grants), and was the major contributor to the awards for research grants and contracts. The fact that the state's input was through a number of different channels may have disguised its overall significance, but this was a financial takeover on a grand scale.

It would be unwise to draw the conclusion that those principles which limited the state's financial input (restrictions on the relative size of the UGC's grant and the notion that it met the essential needs of the universities that their own resources were insufficient to cover) were abandoned, while those which appeared to protect more directly university autonomy (the block grant and the quinquennial system) were retained. In contrast to the inter-war years, after 1945 the UGC moved firmly into the business of awarding earmarked grants. As Carswell (1985) has noted, this enabled the UGC at the very least to influence the course of academic development, for the Committee had to approve the capital programmes that made such development possible. The way was open for the UGC to issue guidelines on university development and to form its own judgements on the various programmes that were submitted to it for funding. The UGC's earmarked grants were in effect grants for approved academic developments, which at the very least eroded the notion that the universities spent their UGC grants at their own discretion. This is not to suggest that the UGC's approach was anything but discreet, but rather to make the point that resources could be made available on a different basis.

How were the universities to respond to this new situation? In fact, far from fearing the expanded financial role of the state, it came to be viewed benevolently by the universities. So strong was the universities' belief in their right to autonomy, that they found it hard to perceive the potential threat inherent in their financial dependence upon the state. The Exchequer had provided in the past without calling the tune and the question was whether an enlarged state input would change matters. If after 1945 the state and universities were partners in national reconstruction, there was little apparent reason why the latter should fear the former. By the mid-1960s, however, the tension in the relationship was there for all to see. The Public Accounts Committee succeeded in gaining access to the books and a Labour government, as if in despair of the universities, created the polytechnics. But Parliament in the short run was to prove a paper tiger, more concerned with careful accountancy than policy matters. It could be argued that the creation of the polytechnics was a monument to university autonomy, for it reflected the political judgement that it was easier to conjure up a new sector of higher education than to require the universities to change in tune with the wishes of government and state.

The failure within Oxbridge to address (at least publicly) financial issues at this time was illustratred beautifully by Oxford's Commission of Inquiry chaired by Lord Franks. Set up in 1964, at a time when the university's financial dependence upon the UGC's recurrent grant was increasing by leaps and bounds, it had virtually nothing to say on the possible implications of this dependence. Its financial concerns were restricted to investigating the exchange of resources between the colleges and the university. Because the university had grown in financial strength thanks to the Exchequer's greatly enhanced input, it was possible for the Commission to advocate that the richer colleges should help to build up the endowments of the poorer colleges rather than to assist the university financially. And yet the Commission remained silent despite the following terms of reference:

> To inquire into and report upon the part which Oxford plays now and should play in the future of higher education in the United Kingdom, having regard to its position as both a national and international University (University of Oxford 1966a: 11).

In retrospect, it seems staggering that the university's affairs could be analysed without any serious consideration of the size and sources of its income. These matters are, however, conspicuous by their absence from the Commission's report. Volume II of the Commission's Report (University of Oxford 1966b) contains a range of invaluable statistics but scarcely anything on university income or expenditure. It is hard not to draw the conclusion that it was believed that the state would continue to support the piper and – crucially – would continue to be equally undemanding. Undoubtedly, these blindspots are explained by the historical context within which the Franks Commission reported and it is inconceivable that any contemporary university inquiry with such wide-ranging terms of reference would treat the financial dimension so parsimoniously.

At the time, however, the new situation did not raise many alarm bells, although a few mavericks started to voice their fears. By and large the universities took the virtual destruction of the traditional basis of their financial relationship to the state in their stride. From the perspective of the 1980s, it was tempting to look back upon this time as a golden age in the development of the British university system. But if it were so, then it was short-lived. Tying the growth of the universities to the benevolence of the Exchequer meant that government economic policy influenced the pattern of university development. Once the universities became significant consumers of state resources, it was inevitable that they would not be overlooked should governments decide to control their own expenditure. Even when the financial scale had been pigmy by comparison, the universities had not escaped the Geddes axe in the immediate post-1918 years Shinn (1986: 116–18). Success at gaining access to the Exchequer's coffers had its price. Carswell (1985: 37), for example, notes that the first post-1945 cutback in the building programme occurred in July 1965, and that the size of the recurrent grant for 1969–70 actually represented a decline over the previous year.

It may seem ironic, but one of the particular problems for university finances was the quinquennial system, which both encouraged long-term planning and distanced the universities from the state. The problem was the rate of inflation, for governments bent on controlling public expenditure were tempted not to make supplementary grants which covered its full effects. The UGC's annual surveys in the early 1970s were filled with references to precisely this difficulty. The course of events assumed a ritual form: the government failed to make full compensation for the effects of inflation, the UGC made representations on behalf of the universities, and then the government would relent, or at least partially so. The UGC's *Annual Survey* for 1973–74 noted that:

> ... at the beginning of December 1973 the Government White Paper on Public Expenditure to 1977–78 (Cmnd 5519) announced that, as a contribution towards economy in public expenditure, the Government had decided to with-hold half the supplementation of recurrent expenditure for the academic year 1974–75 and subsequent years of the quinquennium and not to supplement equipment expenditure for one year's increase in prices (UGC 1973–74: 6–7).

And, optimistically, in the government's view, 'these reductions could be accommodated without detriment to the planned growth of the universities during the remainder of the quinquennium'. But the government was not long in relenting. Apparently, when it had reached its decision in December 1973, the government had underestimated the rate of inflation and so 'in July the Government agreed that additional recurrent grant of £4 million should be made available' (ibid.: 7). At its own discretion, the UGC reluctantly decided to add a further £1.5 million to the recurrent grant by raiding the furniture and equipment allocation. This was crisis management designed to keep the present system ticking over at the expense of new development and refurbishment. Inevitably, to continue in this way would mean a steadily decaying university system. But the final crisis was not long in coming.

Formally, the last quinquennium ran from 1972 to 1977, but as Carswell (1985: 26) cryptically observes, its demise 'had been preceded by four years of financing which it would be polite to describe as annual, so frequent were the interruptions, supplementations and adjustments'. While Command 5519, issued in December 1973, made it clear that for the foreseeable future the state would remain the financial guarantor of the British universities, henceforth resources would be committed initially only on an annual basis and there was no certainty that the universities would be protected from the ravages of inflation. Of the original principles linking the universities financially to the state, only the block grant could be said to remain in place and even that had been eroded.

Except for the aforementioned UGC's general oversight of university development, which emerged as a consequence of its expanded use of earmarked grants, it could be argued that, despite the new financial relationship between the universities and the state, university autonomy remained essentially intact even as late as the mid-1970s. What had changed, so the argument would go, was the willingness of governments to underwrite unfettered university expansion. In other words, the debate was about how much taxpayers' money the universities should receive rather than their right to spend it as they saw fit. In fact, the screw was tightened in areas that were central to the purpose of the universities – admissions, teaching and research. Although the reasons were obviously financial, the first Wilson government's insistence on fee differentiation between overseas and home-based students inevitably affected the admissions process. This particular intervention caused, as Carswell notes, great resentment as the level of fees was 'constitutionally . . . a matter for the universities alone, something which needed the approval of each individual university senate. Yet in this case their approval was taken for granted' (ibid.: 115–16). Universities could refuse to impose the increases, and some did but the UGC adjusted their recurrent grants accordingly – downwards! For both the 1967–72 and 1972–77 quinquennia, the UGC issued a Memorandum of General Guidance which contained student target numbers by subject which, although crude to begin with, were subsequently firmed up, only to be eased again! Finally, the research councils made conscious decisions to promote particular research fields and to encourage bids for certain kinds of projects.

Even the universities' administration and government were attracting the probing eye of the state. In 1956, a committee was set up under the chairmanship of Sir George Gater to investigate the effectiveness of procedures for controlling university expenditure (UGC 1956). The universities were given a revised code of practice to follow in the management of their financial affairs. Following a further enquiry, this time chaired by Sir Arthur Rucker, the procedures were again modified (UGC 1960). The required changes may have made perfect sense, but they also implied that if the universities were to be state-financed bodies, then they had to expect guidelines on how they administered and governed themselves. Internally sponsored reform also anticipated future external scrutiny. Two prominent ex-financial officers of the University of Cambridge have claimed to us that if the Comptroller and Auditor General had examined departmental accounts prior to the late 1960s, 'he would have had a fit' (Interview; 9 April 1988).

In view of the dependence of the universities upon the Exchequer, the above erosions of autonomy can scarcely be described as extensive. So far the developments had had little impact upon how the universities actually conducted their central functions. Parliament could now exercise more financial scrutiny. It was increasingly difficult to portray the UGC as a buffer between the state and government on one side and the universities on the other, for slowly it was being forced more explicitly into the orbit of the state apparatus. The role of government in university affairs was much more visible, even if this visibility was restricted to controlling the financial input of the Exchequer. None the less, the pretence that universities remained in control of their own destinies was harder to maintain. If government decisions can bankrupt universities, then what price university autonomy?

Phase 3, from 1974 to the demise of the UGC: Declining state largesse and the search for market forces

Because the Government wanted to be certain about its future expenditure commitments, from 1975 to 1976 the recurrent grant would include a notional element for inflation so ending the established supplementation arrangements. In the jargon of the day, the universities would be required to work within the confines of cash limits which, as the UGC wryly noted in its *Annual Survey* for 1975–76, would not be such a novelty given the recent failure of supplementary grants to cover inflationary costs in full (UGC 1975–76: 11). The universities could no longer expect retrospective government support to underwrite unforeseen costs that they had incurred. The universities moved from a demand-led to a cash-led system. Not only did the economic crisis of the mid-1970s bring an end to the quinquennial arrangements, but it also imposed cash constraints upon the state's support for higher education. Thus the Exchequer had moved from underwriting those basic needs that the universities themselves could not finance, through supporting almost single-handedly a system whose expansion it could not control, to the imposition of cash limits.

Was this a temporary situation brought about by the contemporary economic constraints or had there been a fundamental change in the fortunes of the universities? The UGC had no doubts and argued in its *Annual Survey* for 1979–80 that the universities were in 'a new situation'. It was possible to point to demographic trends, falling age-participation rates, and declining political sympathy for higher education to support such a pessimistic prognosis. Of course all these variables could be turned around, but undoubtedly the short-term outlook was bleak. The UGC's assessment was dramatic for it suggested that the trials and tribulations of recent years were not a temporary aberration; that the universities should recognize the world they had known since at least 1945 had disappeared.

The worst fears of many were soon realized. Early in 1981, the UGC was told by the government that 'it should plan on the basis that by 1983–84 the recurrent grant for home students would be reduced to a level 8½ per cent below that given in the 1980 Public Expenditure White Paper (Cmnd 7841)' (UGC 1980–81: 5). The UGC calculated that along with the withdrawal of the subsidy for overseas students, the total fall in income between 1980–81 and 1983–84 would be 'not less than 11 per cent' (ibid.). Given that the cuts in recurrent grant were inevitable, then the question was how to impose them. Integral to the UGC's strategy was the decision to make differential cuts; all would suffer but some would suffer more than others.

Obviously the figures for 1982–83 and 1983–84 were projections, whereas in fact between 1980–81 and 1983–84 the percentage decline in UGC funding in real terms was 8.2 per cent for Cambridge and 9.5 per cent for Oxford (*Hansard* (Commons) 1986a). Although Table 3.3 reveals very sharp declines in the recurrent grants of Oxford and Cambridge, other universities were to suffer more. Of the 51 institutions in receipt of a recurrent grant from the UGC, the University of Cambridge had received the 11th smallest percentage cut by 1983–84 immediately followed by Oxford in 12th place. Although better placed than most other institutions, these are not the kind of figures which lend support to those who may believe that Oxbridge occupied a privileged position in the inner sanctum of the UGC.

Following the cuts in recurrent grants imposed from 1981–82 to 1983–84, the UGC had expressed the hope that for the rest of the decade the government would maintain 'truly level funding' (UGC 1984: 27). But as its Circular Letter 22/85 makes clear, this was to prove wishful thinking. The Public Expenditure White Paper of January 1985 (Cmnd 9428) provided figures for the annual grants to cover the years 1985–86 to 1987–88 which allowed for 'increases in universities' costs that are on average 1.5 per cent below the Government's own assumptions about general inflation over three years' (UGC 1985: 1). In the light of this information, the UGC 'decided on a working hypothesis of an average annual decline in the recurrent grant for each institution of 2 per cent in real terms – taken here to mean an annual increase of about 2 per cent below the general rate of inflation' (ibid.: 2).

What was the UGC to do now? In *A Strategy for Higher Education into the 1990s* (UGC 1984: 28), it had contemplated on the alternatives:

1. To let the cuts fall equally.
2. To distribute the cuts unequally as in 1981, though not necessarily following the same pattern.
3. To remove one or more institutions completely from the grant list.

Table 3.3 Recurrent grants at 1981–82 price base (£m)

	1981–82	*1982–83*	*1983–84*	*% decline*
Cambridge	30.03	29.39	28.91	3.7
Oxford	31.33	30.41	29.74	5.1
Total recurrent grant	879.62	838.65	808.07	8.1

Sources: Hansard (Commons) (1981).

Whatever line was pursued, the UGC argued that it would be no more than 'damage limitation'. However, having ruled it out in 1981, it could scarcely take the first line and it believed that the third possibility required a political decision that only the government could make. Thus by default the strategy was again to be selectively applied misery. However, the UGC recognized that all universities were in financial trouble, so no institution was to face 'cuts in real terms of more than 1.5 per cent greater than the average loss' (THES, 1986: 8). While the misery was not being shared equally, the UGC was not discriminating too rigorously between institutions. Presumably, had it done so, then it would have forced if not closures then bankruptcies, and perhaps it wanted to avoid having too much blood on its hands! In this round of cuts, the Universities of Oxford and Cambridge were hit harder than in the previous round. While from 1985–86 to 1986–87 the total recurrent grant had increased by 1.0 per cent, at Oxford it had remained static and at Cambridge it had increased by only 0.7 per cent. By comparison, the most favoured institution, Warwick, achieved a 4 per cent increase. Between 1980–81 and 1986–87, the UGC's recurrent grant to Cambridge had fallen in real terms by 12.5 per cent and to Oxford by 14.4 per cent (*Hansard* (Commons) 1986b).

The only relief to the unmitigated gloom was the launching of a number of special programmes to which both the Universities of Oxford and Cambridge responded adeptly. The most significant of these was the creation of 'new blood' posts. Funding was made available for the recruitment of some 230 lecturers in 1983–84 of whom 200 were expected to be in the natural sciences, technology or medicine. The exercise was repeated in the two subsequent years with approximately the same number of appointments and a similar subject bias. A smaller initiative for the appointment of posts in information technology (IT) was also launched (UGC 1982–83: 9–11). Furthermore, in 1985, the UGC agreed to contribute £12 million to a £43 million programme designed to fund additional students in engineering and technology, with the balance of the funding coming from other government departments (UGC 1984–85: 6–7), and both the Universities of Oxford and Cambridge have taken advantage of this programme (Cambridge was one of the original participating universities). Table 3.4 shows their success in the distribution of the first round of 'new blood' and IT posts.

Table 3.4   Distribution of first round 'new blood' and information technology posts in relation to recurrent grant size

	New blood posts	IT posts	Costs per £1m of Recurrent Grant
1. York	6	3	0.90
2. Cambridge	18	6	0.61
3. Sussex	4	3	0.55
UMIST	4	4	0.55
5. Oxford	17	4	0.52
6. Imperial College	10	3	0.48
Warwick	5	2.5	0.48
All universities	242	70	0.29

Source: University of Sussex (1983: 1).

In cash terms, the figures are perhaps even more interesting. Between 1980–81 and 1986–87, the percentage change in UGC funding for the University of Cambridge in real terms was −12.5 per cent without resources for 'new blood' and information technology posts and −10 per cent with them. The respective figures for the University of Oxford were −14.4 per cent and −12.4 per cent. Of all the institutions on the UGC's grant list, excepting the University of York, these special programmes had the largest impact on the University of Cambridge's recurrent grant figures. Besides the Universities of York and Cambridge, only the Universities of Bath, Essex, Sussex, Warwick and Heriot-Watt fared better than Oxford. All the evidence suggests, therefore, that the ancient universities have proved capable of tapping into new initiatives. It should be remembered that as important as these programmes were for particular departments and individuals, they made only a marginal difference to the overall financial position of the universities. For the University of York, they turned a small deficit in the recurrent grant into a small gain; all other institutions on the UGC's list suffered cuts in the value of their recurrent grants between 1980–81 and 1986–87 except the London Business School. In the major financial review of 1981–82, the Universities of Oxford and Cambridge were treated more favourably than most, but by 1986–87 they were 2 of 28 institutions that had suffered cuts in the real value of their recurrent grant of between 10 and 20 per cent; while 8 fared better, 13 were hit more severely.

Not surprisingly, the most insistent question asked of the UGC during these troubled times was how it had arrived at its pattern of cuts. For 1981–82 to 1983–84, these had amounted at the extremes to 1.7 per cent for the University of York and 42.3 per cent for the University of Salford. The explanatory letter from the UGC's chairman, Edward Parkes, was not very informative. It referred to the Committee's long deliberations and 'the useful information and advice' it had received from a number of sources. In other words, the Committee had exercised its judgement and inevitably those who were hardest hit complained the loudest. Some urged the members of the UGC to resign and force the government 'to do its own dirty work'. The retort was that if the UGC did the job, then the universities would suffer less. There were probably also elements in the UGC which relished their new-found power. But the political visibility of the UGC increased and the demand to make it more accountable intensified. It was supposed to be the body which, among other things, represented the interests of the universities to the government. If its function was simply to impose successive financial cuts, and in a manner which many found both puzzling and reprehensible, then its credibility was undermined and its future threatened.

The proposed solution to the dilemma was to move to a system of formula funding. As long as there could be general agreement that the components of the formula were fair, then any future distribution of resources would be attributable to the operation of the formula as opposed to the machinations of the UGC. This may have saved the UGC from the charge of bias, but it also would seem to have undermined its very *raison d'être*. To relinquish the critical function of exercising its judgement over the distribution of the recurrent grant would leave the UGC as little more than a general lobbying body on behalf of the universities. The government would determine the overall size of the grant and the formula would decide its distribution among the institutions on the grant list. Despite its lack of appeal, this is what happened. The alternatives of resignation, complete absorption into the state apparatus, or constantly having to ward off attacks from aggrieved universities, were even less appealing.

The elements of the formula were spelt out in Circular Letter 22/85, which was sent to the vice-chancellors in November 1985. As expected, most of the resources were to be distributed according to what the jargon described as 'teaching-based criteria' (in essence student numbers by subject) with 'research-based criteria' and 'special factors' accounting for the remainder of the allocation. The judgemental element in the UGC's decisions was not quite at an end, for there was to be some selectivity in the distribution of the resources for research. This led to the evaluation of departmental research records, although in the meantime the UGC felt that it could rely on assessments by peers and 'a variety of performance indicators' to make its recommendations. In Circular Letter 4/86, in which the UGC announced the recurrent grant figures for 1986–87, the committee made a strong defence of formula funding:

> The Committee's approach to the distribution of the grant represents a radical break with tradition. In the past grants have been settled by adjustment to figures rooted in the concept of deficiency funding and representing the accumulation of earlier decisions which, because they were taken at different times and for diverse reasons, may have produced inequities. Universities have rightly complained that the process is obscure and have encouraged the UGC to develop a more rational and systematic approach. The Committee has therefore started afresh

and has devised a method of distributing grant based partly on teaching and research criteria to be applied uniformly to all institutions and partly on selective judgements on research (UGC 1986: 1).

Given the battering of the recent past, the universities may have been forgiven for failing to grasp the special novelty of formula funding. Moreover, it was disingenuous (if to be expected) of the Committee not to mention its own political interest in the development of the concept.

The UGC's decision to build into formula funding rewards for research excellence has worked generally to the benefit of the Universities of Oxford and Cambridge. On the other hand, they faced a real threat from the fact that in calculating total incomes, the UGC worked on the assumption that these included 'estimated fee income from planned numbers of home and EC students'. But this was not the case at either Oxford or Cambridge, as much of the fee income went to the colleges rather than the universities. At a stroke, the two universities stood to lose several million pounds. In a letter to the two vice-chancellors, the Secretary of the UGC, Hardyman, noted that:

> ... the principle of a deduction from Cambridge's [Oxford's] grant on account of College fee income is well-established, as you will know. The issue recently before the Committee was, therefore, how much should be deducted this time, rather than whether there should be a deduction at all (University of Cambridge 1986: 560).

Hardyman's letter went on to refer each vice-chancellor to the principles of formula funding, which included in addition two other variables – 'a common level of resourcing for funded student load in each cost centre' and 'minimum provision for special factors' (ibid.). The message was obvious – it was intended to fund students at the same level regardless of the university they attended. The UGC was of the opinion 'that the time had now come for a fundamental reconsideration of College fee income and that it should consider further the issues involved' (ibid). However in the meantime, a decision had to be made:

> The Committee decided that after a calculation for 1989/90 for Cambridge [Oxford] had been made in the same way as for other institutions it should be reduced by 50 per cent of the estimated College fee income in that year. The reduced sum should then be used to arrive at the 1986/87 grant by interpolation (ibid.).

Although the outcome was financially damaging to the Universities of Oxford and Cambridge, it could have been a more severe crisis. One may wonder why the reduction was to be limited to only half of the estimated college fee income and why it should be phased in gently over 4 years. In fact after negotiations, both universities succeeded in mitigating the damage still further. The consequence is that even without taking into account the colleges' own resources, teaching at Oxbridge remains more generously funded by the state than at other universities.

Despite all of the dramatic changes to university funding that took place in the 1980s, the UGC insisted on retaining a measure of optimism. We have already noted its bullish defence of formula funding. It persisted in claiming that the principle of the block grant remained intact. Thus Circular 22/85 boldly asserted that 'The purpose of the allocation process is to enable the Committee to settle the grant to be made available to each university, not to determine how the university should spend it' (UGC 1985: 1), and the same point was re-affirmed in Circular 4/86: 'Responsibility for deciding how the grant should be spent continues to rest with the universities in the light of their own circumstances . . .' (UGC 1986: 2). These are statements that the UGC could have made at any time in its history. But Circular 4/86 did add the crucial rider – 'and of any guidance which the Committee may provide'. Of course, the most concrete form of guidance was the various special programmes that the Committee had launched but, as these were only a small fraction of its overall budget, it could be argued that such explicit direction was limited. What comfort it was to the universities to know that they remained the real masters of their destinies when confronted with income cuts which brought many of them to the verge of insolvency is another matter. To reiterate the ideology of the past when so much of the substance of the past has been destroyed is to mock rather than to reassure.

The evidence demonstrates that neither the University of Cambridge nor the University of Oxford were immune to the effects of this maelstrom. The 1981 cuts did not hit them as severely as most other British universities, but by 1986–87 their relative position had deteriorated. They took full advantage of the special programmes mounted by the UGC, but these made no more than a marginal contribution to their overall financial positions. The move towards formula funding had brought into the open the fact that both universities were in receipt of a double payment of fees and, although they were able to mitigate its full potential effects, the change-over eroded somewhat their established advantage. Even the selectivity built into resources awarded for 'research-based criteria' did not always benefit them. A Notice on the University of Cambridge's Finances revealed that 'the grant for 1988–89 is some £607 000 less than had been anticipated from the previous grant letter . . .', while the projected figure for 1989–90 was £951 000 below expectations (University of Cambridge 1988b: 447). This was partly because of the recalculation of student numbers in modern languages, and – more interestingly – because of reductions in the block grant for overheads on research grants and contracts. Although Cambridge's research income was expanding, it was not growing at the rate of other universities, and thus the reduction in the figure for overheads! Once the formula was in place no target was sacroscant.

The scale and pace of the reduction in the UGC's recurrent grant meant that at least in the short-run the universities had to reduce their commitments. They were assisted by grants from the UGC specifically for the purposes of restructuring their institutions, but in view of faculty tenure there was particular pressure not to fill vacant posts. Neither Oxford nor

Cambridge have been exempted from this process, as a letter to *The Times* from the vice-chairman of Oxford's General Board of the Faculties made clear:

> Faced with the prospect of being able to refill only 25 posts out of some 112 vacancies at October 1989, the University has to subject every faculty, individual post, to the severest scrutiny. Some posts will need to be filled immediately, others will be suspended, others abolished. Each decision is tough, and every one is taken not arbitrarily but on the advice, on the purely academic priorities, of the faculty board concerned' (*The Times*, 31 May 1988).

The vice-chairman's letter was a response to criticism of a decision not to fill, once their present incumbents had retired, the Regius Chairs of Greek and Ancient History. Although Cambridge intended to fill its regius chairs should they become vacant, the recently retired Vice-Chancellor Michael McCrum has stated that 'in recent years our main way of balancing the books has been leaving vacant posts unfilled, and allowing almost no new development' (McCrum, n.d.: 16).

The vice-chairman of Oxford's General Board in his above letter to *The Times* (1988) had suggested that there was some positive planning in the decision-making process: '. . . the position as regards modern history is that after careful consideration of the academic case, two other prestigious history chairs were accorded higher priority than the Regius Professorship'. In other words, there was a measure of selectivity in the exercise. As the posts were already vacant, it was possible to act in this manner, but it has proven more difficult to make future plans which have built into them the assumption that some academic areas could expect to expand while others could expect to contract. For example, built into Cambridge's Academic Plan for the period 1987–90, was a 5 per cent saving in expenditure by 1990 with targets for the various bodies determined by '. . . the percentage deviation of the average cost per FTE student at each cost centre in Cambridge from the national average for those cost centres' (University of Cambridge 1988a: 273). But in a short space of time, as the 'Notice on the University's Finances' later in 1988 revealed, owing to an 'unexpected reduction in grant income', the savings target was revised upwards to '7 per cent or more, with a consequence increase in the number of posts that must be left unfilled or suppressed' (University of Cambridge 1988b: 448). This is a good example of using national averages to spread the misery equally, as opposed to making selective cuts that would require even tougher decisions.

Accompanying the short-term measure of pruning posts was the equally inevitable decision to run down reserves and/or accumulate deficits. The following note of weary resignation was struck by Cambridge's Academic Plan for 1987–1990:

> Given the anticipated deficits of 1.5 per cent to 2 per cent a year over the next three years an overall savings target of 5 per cent has been set by the central bodies for achievement by 1989/90. On the above assumptions there are likely to be deficits of the order of £600 000 in

each of the years 1987/88 and 1988/89, which will exhaust our reserves, currently about £1m. The aim is to bring the accounts back into balance by 1989/90 or soon after when the economies come fully into effect (University of Cambridge 1988a: 271).

In each of the 5 years from 1983–84 to 1987–88, Oxford's accounts were also in deficit, ranging from £118 000 to close to £2 million (University of Oxford 1988: 22). The failure to guarantee level funding after the cuts imposed between 1981–82 and 1983–84 led Oxford to the conclusion that it could only maintain its academic activities at an acceptable level by 'a massive drain on reserves which are already too small for safety' (Aspen 1985: 3).

The response of shedding posts and running down reserves obviously could not go on indefinitely; either the Exchequer would have to relent or the universities, including Oxford and Cambridge, would simply melt away. And yet it was clear that the government had no intention of relenting. The only option open to the universities, therefore, was for them to find alternative sources of income to the UGC's recurrent grant. In several respects, the Universities of Oxford and Cambridge were better placed than other British universities to loosen the financial stranglehold of the state. In the inter-war years, their endowment income constituted a significant percentage of their total income. Although it declined to relatively insignificant proportions after 1945, none the less it remained a more substantial figure at Oxford, amounting to 6.3 per cent of total income in 1980–81 compared to 0.9 per cent for all British universities. The figure for Cambridge was significantly lower at 2.2 per cent, but it was still the second best endowed university in the country (UGC 1980b: 12–13). Secondly, as collegiate universities, Oxford and Cambridge have been able to turn to their colleges for help. For example, the colleges have been prepared to put more resources into university teaching, which at Oxford has meant a larger college financial input into the CUF lectureships and at Cambridge the creation of college-financed non-university teaching officers (NUTOs). Trinity College, Cambridge, has established the Isaac Newton Trust Fund which assists the university financially, while certain Oxford colleges have subscribed to the university's appeal, the 'Campaign for Oxford'.

Given the prestige of Oxford and Cambridge, it is not surprising that they have launched campaign appeals. As the present Chancellor of Oxford, Lord Jenkins of Hillhead, forthrightly observed: 'They have richer alumni, more glamour and therefore greater money-pulling capacity' (THES 1988: 2). The problem is that higher education in Britain has not attracted much charitable interest, comparing very unfavourably with US universities. Moreover, the tax system is not as supportive of charitable contributions as it might be. The one significant exception to this generalization has been the ability of the Oxbridge colleges to attract endowments which, ironically, could work against the interests of the universities. It is possible that the bulk of institutional money will find its way into the university appeals while personal contributions are made to the colleges. To date, Oxford's campaign has a larger budget, more administrative support, and has generated the greater publicity. It has been conceived as a 5-year operation which aims to raise £220 million, and although contributions can be made for specific purposes, it is a general appeal fund whose purpose is to increase the university's endowment. The Cambridge Foundation, the trust established to manage Cambridge's appeal, is directed more at raising funds for specific targets which have been agreed in advance. It is too soon to judge the success of the appeals. The 'Campaign for Oxford' was officially launched on 26 October 1988 and as late as 15 November of the same year Cambridge was discussing whether the creation of a trust was indeed the most appropriate umbrella under which to run its appeal! What both universities really want are either endowments that generate unfettered income or, should contributions be for specific purposes (e.g. establishing new professorial chairs or building new premises), then there needs to be an endowment component that meets future overheads. There seems little point in extending the activities and infrastructure of the universities if this is going to result in their incurring additional costs. What we suspect will happen, despite Oxford's own commitment to a 5-year campaign, is that such efforts will become a permanent feature of university life, although the form they take could change over time. Oxford may conclude its present campaign but none the less continue its fund-raising activities.

The Universities of Oxford and Cambridge, as well as their colleges, possess tangible assets – that is, in addition to their prestige – which could be loaned or sold to generate income. To date, the most publicized move in this direction was the suggestion that Oxford University Press should be turned into a public company with the university retaining 51 per cent of the shares (THES 1987: 3). This particular proposal was scotched, but it none the less does raise the possibility that perhaps it would be in the best long-term interest of the universities to realize some of their assets and redeploy the acquired capital. One tangible asset which the colleges have used repeatedly to their financial advantage is their land holdings. The colleges are larger landowners than the universities and, moreover, the latter have faced the problem that their property is more likely to have been acquired with public funds which makes it harder to dispose of. In its *Annual Survey* for 1984–85, the UGC laid down guidelines by which universities can dispose 'of sites or properties' and retain at least a proportion of the proceeds (p. 15). Invariably, moves to develop or dispose of assets bring forth charges of 'asset stripping', 'selling the family silver' or 'vandalising the cultural heritage' – which carry considerable weight in Oxbridge circles – but this has been done in the past and there is no absolute bar at present.

While the campaigns to raise money in the marketplace may be successful in the long term, in the meantime both Oxford and Cambridge have taken more immediate income-generating steps to lessen their dependence upon their recurrent grants. Notably, in common with other universities, they have expanded the number of overseas students who pay full-cost fees and have attracted more research contracts and grants. By 1988–89, the recurrent grant for Oxford amounted to 43.6 per cent of total income compared to 48.2

Table 3.5 Selected income sources as a percentage of total income, 1988–89

	Grant	Fees	Endowments	Research	Services
Highest %	75.2	22.0	5.5	30.9	16.0
Lowest %	43.6	9.5	0.1	4.9	1.4
Oxford	43.6	11.3	5.5	30.9	3.7
Cambridge	48.2	13.9	2.8	26.5	2.9
Total (UK)	53.0	12.5	1.5	20.0	6.9

Note: The fees are total fee income. The London and Manchester Business Schools have been excluded from the calculations and all the Welsh institutions form one category.
Source: UFC (1990b: 10–11).

per cent at Cambridge and to a figure for the UK as a whole of 53.0 per cent (UFC 1990b: 10–11). Putting to one side the rather special cases of the London and Manchester Business Schools and the University of Wales' College of Medicine, of all the institutions on the UGC's grant list, Oxford received the lowest percentage of its total income from its recurrent grant in 1988–89. Although by comparison Cambridge has remained more dependent upon its recurrent grant, it has moved in the same direction as Oxford and its dependence is less than most other British universities.

The most obvious conclusion to draw from the above evidence is that in the 1980s the dependence of the universities upon the UGC for their recurrent income was on the decline, falling steadily throughout the decade. This declining dependence has been replaced by an increasing diversity of the funding sources of the institutions in receipt of Exchequer grants. In the wake of the expansion of the UGC's input into the universities, other sources of income paled into insignificance; as the UGC's input has declined, so a range of other sources have increased in importance. The implication is that the dwindling financial importance of the UGC has encouraged the diversification of the character of higher education in the UK. Table 3.5 illustrates the extent of the varying dependence on the differing sources of income.

Within itself such differentiation is not conclusive proof that the individual institutions on the UGC's grant list are evolving their special characters but it points strongly in that direction. For example the variations in the incomes for research grants and other services rendered suggest that the concentration, and presumably the visibiltiy, of such activities varies widely from campus to campus. All, for example, may do some funded research but how much is quite a different matter. Do we now have a university system or do we require a different label to conceptualize the sum of its parts?

Conclusions

Since the creation in 1919 of the UGC, there have been three main phases in the financial relationship between the state and the universities. The first phase, the inter-war years, was one in which a comparatively stable university system received approximately one-third of its annual recurrent income from the UGC. The UGC's grant was a block grant awarded on the assumption that it underwrote those basic needs that the universities lacked the resources to fulfil. The UGC's grants were determined quinquennially, which distanced the state from the day-to-day affairs of the universities, while allowing them to undertake long-term planning with a measure of certainty. Over time, these various facets of the financial relationship of the state and the universities assumed the status of sacred principles which ensured – allegedly – the autonomy of the universities. On the contrary, we have argued that they were pragmatic guidelines that enabled institutions to establish working relationships. Inevitably, as the UGC's financial input expanded rapidly in the second phase (approximately 1939–74) and went into reverse in the third phase (from approximately 1974), so the realities of the financial relationship changed sharply, although the so-called principles upon which that relationship was supposedly based showed remarkable resilience. To the very end of its existence, the UGC was claiming that it merely made resources available to the universities which determined how they were spent.

For the most part, the evidence suggests that both the Universities of Oxford and Cambridge followed the general trend in the financial relationship between the state and the universities. In the inter-war years, their endowment incomes were more substantial elements in their budgets and, although in comparative terms this continued after 1945, their dependence on the UGC's recurrent grant was overwhelming. In the company of a number of other universities, they led the way in increasing the relative input of their research income which has continued to grow, especially at Oxford, ever since. It would be a grave mistake to assume that they were shielded from the effects of the serious decline in the UGC's recurrent grant which began in earnest in 1981. Although in the 1981–84 phase their loss of UGC income was comparatively less severe, by the latter half of the decade their relative position had declined to a point where it was scarcely better than that of any other university. The advent of formula funding posed them with a real threat and, although this was mitigated after negotiations, none the less it was still a nerve-racking time. Other universities might argue, and perhaps justly, that the screw should have been turned even tighter, but this is not to deny the trauma experienced by Oxford and Cambridge. Both the Universities of Oxford and Cambridge showed their ability to relieve the worst effects of the crisis by picking up the financial morsels that the UGC made available in the form of its special programmes. But there was no way either university could avoid the necessity of draining their reserves and cutting their commitments. In the meantime, the generation of new resources was under way. In the short term, the increase in income from research grants and contracts has been most impressive, and in the long run it is just possible that their respective appeals will show that the market is prepared to underwrite university expenditure – something that the historical evidence would seem to deny. Of course, what it may demonstrate is that the market is prepared to support Oxford and Cambridge rather than British universities in general, thus intensifying the diversity of university income sources that accompanied the decline in the financial dominance of the UGC.

With the demise of the UGC, and its replacement by the UFC, another phase in the financial relationship between the universities and the state has commenced. To the bitter end, the UGC clung to the idea that the universities were in control of their own destinies, that it remained essentially a mechanism by which the financial needs of the universities and the resources of the Exchequer could be linked. The fact that the universities continued to receive the bulk of their resources from the UGC in the form of a block grant – albeit one that was cash-limited, determined by formula funding and unlikely to be protected fully from inflationary pressures – enabled the UGC to argue that the basis of the original relationship between the universities and itself remained substantially intact. The block grant, in other words, was the best defence of university autonomy. Although the financial relationship of the UFC to the universities will be on a different footing from that which linked the UGC to the universities, it is as yet unclear as to precisely what form it will eventually take. Initially, it was proposed that the universities would derive most of their income by submitting offers to teach stated numbers of undergraduate and postgraduate students in defined academic subject groups (20 such groups were listed). The universities were to bid against one another in their offers to teach students at designated guide prices, although they could offer to teach all or some of those students below the guide prices or, in special cases, above the guide prices. In medicine, dentistry and veterinary science, the number of student places available would continue to be determined by the government and were to be funded only at the guide prices (in other words, competitive bidding was not to be permitted for these subjects). It is now history that the UFC has abandoned these procedures and in what form they will be resurrected (if at all) remains to be seen. Meanwhile, the UFC has introduced even more selectivity in awarding research funds, although as before these are calculated on the basis of a formula (UFC 1989).

Clearly, what the government wanted was a decline in the unit costs of teaching and believed that this could be achieved by requiring the universities to bid for students in relation to guide prices. The bidding system was frustrated by the failure of the universities to make many bids below the recommended guide prices but, as the universities have learnt to their cost, there is more than one way of skinning a cat. There will also be more competition for research grants and contracts as the ability to increase income from these sources will influence how the UFC distributes that proportion of its grant earmarked for research. Moreover, the UFC has not abandoned the obligation of the universities to produce academic plans, now to be constructed on a 4-year cycle. The concoction is an interesting, if somewhat curious, mixture of state supervision coupled with an attempt to encourage inter-university (and intra-university) competition through the manipulation of bureaucratically determined criteria. For example, in the defunct bidding system the guide prices of the various academic subjects were decided not by market forces but arrived at by calculating the historic costs to the Exchequer. In the sense that the universities were to determine their own bids, they remained autonomous institutions. The question is whether the constraints upon autonomy, inherent within such a system, were likely to be greater or less than the constraints that developed over time out of the financial relationship between the UGC and the universities. Is the government striving for more efficient mechanisms of controlling universities' costs, and influencing the course of their academic development, while allowing them to continue to make their own academic plans? In our final chapter, we return to these issues.

Although the creation of the UFC, and the associated struggle for different operating principles, is the clearest manifestation that a new financial era has commenced, other developments are also worth a mention. The age of student loans is upon us and the pressures to lessen the state's responsibility for student maintenance are likely to intensify. The repercussions, if any, of this for student demand has yet to be gauged, but the potential impact is considerable. In future, the research councils will handle a larger percentage of the government's input into university research, which will reinforce the UFC's own moves towards greater selectivity in the allocation of research funds. While the competition for research funds will increase, so the differentiation in the research character of universities and their individual departments will widen. So far, the government has resisted pressures for a student voucher scheme, although it has increased the percentage of income that universities will receive from fees. Whether this will make the universities more sensitive to student demand remains to be seen. Obviously, student demand will become a critical factor should universities take the opportunity – as government ministers and some vice-chancellors have urged – of increasing their incomes by charging supplementary fees. It may have potentially attractive financial pay-offs, but with it go all the uncertainties of marketplace pressures that the British universities have found so unappealing. The inhibition against too explicit inter-university competition remains strong. It is hard to imagine that Oxford and Cambridge would *not* benefit financially from such a move, but to date they have not broken ranks and neither do they seem likely to. For many Oxbridge people, the idea that the Universities should cash in on their status, while not anathema, has little appeal.

4

Colleges and the Blessings of Endowment Income

Constraining the colleges

Prior to the twentieth century, wealth, power and prestige at both Oxford and Cambridge resided in the colleges rather than in the universities. Neither university had much of a separate identity or control of its own affairs, so firm was the hold of powerful college interests. A central purpose of parliamentary intervention in the nineteenth century was to redress the balance of influence between university and colleges, to establish a model of a collegiate university in which the university could pursue its own interests without being totally at the mercy of the colleges. To accomplish this goal, resources had to be redirected from the colleges to the universities. Fearing that this would be one of its recommendations, it is not surprising that the colleges should boycott Russell's Royal Commission. Whether the colleges objected more to compulsion than augmenting university coffers is a matter of debate; however, what cannot be denied is that by 1919 the principle of transferring resources was firmly established. Indeed, the formal legitimation for Asquith's Commission was to enquire whether there were sufficient resources within the Oxbridge colleges to negate the universities' need for recurrent Treasury grants.

The recommendation of the 1850 Royal Commission that the richer colleges should support various university posts was given statutory backing in 1853, and the Oxford and Cambridge Act 1877 created college contribution schemes whereby the colleges were in effect taxed on their endowments for the benefit of the universities. In his evidence to the Franks Inquiry, Mr Keen, then secretary to Oxford's Curators of the Chest, claimed that the college contributions scheme 'was regarded as the cornerstone of a tripartite treaty between the University, the colleges and the UGC', which would make it difficult to change its purpose (University of Oxford 1965: Pt 2). Whatever the difficulties perceived by Keen, this is precisely what the Franks Report recommended. After the Franks Report, the Oxford colleges were taxed on a different basis and the sums raised augmented the endowments of the poorer colleges rather than the general income of the university. The

University of Cambridge has moved in the same direction. Between 1967–68 and 1985–86, the maximum sum from college contributions that could be devoted to the general purposes of the University of Cambridge was reduced gradually from £190 000 to £10 000, since when college contributions have not been put to the general purposes of the university but go into a fund which essentially serves the colleges.

What made this redirection of college resources possible was the massive post-1945 increase in the size of the UGC's recurrent grants. It became increasingly difficult to see the two universities as the poor relations of their colleges. Thus there were internal pressures to redirect college contributions to the poorer colleges and there does not appear to have been any significant objection to the move from either the UGC or the DES. While the notion that the colleges should make a significant financial input into the universities is dated, the balance of financial power is far from static and in their recent crises both Oxford and Cambridge have looked to their colleges for assistance. While this has been forthcoming, it seems unlikely that the college contributions schemes as originally designed will be resurrected. Initially, therefore, the state looked to the colleges to provide the universities with financial sustenance but then increased its input to the point where the resources of the richer colleges could be used to the benefit of the poorer colleges rather than the universities. Now the various parties – colleges, universities and the government – are pinning their hopes on the market as the great benefactor of the future.

If the first concern of government was to redirect resources from colleges to the universities, then the second was that the colleges should keep their costs under control. In recent years, this interest has been linked closely to the political desire to control state expenditure on higher education, but at the time of the Asquith Commission, when the state was starting to make both a regular and significant input into university incomes, the pressure upon colleges to control their costs stemmed more from the wish to place an Oxbridge education within the bounds of poorer scholars. Thus the Commission showed considerable interest in catering costs with much discussion of the feasibility and desirability of centralizing the purchase of supplies (Royal Commission on Oxford and Cambridge Universities 1922b: App. 10). In a contemporary debate in the House of Lords, Viscount Haldane contended that only one-third of the costs of keeping a student at 'the ancient universities' were met by privately paid fees (*Hansard* (Lords) 1923: 745). The implication was that other sources of college income were being used to subsidize the education of students who could well afford to do without such assistance. The Asquith Commission concluded that college fees should be set at a level which met the full cost of board and lodging (Royal Commission on Oxford and Cambridge Universities 1922a: 200). This may have helped to swell colleges' incomes, and prevented colleges from subsidizing the costs of their richer students, but it is difficult to see how it would have aided poorer students unless the released resources were directed towards them.

The attention periodically devoted to the costs of college life has betrayed as much interest in curbing the over-indulgence of the idle rich as with promoting the cause of the worthy poor. The Franks Inquiry, for example, was anxious that Oxford should not be seen as encouraging too much gracious living, and like the Asquith Commission before it, raised the question of whether colleges could cut their costs by co-ordinating their purchase of supplies. *Brideshead Revisited* is not an Oxford image that many of today's dons find attractive; scholarship may require its comforts but excess is to be avoided.

If the colleges were to be cost-conscious institutions, then it was necessary for them to publish intelligible accounts that demonstrated their probity. To this end, the accountants Messrs W.B. Peat drew up a model form of accounts for the Asquith Commission, which are reproduced in its evidence (Royal Commission on Oxford and Cambridge Universities 1922b: 332–41). With minor modifications, the Cambridge colleges have used it ever since, whereas the Oxford colleges now present their accounts in a form recommended by the Franks Inquiry (University of Oxford 1966a: 164–9). After the Asquith Commission, the college accounts were required to carry the W.B. Peat seal of approval:

> We hereby certify that the Accounts of the College are duly kept in the form prescribed by Statute, that the foregoing Revenue and Capital Accounts and the Balance Sheet are correct and that such Balance Sheet represents a true statement of the affairs of the College according to the best of our information and the explanations given to us and as shown by the Books of the College (Royal Commission on Oxford and Cambridge Universities 1922b: 340).

Henceforth, if colleges were not displaying the frugality that was widely considered necessary, then presumably the accounts could be expected to reveal their excesses.

Although over the past century the financial affairs of the Oxbridge colleges have been more closely regulated, none the less the colleges have remained very much in control of their own monies. The clearest manifestation of this financial independence is that endowments, and the income they generate, continue to be seen as resources which belong to the individual colleges. The Asquith Commission heard evidence for the pooling of endowments; that they should be managed by one central body within each university and the income derived from them should be distributed among the colleges according to an agreed formula (ibid.: 13–14). The Commission firmly rejected this line of argument and claimed that there was a relationship between the overall well-being of collegiate universities and the independence of their colleges. If endowments could not be made to individual colleges, then it was possible that they would not be made at all. Moreover, endowments allegedly helped to create the special character of colleges and to pool them would undermine these particular identities. These were arguments to be repeated in the report of the Franks Inquiry over 40 years later. How much of this is rationalization rather than reality is hard to say, for presumably colleges would control how they spent their share of a pooled endowment income. Whatever the truth may be, it is evident that the internal political opposition to pooling arrangements would be very fierce indeed, and that the understanding of college independence – still a highly prized Oxbridge value – continues to incorporate the idea that colleges manage their own endowments.

The fact that colleges are independent institutions has not prevented the growth of a wide measure of inter-collegiate cooperation at both Oxford and Cambridge. There are, for example, inter-collegiate bodies for admissions, teaching and financial matters and, as we will show, their creation owes much to external pressure. Up until now, these are not bodies which can impose binding decisions, but rather work by establishing common denominators and building consensus around them. There is always the risk that their work can be jeopardized by the strong-minded maverick. One of the central recommendations of the Franks Inquiry was that the Oxford colleges should form a Council of Colleges which was to be composed of the vice-chancellor and one person appointed by each college. This proposed body was 'to consider all matters affecting the colleges' and that 'every college and other society ... shall be bound by decisions taken by an absolute majority of the members of the Council of the Colleges' (University of Oxford 1966a: 338). At about the same time, Bridges' Syndicate recommended that Cambridge should establish a Board of Colleges (University of Cambridge 1962: 1101–1103). It was intended that this should be a small body composed of representatives of the colleges who would make appointments in rotation, as well as members nominated by the Council of the Senate. Significantly, it was *not* proposed that it should arrive at its decisions through majority voting or that those decisions would be binding upon the colleges. Optimistically, Bridges' Syndicate expected the board of colleges to be 'a body which would seek a solution which represented the general sense of the meeting rather than a compromise between sectional interests' (ibid.: 1101).

But the best laid plans can go astray. Oxford rejected the proposals for a Council of Colleges, although it has a Conference of Colleges to which each college can send two representatives, but votes are not taken and it has no authority to bind individual colleges to a particular course of action. Opinion as to its merits are divided; for the most part, it seems to have been little more than a talking shop, but it has taken important initiatives on college fees, a matter we will come to shortly. The recommendation to create a board of colleges at Cambridge, like so many of the proposals of Bridges' Syndicate, ran – in the words of Lord Annan – 'into the sands' (Interview: 2 April 1986). Cambridge does have a Colleges' Committee which is composed of the heads of colleges, but it is scarcely more effective than Oxford's Conference of Colleges. Should, however, college government be reformed in the light of the Wass Report (see Chapter 9), then the status of this committee could be upgraded. The recent history of college government would suggest, therefore, that while the colleges have extended cooperation and implemented common programmes of action, they are distinctly unwilling to be bound by bodies that wield executive authority and arrive at decisions through majority votes. The desire of the colleges to retain the ultimate formal control of their affairs remains as strong as ever.

However, although there has been little support for proposals either to deprive colleges of their endowment income or to weaken how they manage their financial affairs, this is not the same as saying that they are financially independent institutions. The expansion of student numbers, coupled with the commitment of the state to pay tuition fees, has meant an inevitable increase in the flow of resources from the Exchequer into the colleges. In other words, the debate about what happens to university autonomy if the Exchequer should become the paymaster is also applicable to the colleges. As with the universities, there are two broad considerations: the threat to the financial welfare of colleges should governments decide to reduce their level of support for college fees, and the possibility that the state, in return for the Exchequer's input, would try to influence college policy in both financial and academic matters.

The various college charges, primarily fees to cover tuition costs as well as board and lodging, can be seen as payments for services rendered. At the same time, the Exchequer's input into the colleges discharges a statutory obligation, for it was Parliament that agreed to meet the full tuition costs of home-based students and to make means-tested grants. With respect to collegiate universities, and Oxford and Cambridge in particular, the state's commitment to pay fees results in two interrelated problems. In the first place, in a collegiate university, the state incurs higher tuition costs than in the unitary universities. The accounts of the Cambridge colleges neatly illustrate the point. They contain a 'tuition account' which invariably on the income side consists of just two items: university dues (i.e. university fees which are collected by the colleges on behalf of the university) and fees for college tuition and supervision. Historically, the UGC's recurrent grant was adjusted to take into account this payment of two sets of fees, but not to the point where it could be said that no financial advantages accrued to Oxford and Cambridge. Secondly, and this is a more contentious point, it is necessary to consider what college costs are built into 'the board and lodging' account. The statements of the accounts of both the Oxford and Cambridge colleges contain an internal revenue account, that is Account 11 for the Cambridge colleges and Account V for the Oxford colleges. At Oxford, the kitchen account is incorporated in its internal revenue account but it is listed as a separate item in the accounts of the Cambridge colleges. As expected, the largest item of expenditure is on the wages of college staff followed by expenditure on catering supplies. In addition, however, the internal revenue accounts include items such as insurance premiums, and repair and maintenance charges. The accounts of the Oxford colleges indicate that there are also transfers from the 'education and research account' (broadly equivalent to Cambridge's tuition account) to help meet these items of expenditure. By paying maintenance grants, and the Oxford college accounts would suggest also through the payment of tuition fees, the Exchequer is helping the colleges to maintain themselves as viable institutions. There is nothing startling about such revelations, for inevitably students will cause wear and tear and the colleges can be expected to build into their fees a charge to cover overheads. The question is whether the Exchequer is helping to maintain colleges that provide 'board and lodging' at an unacceptably high price. For example, given their many ancient buildings, the colleges are likely to have high maintenance bills and some would consider that not all of their buildings (e.g. the chapels) are essential to an educational institution. Be that as it may, the state has been prepared to pay both extra tuition fees and in the past higher maintenance grants for students at both the Universities of Oxford and Cambridge, although the screw has been tightened in recent years.

In Chapter 3, we showed how the financial dependence of the British universities, including Oxford and Cambridge, upon the UGC's recurrent grant increased dramatically after 1945. Although universities retained a variety of other income sources, the relative importance of these declined to the point where it can be said that the Exchequer, through the UGC and to a lesser extent the research councils, was the paymaster. As Oxford and Cambridge are collegiate universities, we need to know whether their colleges followed the same path. Was the essential precondition of autonomy (i.e. financial independence) also eroded within the colleges?

College accounts are drawn up to show the income and expenditure of the colleges and do not reveal the capital that colleges possess (Boys Smith 1959: 3). It is impossible therefore to discern accurately their wealth from the accounts, although it would be possible to hazard a guess as to the size of their resources from the income they generate. However, there are college resources – books, paintings, silver – that do not earn income, and because they need to be insured, protected and occasionally restored, on the contrary may incur costs. In our analysis of college accounts, we have restricted our attention to income rather than wealth. Wealth is of importance because it enables the colleges to conjure up the means to meet their recurrent obligations. It is the ability to generate their own income that enables institutions to maintain the preconditions that ensure their autonomy.

The best measure of a college's financial independence is its endowment income, which is composed primarily of rents on agricultural and commercial property, and of interests and dividends. Not all of a college's endowment income is available for its own purposes; some resources may be needed to retain the endowment, and the income – as we have discussed – is taxed to assist the poorer colleges. It is possible to obtain, however, comparable figures of gross endowment income and, although these figures obviously inflate the income at the disposal of the individual colleges, they will give an accurate picture of their relative standing. Moreover, to have calculated a figure for net endowment income would have made comparisons more difficult. The two universities permit different deductible items from the gross endowment incomes of the colleges before they are taxed, and following the

Franks Inquiry the Oxford colleges have been permitted fewer deductions. Furthermore, it should not be assumed that the colleges derive no benefits from their endowment incomes until they have been taxed. Thus it would have been more complicated to have calculated net endowment incomes and it would have resulted in figures that did not represent the full resources available to the colleges as a whole. We have, therefore, decided to compare gross endowment incomes and total incomes and the reader should consult Appendix 1 to learn how these have been calculated.

We have examined the following 20 Oxford and 17 Cambridge colleges for which records of their accounts are available back to 1920:

- *Oxford*: All Souls, Balliol, Brasenose, Christ Church, Corpus Christi, Exeter, Hertford, Jesus, Lincoln, Magdalen, Merton, New, Oriel, Pembroke, Queen's, St John's, Trinity, University, Wadham, and Worcester.
- *Cambridge*: Christ's, Clare, Corpus Christi, Downing, Emmanuel, Gonville and Caius, Jesus, King's, Magdalene, Pembroke, Peterhouse, Queens', St Catharine's, St John's, Sidney Sussex, Trinity, and Trinity Hall.

The most important omission is the women's colleges (most of which of course are now mixed colleges). Their accounts used to be more inaccessible and were not presented consistently in the same form as the accounts of the men's colleges, so making comparisons more hazardous. The women's colleges, like the other excluded institutions, tend not to be as well endowed as the colleges whose accounts we have examined. This, and other possible modifications, to the perspective created by the 37 colleges under examination, are discussed in the text.

Sources of college income: The tranquil years

Table 4.1 presents the gross endowment income figures for the financial years 1919–20, 1929–30 and 1939–40. What is most remarkable about Table 4.1 is the stability over time of both the relative position of individual colleges and the overall size of their endowment income. At Oxford in 1920, Hertford College was the least well-endowed college, with an endowment that generated an income of less than £1000, a position the college retained for the next 20 years. Of the next four most poorly endowed Oxford colleges in 1940 – that is, Exeter, Pembroke, Wadham and Worcester – all four also had had endowment incomes of less than £10 000 in 1920. At the other end of the Oxford continuum, Magdalen and Christ Church had the highest endowment incomes in both 1920 and 1940. What was true of Oxford was also true of Cambridge. The least well-endowed five colleges across the 20-year period were Downing, Magdalene, Queens', St Catharine's and Trinity Hall, while Peterhouse and Pembroke took turns to fill the sixth least favourable spot. At the other end of the scale stood Trinity College, clearly and consistently the best endowed of the Cambridge colleges. In fact, Trinity

Table 4.1　Oxford and Cambridge colleges: Gross endowment incomes, 1920–40

	Number of Colleges					
	1919–20		*1929–30*		*1939–40*	
	Oxford	*Cambridge*	*Oxford*	*Cambridge*	*Oxford*	*Cambridge*
Under £5 000	2	2	1	0	1	0
£5 001–£10 000	4	4	6	1	4	0
£10 001–£20 000	5	7	3	7	5	6
£20 001–£40 000	5	1	4	5	3	7
£40 001–£60 000	2	2	4	1	4	1
£60 001–£80 000	0	0	0	2	1	1
£80 001–£100 000	2	1	2	0	2	1
Over £100 000	0	0	0	1	0	1
Total number of colleges	20	17	20	17	20	17

Sources: Royal Commission on Oxford and Cambridge Universities (1922b: 325–32), University of Cambridge (1931, 1941), University of Oxford (1930, 1940).

College probably remains the most favourably endowed educational institution in the UK. St John's and King's College competed keenly for the second spot followed at some distance by Gonville and Caius, and then Emmanuel.

In 1920, the total gross endowment income of the 20 Oxford colleges was £513 256; by 1930 it had reached £529 224 and by 1940 rose to £619 504. Over the 20-year span this was an increase of 20.7 per cent. The 17 Cambridge colleges did somewhat better, raising their total gross endowment income from £373 700 in 1920 to £628 101 in 1940, an increase of 72.7 per cent. We have no way of accounting for the better record of the Cambridge colleges; either they were underperforming in 1920 and/or managed their financial affairs more competently or with a greater slice of luck than the Oxford colleges in the inter-war years. Allowing for the relative stability in the value of money (the retail price index rose sharply between 1914 and 1920, from 100 to 225, but had declined to 159 by 1938) these are no more than respectable rates of growth.

The Cambridge colleges also had a narrower range of endowment incomes than the Oxford colleges. While one or two Cambridge colleges could be said to have outstandingly generous endowment incomes, the more typical college was moderately endowed: 11 of the 17 colleges had endowment incomes of between £5000 and £20 000 in 1920, and 12 of the 17 in 1930 and 13 of the 17 in 1940 had endowment incomes of between £10 000 and £40 000. By comparison, there were more poorly endowed Oxford colleges to contrast with the much wealthier colleges of Magdalen and Christ Church. Thus the 1930 and 1940 figures show the balance of endowment income at the Oxford colleges as notably lower than at the Cambridge colleges, and while Oxford clearly had more poorer colleges, Cambridge had a somewhat richer head coupled with a less pronounced poorer tail.

It is evident from the gross endowment income figures presented in Table 4.1 that several of the Oxbridge colleges would have remained rather paltry educational institutions if their well-being had depended upon endowment income alone. Put simply, they lacked the resources to be vibrant educational institutions without alternative sources of income. They required a healthy fee-paying student base to make up for their lack of wealth. Nearly all the nineteenth- and twentieth-century foundations (with the clear exception of Nuffield College), including all the women's colleges, fall into this category.

At Oxford, the two extremes were represented by Hertford College and All Souls College: the former because it had no endowment income worth speaking of, while All Souls, because it had neither undergraduate nor postgraduate students, had little else but endowment income! The absence of either a Hertford College or an All Souls College meant that there were less extremes at Cambridge. Only at King's College, and then only in 1940, did a Cambridge college have a gross endowment income that constituted over 80 per cent of its total income. In conjunction with the comparatively moderate increases in the total amounts of endowment income, the stability of these distributions reflect the overall steady state of the two universities. Between the wars, there was not a sufficiently large enough expansion of student numbers to upset the relationship that had existed in 1920 between the major sources of college income. Between 1920–21 and 1938–39, Cambridge increased its total full-time student numbers from 5187 to 5931, while Oxford grew from 4205 to 5023 (UGC 1936: 52–3; 1938–39: 7).

Not only is the overall picture very stable, but the same is true of the individual colleges. At Oxford, of the 10 colleges whose gross endowment income made up at least 60 per cent of their total income in 1920, only Jesus College had fallen below that figure by 1940; while at Cambridge, of the 17 colleges 13 remained in the same categories used in Table 4.2 throughout the 20 years, with two colleges becoming more reliant on non-endowment income and two less reliant. However, the continuity of the balance between income sources is partly dependent upon the size of the categories employed in Table 4.2, that is the categories are too large to detect a small but evident shift towards a generally greater dependence on non-endowment income. If the two extremes of Hertford College and All Souls College are excluded from the Oxford calculations, then gross endowment income as a percentage of total income increased for 7 colleges but declined for 11. In similar fashion at Cambridge, it increased for 7 of the colleges but declined for 10 of them. However, where endowment income did decline as a percentage of total income, the decreases were small: only Christ Church and Exeter Colleges at Oxford experienced a decline in its relative importance of more than 10 per cent; at Cambridge, Downing College experienced the largest shift of 16.1 per cent. The changes were not so marked to undermine the overall picture of stability.

The college income figures for the inter-war years are, therefore, remark-

Table 4.2   Oxford and Cambridge colleges: Relationship of gross endowment income to total income, 1920–40

| | Number of colleges | | | | | |
| | 1919–20 | | 1929–30 | | 1939–40 | |
	Oxford	Cambridge	Oxford	Cambridge	Oxford	Cambridge
Less than 10%	1	0	1	0	1	0
10–20%	0	0	0	0	0	0
21–40%	7	1	6	3	5	2
41–60%	2	8	5	8	5	6
61–80%	7	8	6	6	7	8
Over 80%	3	0	2	0	2	1
Total	20	17	20	17	20	17

Sources: See Table 4.1.

ably similar to those of the two universities. The Universities of Oxford and Cambridge were no more dependent upon the UGC's recurrent grant in 1940 than they had been in 1925–26 and they continued to attract their income from a variety of sources: their endowments, the UGC, government departments, as well as fees from their students. The same pattern was repeated in the colleges and as late as 1940 *net* endowment income was approximately half of total income in most of the Oxbridge colleges. For the colleges, although a somewhat greater dependence upon fee income over time may have restricted their freedom of action, the state could by no means be considered as a highly intrusive new partner. Moreover, it has to be remembered that between 1920 and 1939, college dues and fees were not universally underwritten by the public purse. The Asquith Commission referred to the growth of both local authority and state scholarships but students, besides meeting their own fees, also received assistance from private educational charities as well as the colleges themselves.

Sources of college income: Elite colleges in the age of expanding higher education

Although the Universities of Oxford and Cambridge shared in the growth of British higher education that occurred after the Second World War, the size of their presence within the overall picture declined. It was particularly difficult for the older colleges with their locations in the centre of the cities to expand greatly on their original sites, even assuming that they wanted to. However, this has been partly compensated for by a remarkable growth in new foundations at both universities. Indeed, the post-1945 years have seen a boom in the foundation of new colleges, although this may now have come to at least a temporary halt. While some of the newer colleges serve broad educational purposes (St Catherine's at Oxford, Fitzwilliam and Robinson at Cambridge), others have more specialized goals such as the training of postgraduate students (e.g. St Antony's at Oxford and Wolfson College at Cambridge) or recruit students in specialized subjects (teacher education at Homerton College, Cambridge – strictly speaking 'an approved society' of the university rather than a college). Inevitably, what such expansion has meant is the infusion of more fee income into the colleges, for new foundations could not be expected to match the endowments of some of the older institutions. Lacking endowment income, of necessity most of the new colleges have been more dependent upon fee income for their survival. Therefore, our continuing concentration upon the 17 Cambridge and 20 Oxford colleges that formed the basis of Tables 4.1 and 4.2 presents a less accurate picture of the overall situation in the post-1945 years than it did of the inter-war years. As well as excluding the women's colleges, as in Tables 4.1 and 4.2, Tables 4.3–4.5 also exclude several recently founded colleges.

Of course, to maintain the same basis to the tables, permits easier comparisons over time. Moreover, as these colleges could be said to comprise the traditional hearts of the two universities, we are examining what is happening at the very centres of their collegiate identities. The reader will recall that, although the Universities of Oxford and Cambridge remained after 1945 the best endowed British universities, and indeed the value of those endowments expanded, the relative importance of the different sources of income changed rapidly. The sheer scale in the increase of the UGC's recurrent grant was such as to obliterate the previous fine distinctions. To what extent did the colleges follow the same route?

The most obvious initial comment on Table 4.3 is that the decline in the value of the currency has made it more hazardous to make comparisons over time. Up to 1970, the gains in endowment income were substantial: for these 20 Oxford colleges, total endowment income rose from £770 994 in 1950 to £3 401 353 in 1970, an increase of close to 350 per cent; for the 17 Cambridge colleges, the growth was from £873 101 to £3 095 814 or over 250 per cent. Despite inflation, the post-1970 totals remain impressive with the 1990 Oxford figure reaching £35.5 million and the Cambridge colleges doing even better with a total figure of over £40 million. Evidently, the investments and property holdings of colleges have served them well in recent years. Of course, the gains are less impressive in the light of a retail price index that had risen by approximately 14 times between 1947 and 1987, but the overall endowment income of the colleges has kept comfortably ahead of inflationary pressures.

As in the inter-war years, the variations in the endowment incomes of the colleges create a number of different groupings, although these tend to overlap in membership rather than form distinctive cliques. At Oxford, Christ Church is always one of the top three best endowed colleges, to be joined regularly by All Souls and St John's, and at the other end of the scale

Table 4.3 Oxford and Cambridge colleges: Gross endowment incomes, 1950–90

	Number of colleges									
	1949–50		1959–60		1969–70		1979–80		1989–90	
	Oxford	Cambridge	Oxford	Cambridge	Oxford	Cambridge	Oxford	Cambridge	Oxford	Cambridge
Under £10 000	3	0	1	0	0	0	0	0	0	0
£10 000–£25 000	7	6	5	1	0	0	0	0	0	0
£26 000–£50 000	3	6	7	5	2	2	0	0	0	0
£51 000–£75 000	2	2	1	3	2	3	0	0	0	0
£76 000–£150 000	5	1	3	5	7	6	0	0	0	0
£151 000–£250 000	0	2	3	2	4	3	3	3	0	0
£251 000–£500 000	0	0	0	1	5	2	5	5	1	0
£500 000–£1 million	0	0	0	0	0	1	9	5	3	6
£1–2 million	0	0	0	0	0	0	3	3	11	5
£2–5 million	0	0	0	0	0	0	0	1	5	5
Over £5 million	0	0	0	0	0	0	0	0	0	1
Total number of colleges	20	17	20	17	20	17	20	17	20	17

Sources: University of Cambridge (1951, 1961, 1971a, 1981, 1991c); University of Oxford (1950, 1960, 1970c, 1980c, 1990b).

are to be found Hertford, Worcester and Pembroke. The Oxford groupings have remained remarkably stable over time, although some of the changes in the position of individual colleges are worth mentioning, especially the improvement of both Hertford and St John's and the decline of Magdalen. Since the Second World War, Magdalen College has not appeared consistently in the top four colleges with the highest endowment incomes, whereas St John's now appears regularly in that slot. Although Hertford remains by comparison a poorly endowed college, by 1990 it was in fact showing a higher endowment income than Exeter, Oriel, Pembroke and Worcester, a quite remarkable transformation since the pre-1939 years. But these individual fluctuations are eddies rather than currents and the pre-1939 college hierarchy at Oxford still remains substantially intact.

Likewise, the pre-1939 pecking order also persists at Cambridge. Trinity College continues to dominate the other Cambridge colleges to an extent that none of the colleges, not even Christ Church, have achieved at Oxford. Approximately one-third of the total endowment income of the Cambridge colleges is earned by Trinity College. King's, St John's, and Gonville and Caius still vie for the second spot. While their individual ranking has varied over time, the six colleges with the lowest endowment incomes remain Downing, Magdalene, Pembroke, Queens', St Catharine's and Trinity Hall. The traditional order is thus reaffirmed. The business of generating endowment income appears to confirm fully the old maxim of 'to him that hath shall be given!' This is not to say that there have been no changes at Cambridge. While remaining a comparatively poorly endowed college Trinity Hall, like Hertford College at Oxford, has improved its relative position, and Peterhouse is now a more secure member of the moderately endowed group within which the position of Clare and Corpus Christi has become more ambivalent. But as at Oxford, the general contours of the hierarchy remain undisturbed.

Despite the comparative stability of the hierarchies at the two universities, it should be pointed out that the differences in gross endowment income at Oxford are by no means as steep as they used to be. Taking the average college endowment income at Oxford and distributing the colleges on the basis of those with either less than half that income or more than half as much again, the pattern in Table 4.4 emerges.

Although the picture would be modified by including the women's colleges (both remaining and former) and the newer foundations, the general trend is evident. There are, comparatively speaking, only a few very wealthy Oxford colleges, and one or two very poor ones, while most of them are now comfortably endowed. The internally sponsored efforts aimed at redistributing college wealth appear to have borne fruit. As a consequence, the richer have relinquished some of their development possibilities, but correspondingly it would be fair to say that the college system as a whole at Oxford has benefited.

Interestingly, this narrowing of college endowment income has not occurred at Cambridge. Using the same income categories as for the

Table 4.4   Distribution of Oxford college income

	Number of Oxford colleges			
	1919–20	*1939–40*	*1959–60*	*1989–90*
Less than half average income	9	10	8	2
Average income category	6	4	6	14
More than 1½ times average income	5	6	6	4
Total number of colleges	20	20	20	20

Oxford colleges, the distribution of colleges was almost the same in 1990 as it had been in 1930 – that is, nine colleges in the average income category (as in 1930) with two above it (one less than in 1930) and six below it (one more than in 1930). The Cambridge colleges had established a more even endowment income scale than the Oxford colleges before the Second World War, but thereafter it has remained more stable. So great are the endowment resources of Gonville and Caius, King's, St John's and, above all, Trinity College in comparison with most other Cambridge colleges, that short of a really draconian redistribution of wealth this would be impossible to change. In 1990, these four Cambridge colleges produced approximately 60 per cent of the total college endowment income between them. At Oxford, the redirection of resources from the richer to the poorer colleges has been going on for a longer period of time than at Cambridge, and possibly this accounts for the ability of the poorer Oxford colleges to increase their endowment income at a faster rate than the richer colleges.

Although the evidence demonstrates the remarkable ability of both the Oxford and Cambridge colleges to sustain the value of endowment income, the question is whether its relative importance in the total incomes of the colleges has remained equally impressive. As Table 4.5 shows, since 1945 the relative importance of non-endowment income in the finances of both the Oxford and Cambridge colleges has scarcely increased. Of the Oxford colleges, Christ Church, Queen's and St John's besides All Souls were obtaining more than 80 per cent of their income from endowments by 1990. Up until 1980, what appears to have been happening at Oxford was a substantial narrowing of the differences between colleges in terms of the relative value of the sources of their incomes. The poorer Oxford colleges became better endowed while the richer colleges – with the exception of All Souls, which has continued successfully to resist the entry of either undergraduates or postgraduates – became more dependent upon fee income. In the 1980s, the trend was reversed with a substantial surge in the relative importance of endowment income. The key difference between the Oxford and Cambridge colleges is the remarkable stability of the latter's income pattern since 1945. Our figures show that between 1950 and 1990, the relative importance of

Table 4.5 Oxford and Cambridge colleges: Relationship of gross endowment income to total income, 1950–86

	Number of colleges									
	1949–50		1959–60		1969–70		1979–80		1989–90	
	Oxford	Cambridge	Oxford	Cambridge	Oxford	Cambridge	Oxford	Cambridge	Oxford	Cambridge
Less than 10%	1	0	1	0	0	0	0	0	0	0
10–20%	0	0	2	0	2	0	0	0	0	0
21–40%	10	6	7	6	4	5	9	5	4	4
41–60%	3	6	5	6	7	7	7	7	9	8
61–80%	5	4	4	5	6	5	3	5	3	4
Over 80%	1	1	1	0	1	0	1	0	4	1
Total number of colleges	20	17	20	17	20	17	20	17	20	17

Sources: See Table 4.3.

endowment income for the Cambridge colleges as a whole remained virtually unchanged. The big increase in the input of non-endowment income occurred at Cambridge in the decade between 1940 and 1950. In those years, the number of colleges whose total incomes consisted of between 61 and 80 per cent of endowment income declined from eight to four. During the same decade, there was an identical increase in the number of colleges which obtained between 21 and 40 per cent of their total incomes from endowments. Thereafter, the picture has remained virtually static.

While certain colleges are richer than others, what is most striking about these figures is the overall financial independence of these 17 Cambridge and 20 Oxford colleges. In the post-1945 years, the Universities of Oxford and Cambridge followed, in conjunction with all other British universities, the route that led to virtual financial dependence upon the UGC's recurrent grant. These colleges, however, have continued to retain a considerable measure of financial autonomy. Some colleges are more dependent upon fee income than others, and thus the prerequisites of their autonomy are weaker than the less dependent colleges, but the overall financial independence of the college system contrasts remarkably with the financial dependence of their universities.

We have dealt with the traditional collegiate heart of the two universities. Other colleges have been founded, and one or two have substantial endowments, but these 20 Oxford and 17 Cambridge colleges can claim to be the traditional centres around which their respective universities have revolved. Although the newer institutions may be formally collegiate institutions, to what extent they are all also collegiate in character is open to debate. With notable exceptions, our analysis revealed that the financial profiles of these particular colleges were converging, but whether this would also extend to the outer collegiate circle is another matter. What can be said is that several would lack significant endowment incomes with the inevitable consequence that they are more dependent upon fee income. The conclusions we have reached must be tempered by this consideration. The question for the future is whether the redistribution of the taxed endowment incomes of the richer colleges will draw the newer foundations towards the traditional collegiate centre in the same way as it appears to have assisted that process in the past.

Cash limits and fee income: An ambivalent view of the colleges

What makes Oxford and Cambridge unique universities are their colleges. But as the Franks Inquiry recognized: 'The college system is expensive, and there has been some criticism of it from this point of view' (University of Oxford 1966a: 156). The conclusion of the Inquiry, however, was to exonerate the colleges: the expense was not the consequence of purposeful extravagance, but quality education was inevitably costly (ibid.: 156–63). Despite the additional expense to the Exchequer, it was not until the 1970s that the issue stirred much public interest. If the college fees at Oxford and Cambridge (and less significantly at Durham, Kent, Lancaster and York) had been added together, they would have amounted to only a comparatively small item in a rapidly expanding higher education budget. Moreover, adjustments to the UGC's recurrent grant were supposed to take care of these double fee payments. There was also considerable sympathy in many quarters for the collegiate model of the university. The post-1945 expansion of higher education had brought onto university campuses a generation of students many of whose families had no experience of university education. Colleges and halls of residence allegedly created appropriate social environments for the culturally uninitiated.

The initial official concern with college fees was motivated more by financial rather than ideological considerations. The issue was the costs of college residence rather than its desirability or otherwise. For example, if one takes the colleges that formed the basis of the tables in this chapter, the average college undergraduate fee rose from £588 at Cambridge and £719 at Oxford in 1975–76 to £1786 at Cambridge and £2150 at Oxford in 1985–86, increases in each case of approximately 200 per cent (DES 1975–76, 1985–86), and fees can now amount to close to £3000 at some colleges. There is limited evidence to suggest that the rises in the first half of the 1970s had been even steeper (DES, n.d.). In the light of inflationary pressures, such increases may have been reasonable, especially as colleges are labour-intensive institutions, but as the universities moved inexorably into the era of cash limits, so the colleges were drawn into the same net. The reaction was an impressive growth of inter-collegiate activity at both Oxford and Cambridge and a measure of cooperation between the colleges of the two universities in their approach to the state. The colleges of the two universities have created their own fees committee, which at Oxford is formally subject to the authority of the Conference of Colleges while at Cambridge it falls under the auspices of the Bursars' Committee. These committees agree upon the fees for their respective colleges which will vary according to the particular circumstances of each college, while the two committees send a joint delegation to the DES to agree an overall figure. At both Oxford and Cambridge, these are matters for those who are most intimately concerned with the financial well-being of the colleges, that is the bursars – some of whom, it should be remembered, still have academic responsibilities.

The creation of committees to regulate the fees that colleges can charge is an excellent example of institutional flexibility in response to external pressure. When it was first created, Oxford's Conference of Colleges was despised by many as a mere talking-shop, but it has since spawned this committee which carries out vital functions on behalf of the colleges. While formally these committees may lack executive authority, it is difficult to imagine that their decisions would be thwarted. Agreement is reached with the DES on the overall percentage increase in the total allocation for fees. What the committees then have to do is to agree percentage fee increases for their individual colleges. Obviously, certain colleges may request readjustments but this can only be pursued through the committee, for there is a clear need to balance the interests of all the parties. Individual colleges cannot act unilaterally, for the colleges as a whole have to operate within the boundaries negotiated with the DES. To apply cash limits also meant that the colleges had to be allocated quotas of students, and clearly it made sense to negotiate these through the committees that handled fee increases. The financial constraints imposed by the state brought to an end any ideas of unregulated expansion that college heads may have entertained.

The introduction of formula funding in the mid-1980s raised not so much the question of what should be the level of college fees, but whether the Exchequer was obliged to pay them at all. The collegiate universities may offer a quality education but should the state meet the additional costs that they generate? The initial stance on formula funding was that the UGC would make a standard payment for each student, varied according to the student's course. This was to cover teaching costs and there was to be no variation to support so-called quality education, i.e. the educational experience apparently on offer in the collegiate universities. Besides the UGC's grant for each student, the universities also received a fee for each student paid for by the student's LEA (the LEA in effect handed over money it had received from the DES for this purpose). The UGC would deduct from the university's total teaching grant the full amount received in fees from the LEAs. The assumption was that all monies received from the LEAs could be assumed to be part of the university's total income, but clearly with the Oxbridge colleges receiving fees from the LEAs this was not an assumption that fitted the circumstances of either the Universities of Oxford or Cambridge. And yet the UGC's apparent attack was tentative: only 50 per cent of total college fee income would be deducted from the UGC's annual grant to the Universities of Oxford and Cambridge and then only in stages over a 4-year period. Furthermore, after negotiations, the reductions were reduced to 42 per cent for Oxford and to 38 per cent for Cambridge, still large cut-backs but not quite so bad as first feared.

This little tale illustrates both the continuing sophistication of the collegiate universities in defending their interests and the perpetual ambivalence of the state towards them. Evidently, the desire to act fairly had to be balanced by the need to preserve the best. Or was it more a question of a powerful lobby thwarting bureaucratic rationality? But with the ever-increasing emphasis upon unit costs, the question of college fees is unlikely to go away. For example, the research councils have also in the recent past considered whether they should continue to pay college graduate fees as well as the standard tuition fees to the universities (THES 1985: 3). Do graduate students, as one former head of college put it to us, need to reside in an institution that feels it necessary to maintain a chapel? Be that as it may, representatives of the colleges have met with the research councils and convinced them that the Oxbridge colleges are providing value for money and the college fees are still being paid. Inter-collegiate structures have enabled the colleges to formulate common responses to external threats, both political and bureaucratic, to the idiosyncrasies of the collegiate universities. It will be interesting to see for how long the state will be prepared to pay Oxford and Cambridge what amounts to a 'top-up' fee? Alternatively, will the colleges be forced to charge their own 'top-up' fees with, presumably, remissions for needy students?

Conclusions

Despite all of the problems faced by British universities in the past decade, including the Universities of Oxford and Cambridge, the Oxbridge colleges have remained in a comparatively secure financial position. The value of their endowment incomes has continued to grow (the 1980s was a particularly good decade), and not content to rest on their laurels, many colleges remain actively engaged in increasing their endowments by employing more aggressive fund-raising techniques (*The Times*, 11 March 1987). For the present, they have succeeded in seeing off the various threats to their fee income. So after a protracted period of time in which, thanks to the financial input of the Exchequer, the universities appeared increasingly dominant *vis-à-vis* the colleges, the roles – at least temporarily – have been reversed and the colleges are once again coming to the financial aid of their universities and, fortunately, more willingly than in the past.

It is our contention that the key to understanding this changed situation is that the colleges, unlike the universities, maintained a considerable measure of financial distance from the state and thus were better placed to weather the cutbacks in expenditure on university education. While the universities were, for understandable reasons, increasingly dependent upon the UGC's recurrent grant, the colleges succeeded in expanding their endowment income and maintaining its relative value. This has been coupled with a sophisticated defence of their fee income, as seen in successful negotiations with both the DES and the research councils. The inter-collegiate committees have been able to increase the clout of the colleges by presenting a united front to the various funding agencies, including the DES.

One certain conclusion is that the external pressure on fees has greatly enhanced the inter-collegiate identities of both Oxford and Cambridge. The interesting question, to which there is no certain answer, is when do the two universities become inter-collegiate – as opposed to collegiate – institutions? We have argued that one critical ingredient in the maintenance of collegiate identity was the preservation of individual college control over their endowments, that if this were to be centralized then the collegiate character of the two universities would change irrevocably. For colleges to control their own financial resources is a concrete manifestation of their autonomy. The differential financial status of the colleges leads to a measure of diversity in their individual characters which is one of the more interesting features of the collegiate universities. The idea of a college also incorporates the notion that its benefactors have established personal ties with it; colleges represent an institutional link between the past, the present and the future. Thus inter-collegiate action may be necessary to co-ordinate responses to external pressure, but it has to be careful not to infringe the individual college's property rights.

A clear constraint on inter-collegiate action is the kind of authority that inter-collegiate institutions exercise. Although in practice their authority may be binding, it is not obligatory. The inter-collegiate institutions, therefore, have to establish a wide measure of consensus before they can act, which perhaps means that they have to proceed at the pace of the slowest. Even today, colleges are reluctant to concede their formal freedom of manoeuvre. It is no surprise that the Oxford colleges resisted the Franks' proposal for a Council of Colleges which was to be permitted to take votes if necessary and to make binding decisions. Traditionally, the institutional form that inter-collegiate action takes is to create a small committee of college representatives which reports back to a larger committee on which all the colleges are represented. The various representatives will take soundings, both formally and informally, in their colleges, which can mean that some are little more than delegates. If the dons still exercise influence, in other words if donnish domination has not declined, it is much more likely to be felt in the politics of the colleges than in the politics of the two universities.

The current ambivalence towards the collegiate universities stems from the fact that on the one hand the political pressures are in favour of a diversified university system in which high-status institutions like Oxford and Cambridge will have a significant part to play, while on the other the bureaucratic pressures favour the standardization of the state's financial input so that all universities – regardless of the assumed quality of their product – receive identical resources for the same service. To date, both Oxford and Cambridge have succeeded in retaining some of their advantages with respect to state funding; in other words, the standardization of the state's input has not been carried to its logical conclusion. If the political pressure is in favour of diversification, then the effort involved in challenging college fees may simply not be worth the costs it incurs. However, if it is the colleges which, in the words of the former vice-chancellor Sir Patrick Neill, 'provide the basis for Oxford's excellence, particularly in teaching' (*The Guardian*, 29 May 1986), then it would be interesting to know what price the market would put on that assumed excellence!

To diversify university education means creating different status levels. Undoubtedly, a disproportionate percentage of resources, including the most talented people, will gravitate towards what are considered to be the most prestigious institutions. Within the UK this has been, and still is, the traditional collegiate model as represented by Oxford and Cambridge. The question for the future is not so much whether this will change – for it will not – but rather who will finance it. Should the present political will for diversification be matched by a more potent future concern for an even-handed parsimony, then the colleges have demonstrated amply their ability to maintain the financial basis of their autonomy. The market may not give either Oxford or Cambridge all that they want, but it would surely give – as it has given in the past – their colleges the resources to survive with a certain amount of style.

Part 3

The Organization of Knowledge:
Control, Change and Access

traditions — Lit hist'y
Ac L in elis'ty   formal v informal
                         ability to create
                   history   a following.
On leadership — theory
                    L & A.
On L & M
On organisational context
On change.
L in   VC in context
practice HoD " "
          PVC " "
          SMT "
knowl. skills & charac.
Devt

5

Oxford, Cambridge and the Changing Knowledge Maps

Introduction

The most important function that universities perform is the control of what is to count as high-status knowledge, both what is to be taught and what is to be researched. In undertaking this task, they have been remarkably free in the twentieth century from direct interference either from the state or from society. It is evident, however, that British universities have changed their knowledge maps in response to external pressures. For example, in the nineteenth century the study of law and medicine were rejuvenated in both the Universities of Oxford and Cambridge partly in response to pressure from the Russell Commission, and several of the civic universities have always offered courses, often in one of the branches of engineering, geared to the interests of important local industries. It is not too great an exaggeration to see the Universities of Oxford and Cambridge as national institutions that for much of their histories have served the Church and thus the state, while the civic universities were founded to service regional interests, especially the needs of local industry. As Oxford and Cambridge became more secular institutions, controlled by their resident dons, so their primary function became the regulation of knowledge. Meanwhile, the civic universities slowly became national institutions that transcended their local origins and established traditions of teaching and research that were more in tune with the Oxbridge model of the university.

Although in the twentieth century it has been expected that universities will respond to national needs, it is also recognized that the universities have considerable authority in deciding the precise form that response should take. Emerging professions gain status by incorporation within the university's curriculum; if the university lacks the authority to influence, at the very minimum, the terms of incorporation, then it has no status to confer. Autonomy gives institutions both authority and status, and to control them too closely is to risk destroying the legitimacy that they may confer on those who seek entry. Thus the state, like society, has genuflected to the university's control of knowledge. Inevitably, the state has couched its demands in very general terms, offering universities incentives to change as opposed to issuing specific threats should they fail to adapt. In this century, the state – mainly through the reports of the UGC – has pressured the universities' established knowledge maps in four interrelated ways: that they should expand, so providing more of everything; that as they expanded so the relative presence of science should increase; that the applied sciences – along with other vocationally oriented disciplines – should assume a more significant presence; and that the balance between teaching and research should shift in favour of the latter. Our presentation of the changing knowledge maps will refer to the specific manifestations of these general pressures.

This chapter, therefore, presents an overview of the evolving academic characters of the Universities of Oxford and Cambridge. Within itself, this is an important exercise and, furthermore, comparison will enable us to see how the two universities differ from one another as well as how each differs from the national picture. This chapter also provides a context for the subsequent discussion of the organization of academic activities within the two universities. Finally, we need to know whether the knowledge maps of the universities of Oxford and Cambridge have moved in a direction that is consistent with the external pressure for change.

In pursuing these objectives we have relied solely upon student numbers in the UGC's returns, as these provide the best comparative statistics. Faculty statistics are less complete, bedevilled by the confusions engendered by the fact that some dons are employed by the universities, some by the colleges, although the majority now have dual responsibilities. Our focus is purposefully narrow: changes in overall student population numbers, the balance between undergraduates and postgraduates, and distributions by defined subject areas. We have refrained from introducing social variables, such as gender, as this chapter is not meant to be a general demographic portrait of the two universities. But it should be recognized that the shape of the knowledge maps can be influenced by well-established relationships between subjects and the social characteristics of their student base. Thus it is pertinent to ask whether engineering would have had a more significant presence in British universities if it had been less male dominated. And to wonder what would have happened to certain subjects, again mainly those with a technological bias, if they had not succeeded in recruiting large numbers of overseas students. These are matters, however, that demand detailed analysis in their own right. While student numbers do not provide a complete guide to the changing academic characters of universities, they are probably the best single indicator and even research, especially in scientific subjects, has been heavily dependent upon the input of postgraduate students.

The inter-war years: Steady growth and a shift to science?

The continuity of the pressures upon the universities to modify their knowledge maps is well illustrated by the recommendations of the Asquith Com-

Table 5.1 Total full-time student numbers: The inter-war years

	1920–21	*1938–39*
Cambridge	5 187	5 931
Oxford	4 205	5 023
Total (GB)	48 452	50 002

Sources: UGC (1936: 52–3; 1938–39: 7).

mission. The Commission argued that both the Universities of Oxford and Cambridge should become more developed centres of research and graduate study, and recognized that Oxford in particular needed state grants to expand its scientific activities (Royal Commission on Oxford and Cambridge Universities 1922a: 114). Scientific investigation was seen as the means by which the nation could command the resources of nature; by embracing science, the universities could fulfil their obligation to respond to national needs.

The expansion of student numbers in the inter-war years is shown in Table 5.1. Although the figures suggest a period of slow national expansion (3.2 per cent) compared to greater growth at Oxford and Cambridge (14.3 per cent at Cambridge and 19.5 per cent at Oxford), they should be treated cautiously. The growth was by no means uniform, with downturns in the early 1920s and the 1930s; and although the overall picture was always consistent with the distributions in Table 5.1, changing the years of comparison would produce considerable variations. The situation was confused by the dislocation of wartime and the severe economic crises of this period also hampered overall university expansion. Neither Oxford nor Cambridge was stretched to capacity and the problem prior to 1939 was not how to cope with an over-supply of candidates but rather how to fill places. It is accurate to describe this as a steady-state university system, an image reinforced by the financial data presented in Chapter 3.

Traditionally, both Oxford and Cambridge were reknowned as collegiate universities that concentrated their energies upon the the teaching of their undergraduates. Indeed, the Asquith Commission was of the opinion that the commitments of many college teaching fellows were sufficiently demanding to prevent them from engaging in any serious research. It is difficult to say whether the teaching duties of college fellows declined in the inter-war years, but there is some evidence to suggest that postgraduates succeeded in establishing a firmer foothold in both universities. The picture, however, is far from clear, thanks to the imprecision of the labels that the UGC used to describe students (first, advanced and diploma students) and the conflicting figures presented by different sources. If diploma students are excluded (students reading vocationally oriented courses – usually in agriculture, forestry or medicine – of whom some were also classed as advanced students), the first-degree students are classified as undergraduates and the

Table 5.2   Undergraduates/postgraduates as a percentage of total student numbers (excluding diploma students)

	1922–23			1938–39		
	Undergraduates (%)	Postgraduates (%)	Total no.	Undergraduates (%)	Postgraduates (%)	Total no.
Cambridge	92.3	7.7	4 776	91.0	9.0	5 746
Oxford	93.7	6.3	3 870	93.2	6.8	4 730
Total (GB)	94.5	5.5	36 404	92.7	7.3	42 323

Sources: UGC (1922–23: 13–14; 1938–39: 10–11).

advanced students as postgraduates, then the undergraduate/postgraduate profiles were as shown in Table 5.2.

Whereas postgraduates had a greater presence in British universities by the end of the inter-war period, the growth in their numbers was no means startling. British universities remained overwhelmingly institutions for the teaching of undergraduates, and although postgraduate numbers increased at both Oxford and Cambridge, the expansion was limited. The University of Cambridge, however, could be said to be different from Oxford in that it had a higher percentage of postgraduates than was true nationally, and the increase in their numbers was steeper. The contrast is heightened if the expansion of postgraduate and undergraduate numbers is compared. In comparision to both Cambridge and the national trend, Oxford experienced the largest percentage increase in undergraduates and the smallest percentage increase in postgraduates. The conclusion is that during these years, Oxford reaffirmed its traditional identity as a collegiate-centred university whose principal function was the teaching of undergraduates, whereas at Cambridge this model was being slowly eroded.

The most comprehensive Oxford statistics on the distribution of students by subject group during the inter-war years can be found in Volume II of the Report of the Franks Inquiry (University of Oxford 1966b: 17, 23). The drawback in using those statistics is the absence of comparative data and the likelihood that the commission constructed its subject categories differently from the UGC. We will continue, therefore, to use the UGC's profiles but draw upon the Report's tables for additional refinement.

The data in Table 5.3 illustrate vividly the difference between the knowledge maps of both Oxford and Cambridge and the national picture during these years. Throughout these years, Oxford could be described essentially as a university catering for students in the arts and social studies with comparatively small additional academic appendages. This picture was as pronounced at the end of the period as it was at the beginning. Cambridge's profile was closer to the national picture in view of its less visible arts base and the rapid increase in the representation of technology. By 1938–39, the

Table 5.3   Subject group profiles in the inter-war years (all students)

	1922–23			1938–39		
	Oxford (%)	Cambridge (%)	UK (%)	Oxford (%)	Cambridge (%)	UK (%)
Arts/Social Studies	78.2	54.0	40.9	81.4	58.2	44.7
Science/Mathematics	10.2	27.8	17.4	11.4	19.7	15.3
Medicine/Dentistry	3.5	8.5	26.6	4.6	8.3	27.3
Technology	2.0	3.6	12.5	1.0	11.0	10.6
Agriculture	6.1	6.1	2.7	1.7	2.8	2.1
Totals[a]						
Percentages	100.0	100.0	100.1	100.1	100.0	100.0
Numbers	4426	4488	44 619	5023	5931	50 002

[a] A total of 311 Cambridge students who could not be allocated to a subject group were excluded from the 1922–23 distributions.
Sources: UGC (1922–23: 14–15; 1938–39: 12–13).

inbalances at Cambridge – that is, in comparison to national distributions – centred around the under-representation of students in medicine and dentistry coupled with their over-representation in the arts and social studies. The statistics presented by Oxford's Franks Commission of Inquiry tend to confirm the UGC's figures. The Commission's use of more refined subject categories showed the stability of the student base in arts (consistently close to 60 per cent), coupled with an uneven growth of social studies (from approximately 15 per cent in 1923–24 to approximately 22 per cent in 1938–39). The other interesting trend that the Commission's data revealed was the steady decline of the Pass School (not referred to in the UGC's statistics) – all but a nostalgic memory after 1945.

Because the UGC presented only *total* student numbers by subjects studied, it is more difficult to compare the changing patterns for undergraduates and postgraduates. The Franks data show a decline at Oxford between 1923–24 and 1928–29 in postgraduate student numbers from 439 to 357, followed by an increase to 536 by 1938–39. After considerable stability in the distribution of students in the earlier period, the arts and social studies postgraduates declined from 86.6 per cent of the total postgraduate population in 1928–29 to 72.4 per cent in 1938–39, matched by a commensurate growth of postgraduates in the pure sciences (from 11.8 to 23.5 per cent). The numbers in all other areas were insignificant (University of Oxford 1966b: 4, 17, 23). The information on Cambridge postgraduate students numbers is very rudimentary. Bridges' Syndicate (University of Cambridge 1962: 1146) presented a simple arts/science/other split for 'research students in residence' (see Table 5.4).

Given the distribution of undergraduate student numbers, it is not surpris-

Table 5.4   Cambridge research students: The inter-war years

	1928	1938
Science	135	153
Arts	54	66
Other	15	12
Total numbers	204	231

ing to discover that postgraduate numbers were skewed so heavily towards the arts at Oxford and the sciences at Cambridge. By the eve of the Second World War, Oxford had established a viable research base in the natural sciences but remained virtually a desert for applied science research and teaching. The Cambridge figures are more interesting in that they suggest either that the arts and the sciences would have fundamentally different relationships to research or that science would be the channel through which research first established itself as a serious university activity. Table 5.3 showed that the University of Cambridge was *not* predominantly a science-based university in the inter-war years, but in terms of its postgraduate students it most certainly was. The potential repercussions of this for the intellectual maps created by an expanding university system were simply enormous. Either science would go its own way or it would drag the arts along in its wake.

Within the overall pattern of student distributions, there are two developments worth noting: the expansion of student numbers in technology at Cambridge (up from 3.6 to 11.0 per cent of the total student population between 1922–23 and 1938–39) and the more significant presence of postgraduates in the natural sciences at Oxford (up from 11.8 to 23.5 per cent of the total number of postgraduate students between 1923–24 and 1938–39). By comparison, the national figures over the total time period suggest remarkable stability, although this disguises considerable short-term variations in the number of students in medicine and dentistry. Although by 1938–39 total student numbers had expanded, albeit in a hesitant fashion, it would be impossible to describe the inter-war years as ushering in an age of scientific and technological dominance of the universities. Numbers in these areas had expanded, but so had numbers in the arts and social studies. The knowledge maps at individual universities may have differed widely, but the overall academic character of the universities in Britain was much the same in 1939 as it had been in 1919. The growth in postgraduate studies, for which, significantly, UGC data are hard to come by, was not sufficiently pronounced to upset this generalization.

To suggest, on the basis of this evidence, that the universities were out of tune with national sentiment would be very tendentious. For example, although the Asquith Commission argued that both Oxford and Cambridge required state resources to refurbish and extend their scientific work, there was no suggestion that this expansion should be at the expense of other knowledge areas. Furthermore, there was no discussion, either in the report of the Asquith Commission or the UGC's reports, of what the relative balance among subject groups or between research and teaching within universities should be. In its early years, the UGC came to the conclusion that technological subjects should be part of the university curriculum, but it wanted many of the specializations to be offered by only a few universities (reflecting a concern at their expense), and it was of the opinion that a great deal of current teaching in technology within institutions that aspired to be universities did not belong to a university curriculum (reflecting a concern that universities should impart broad principles). Like Shinn (1986: 193–227), we would describe the UGC's support for technology during these years as at best equivocal.

Regardless of how the UGC may have viewed the academic development of the universities, it was constrained during these years by its terms of reference, reinforced by its own perception of its functions. Its formal task was to make available to the universities an annual grant from the Exchequer, a block grant that the universities spent at their discretion. However, it is naive to imagine that the UGC had no inkling of how the universities were going to spend their recurrent income, and clearly the UGC was in a position to influence the future academic shape of individual universities by refusing to underwrite programmes of which it disapproved. And yet in its annual reports the UGC invariably portrayed itself as a body that was loathe to direct the pattern of change. The spirit of the inter-war years was reflected in the following quote from the UGC's Report for the period 1929–30 to 1934–35.

> We have touched on this problem (of the merits of honours versus general degrees) with considerable hesitation since its solution does not in the main depend on finance, and it therefore falls somewhat outside our immediate province. In seeking to solve it the Universities must work out their own salvation, advice or criticism from outside can seldom be sufficiently well-informed to be helpful (UGC 1936: 25).

If the UGC did not see itself as 'sufficiently well-informed' on curricula matters to offer advice, then the universities could be said to be a law unto themselves in such matters, for who else could claim such competence? But these were matters that were considered to be only *somewhat* outside the UGC's remit, leaving the impression that it would not take much to alter that judgement. Moreover, did the UGC consider itself as offering advice and criticism from 'the outside'? A question that the quote left unanswered and obviously a matter to be resolved by future developments.

Student numbers: The age of expansion

Any interpretation of the data presented in this section of the chapter has to be made within the context of two very important developments. The first is the UGC's new terms of reference which came into effect in 1946. Besides enquiring into the financial needs of the universities, advising government as to the size of the annual recurrent grant, and collecting and publishing a range of statistical information, the UGC also had the authority:

> ... to assist, in consultation with the universities and other bodies concerned, the preparation and execution of such plans for the development of the universities as may from time to time be required in order to ensure that they are fully adequate to national needs (UGC 1948: 7).

In theory, therefore, it was possible for the UGC to engage in a measure of forward planning including curriculum development.

After 1945, higher education within itself was assumed to be in the national interest. The second development, therefore, is that university expansion became an end in itself, with the positive outcomes almost taken for granted and it was no longer simply a means to an end. In the process, there was a subtle but important change in how a university education was perceived, with the emphasis upon the end product rather than the nature of the process. As the system expanded, so the UGC sought continually to balance the old and the new value systems. This is not to say that the autonomy which the universities prized so much was at an end (note that the UGC's terms of reference required 'consultation with the universities'), but that the external pressure upon them was much sharper. It is easier both to plan and to enforce accountability by measuring products as opposed to understanding processes.

The 25 years following the end of the Second World War have been portrayed as a golden age for British universities, one of unparalleled growth and public esteem. The image, however, cannot be sustained by the evidence, and is more a nostalgic reflection on the past from the hard years of the 1970s and 1980s. The Robbins Report showed an increase in full-time student numbers between 1944–45 and 1949–50, but in the next 4 years the numbers actually declined. Thereafter, it was not until 1956–57 that the number of full-time students in British universities exceeded the figure for 1949–50, that is up from 85 400 to 89 900 (Committee on Higher Education 1963: *op.cit.* App. Two (A), 17). To some extent, this pattern reflected the dislocation engendered by the war years. As the war ended, so there was the expected sharp increase in student numbers, and as early as 1945–46 there were more full-time students in British universities than there had been in 1938–39, up from 50 000 to 51 600. But this initial anticipated expansion was not maintained. Was this a consequence of the shortage of resources and the comparatively low priority of higher education within national expenditure plans? Or, alternatively, as the UGC would have us believe, was the downturn a short hiatus between the ending of the Further Education and Training Scheme for ex-national servicemen and the sustained expansion generated by the steadily increasing number of sixth-form leavers? (UGC 1958: 15). Certainly, the decline in total student numbers was not as steep as after the First World War, and when expansion reoccurred it was on a

Table 5.5   Total full-time student numbers: 1949–50 to 1969–70

	1949–50	*1959–60*	*1969–70*
Cambridge	7 986	8 997	10 367
Oxford	7 323	8 893	10 834
Total (GB)	85 421	104 009	219 308

Sources: UGC (1949–50: 10–11; 1959–60: 40; 1970: 18–19, 28–9).

sustained basis, not interrupted by economic turmoil as in the inter-war years. Regardless of what gloss may be put on the figures, it is important to stress that the expansion of higher education in Britain has invariably been uneven and this includes the highly regarded decades of expansion post-1945.

Table 5.5 shows that the increases in full-time student numbers over this 20-year period were as follows: Cambridge 29.8 per cent, Oxford 47.9 per cent and for all British universities 156.7 per cent. Unlike in the inter-war years, excepting the short downward turn in the early 1950s, the expansion of student numbers was continuous. The trend is very much as expected. Although the growth of the Universities of Oxford and Cambridge was impressive, so great was the overall expansion that it was beyond their capacities to accommodate more than a comparatively small percentage. This is in contrast to the inter-war years, where the combination of spare capacity in the colleges combined with a much slower and uneven growth rate made it possible for Oxford and Cambridge to absorb a disproportionate percentage of the expansion. It should also be remembered that there has been a powerful sentiment within many Oxbridge colleges that they should *not* grow too large for fear of destroying the idea of the college as a small and intimate community. On the other hand, some of the more poorly endowed colleges would welcome the increased student numbers because of the fee income they brought with them, and the overall growth in student numbers has stimulated the foundation of several new colleges.

Expansion meant that the presence of Oxford and Cambridge students within the British university system declined over time. Their shrinking representation between 1920–21 and 1969–70 was as follows:

1920–21	19.4 per cent
1938–39	21.9 per cent
1949–50	17.9 per cent
1959–60	17.2 per cent
1969–70	9.7 per cent

The potential repercussions of this were considerable. One of our initial assumptions was that the Universities of Oxford and Cambridge had profoundly influenced the model of the *English* university. This was not based merely on their relative size, but none the less their sheer presence within the overall university system helped to reinforce that idea. As that presence declined, it is pertinent to ask whether their influence upon the general character of British universities also waned. Alternatively, were there other factors that countered this possibility? Inevitably, direct influence declined (e.g. students had more universities to choose from and departmental faculties would be composed of fewer Oxbridge graduates), but the indirect influence was potentially as great as ever if students and faculty – regardless of where they studied or where they were educated – still perceived Oxbridge as *the* university ideal.

As the university system expanded, did its academic orientation also change? The most striking feature of Table 5.6 is the inexorable increase in the University of Oxford's postgraduate student population. The growth was such that the academic map of the university was transformed in a comparatively short space of time. Although the same trend occurred at Cambridge, the post-war expansion of their numbers was neither as large nor sustained as consistently. By 1959–60, it was no longer possible to see the essential academic purpose of Oxford as the teaching of undergraduates; it had become one of the nation's leading research centres. It is interesting to note that this trend commenced before the years of sustained growth in student numbers that occurred from the mid-1950s. At Cambridge, the years 1938–39 to 1949–50 saw the largest expansion in the number of postgraduate students, while proportionally their representation more than doubled. At Oxford, while greater expansion was yet to come, the proportional representation of postgraduates also almost doubled during those same years. The suggestion is that the war years, and the subsequent period of reconstruction, instigated a deep-rooted change of purpose in the ancient universities which was independent of the post-war boom of the 1950s.

Comparisons with the national trend are complicated by the fact that whereas the UGC's returns recorded no part-time postgraduate students (or advanced students) at either Oxford or Cambridge until 1969–70, they did show large numbers of part-time postgraduates in British universities as a whole (expanding from 4080 in 1949–50 to 19 483 in 1969–70). This suggests a less significant drift towards postgraduate studies at Oxford and Cambridge, that is compared to the national picture, than is shown in Table 5.6. The part-time figures reinforce the notion of a general expansion in the presence of postgraduate students in university profiles.

Despite the growth in postgraduate student numbers, the UGC's statistical returns did not give subject group distributions for undergraduates and postgraduates separately until after 1959–60. Initially, therefore, we continue to present subject group profiles for all students during these years. For 1969–70, the differences between undergraduate and postgraduate patterns can be gleaned from the UGC's statistics, while for the earlier years we rely upon internal university sources.

The first observation to make on Table 5.7 is the extent to which the undifferentiated 'arts' subject group category in fact disguised the presence of a large wedge of social studies students. In view of the fame of the PPE

Table 5.6 Undergraduates/postgraduates as a percentage of total full-time student numbers (excluding diploma students)

	1949–50			1959–60			1969–70		
	Undergraduates (%)	Postgraduates (%)	Total no.	Undergraduates (%)	Postgraduates (%)	Total no.	Undergraduates (%)	Postgraduates (%)	Total no.
Cambridge	81.5	18.5	7 658	84.9	15.1	8 921	79.5	20.5	10 367
Oxford	87.6	12.4	7 031	84.9	15.1	8 788	72.0	28.0	10 834
Total (GB)	90.3	9.7	75 962	83.3	16.6	99 732	82.2	17.8	219 308

Sources: UGC (1949–50: 16–17; 1959–60: 50–1; 1970: 18–19, 28–9).

Table 5.7 Subject group profiles: 1949–50 to 1969–70 (all students)

	1949–50			1959–60			1969–70		
	Oxford (%)	Cambridge (%)	GB (%)	Oxford (%)	Cambridge (%)	GB (%)	Oxford (%)	Cambridge (%)	GB (%)
Arts	74.7	55.1	43.6	53.4	39.5	32.8	38.6	32.1	21.4
Social Studies	–	–	–	19.5	14.1	10.1	22.2	18.6	20.0
Science	16.8	22.6	19.8	20.5	25.1	23.8	25.6	25.3	24.9
Medicine/Dentistry	4.8	7.0	19.8	3.4	5.7	14.8	5.4	6.6	9.9
Technology	1.2	9.8	12.8	2.1	12.4	15.3	4.6	10.9	16.1
Agriculture/Forestry	2.5	5.4	3.2	1.1	2.3	2.0	1.0	1.9	2.0
Veterinary Science	–	0.1	0.8	–	0.9	1.2	–	–	–
Education	–	–	–	–	–	–	2.6	2.4	3.9
Professional/Vocational Studies	–	–	–	–	–	–	–	2.2	1.9
Totals									
Percentages	100.0	100.0	100.0	100.0	100.0	100.0	100.0	100.0	100.1
Numbers	7323	7986	85 421	8893	8997	104 009	10 834	10 367	219 308

Notes: (1) The UGC did not distinguish between Arts and Social Studies in its 1949–50 returns. (2) In the 1969–70 returns, Veterinary Science was incorporated with Agriculture/Forestry. (3) Professional/Vocational Studies is composed mainly of Architecture, previously considered to be a technological subject.

Sources: UGC (1949–50: 20–1; 1959–60: 55; 1970: 18–19, 28–9).

degree, this could have been anticipated at Oxford but their presence at Cambridge was almost equally pronounced. Although we can make only limited comparisons between the arts and social studies, the data suggest a steady decline in the former matched by a large expansion of the latter at Cambridge and nationally. The Franks Inquiry did differentiate between arts and social studies students at Oxford in these post-war years, and its data show that social studies remained stable at approximately 20 per cent of total student numbers (University of Oxford 1966b: 17). Secondly, while the combined representation of arts/social studies student numbers at the national level had remained almost unchanged since 1922–23 (40.9 per cent in 1922–23, 41.4 per cent in 1969–70), there had been a steady movement in other directions at both Oxford and Cambridge after 1945. In terms of the combined presence of arts and social studies, by 1969–70 the University of Cambridge's knowledge map was almost identical to the national picture, and the University of Oxford's was moving in the same direction. Technology was one of the clear growth points at the University of Oxford and by 1969–70 it can be described as having a real, as opposed to its prior marginal, presence in the university. By comparison, the presence of technology remained more or less stable at the University of Cambridge at approximately 12 per cent of the total student population, with the decline in 1969–70 numbers compensated for by the fact that architecture (previously classified as a technological subject) was reclassified under professional/vocational studies. There was a consistent increase in the natural sciences and a consistent decline in agriculture/forestry across this 20-year period of expansion at both the national level and at Oxbridge. Finally, the medical student numbers (note neither Oxford nor Cambridge have schools of dentistry) fluctuated at both Oxford and Cambridge but declined sharply at the national level, but again, however, the overall trend was converging.

The extent of this convergence of the relative presence of subject group areas over this period is illustrated by Table 5.8. For the purposes of this table, we have combined the numbers for technology and professional/vocational studies which results in a consistent, if small, increase in Cambridge's technology student numbers. Secondly, we have assumed that the representation of social studies students was lower in 1949–50 than in 1959–60, except in the case of Oxford where we have relied upon a breakdown of arts and social studies numbers provided by the Franks Report. Strictly speaking, Oxford's social studies numbers indicated a very small fluctuating presence at the university, but nowhere on the scale of the student numbers for medicine.

Although both the Universities of Oxford and Cambridge, therefore, continued to present distinctive knowledge maps during these years of expansion, the trends in total students numbers pointed to an erosion of the most extreme differences from the national picture, which was most clearly seen in the steady growth of technology at Oxford coupled with a much sharper decline in its arts base. However, even in 1969–70, student numbers would suggest that *both* the Universities of Oxford and Cambridge were over-

Table 5.8   Subject group representation: 1949–50 to 1969–70

	Oxford	*Cambridge*	*GB*
Arts	CD	CD	CD
Social Studies	SR	CI	CI
Natural Sciences	CI	CI	CI
Technology	CI	CI	CI
Medicine/Dentistry	FR	FR	CD
Agriculture/Forestry	CD	CD	CD

Abbreviations: CD, consistent decline; CI, consistent increase; FR, fluctuating representation; SR, stabilized representation.

represented in arts subjects and under-represented in technology. Consistently Oxford was the more distinctive of the two universities precisely because of the extent to which it differed from national distributions in these subject areas. The other major observation is that whereas there were large changes both nationally and at Oxford, the Cambridge picture remained by comparison relatively stable. In a short space of time, the academic landscape of Oxford was reshaped to produce a radically different university from the inter-war years. Although Cambridge followed the national trend – interestingly not so much by increasing student numbers in the natural sciences and technology but rather by expanding social studies at the expense of its arts subjects – the movements were small by comparison with Oxford. In effect, it could be argued that, with respect to the balance of subject groups, Cambridge represented the model to which British universities in general were evolving! It had a smaller arts base to shed than Oxford but provided a more than respectable home to large faculties in both the natural and applied sciences.

Because of the failure of the UGC to breakdown postgraduate student numbers by subject group in its 1949–50 and 1959–60 returns, we have been compelled to rely on internal university sources for the detailed analysis of undergraduate/postgraduate comparisons prior to 1969–70. Fortunately, presumably in response to the expansion of the postgraduate populations, the internal statistics are more detailed than for the inter-war years. Using UGC data, we will present the patterns for 1969–70 and then in the text use internal university sources to consider the trend towards those patterns. There are three comparisons that are of particular interest: the subject group distributions of the postgraduate students, how those distributions compare to those of the undergraduate students, and the balance within individual subject groups of undergraduate and postgraduate student numbers. On the one hand, there is the question of the general character of the knowledge maps of the universities, while on the other it is necessary to know whether identifiable knowledge areas have their own peculiar features.

As we have noted, during the inter-war years the limited number of postgraduate students at Oxford (a total of 536 in 1938–39 according to the Franks Inquiry) were concentrated in arts, social studies and the natural sciences (University of Oxford 1966b: 4, 17, 23). By 1938–39, students in these subjects comprised over 95 per cent of Oxford's postgraduates, with the trend running in favour of the natural scientists (up from approximately 10 per cent of the total postgraduate student population in 1923–24 to over 23 per cent in 1938–39) and against the arts and social studies (down to a still massive 72.4 per cent of the total number of Oxford postgraduates in 1938–39 from a high of 86.6 per cent in 1928–29). The much more rudimentary Cambridge data suggested a different picture for, although a university in which most students were in arts or social studies, the postgraduates were by a wide margin disproportionately in science. The data agree, however, on the more powerful presence of postgraduates in science at both universities. In 1938–39, of Oxford's 568 students in the natural sciences, 126 or 22.2 per cent were postgraduates, compared to 388 postgraduates or 10 per cent out of a total of 3877 students reading for an arts or social studies degree. What happened to these simple profiles once the numbers started to expand rapidly?

The most striking feature of Table 5.9 is the similarity of the undergraduate and postgraduate profiles. The one exception is education, which is accounted for by the fact that most of its students are taking the Postgraduate Certificate in Education (PGCE) course. Invariably as postgraduate courses expanded in Britain, they did so on the foundations of departments that had a solid basis of undergraduate teaching. With the exception of education, this generalization applied in 1969–70 across the whole range of subject groups at both Oxford and Cambridge. So that at Oxford the strength of its humanities tradition ensured that, even as late as 1969–70, the largest single wedge of its postgraduate students continued to study arts subjects. Given the symbiotic relationship of undergraduate to postgraduate courses, the knowledge maps that were drawn on the basis of total student numbers are not modified substantially by refining the data into postgraduate and undergraduate student numbers. Thus the generalizations that were made on the basis of total student numbers hold good after comparing undergraduate and postgraduate distributions: the distinctiveness of Oxford with respect to its large arts base and the small presence of technology, the almost identical representation by 1969–70 of the natural sciences in Oxford, in Cambridge and in the total student population, and the much closer proximity of Cambridge to the national pattern.

What light do the internal university sources shed upon the evolution of the above profiles? What appears to have happened is that the undergraduate and postgraduate profiles moved over time towards a common model for both the Universities of Oxford and Cambridge. In other words, there was an erosion of their respective peculiarities. The Franks Report showed a small decline in the proportionate representation of the arts/social studies and of the agriculture/forestry subject groups at Oxford at both undergraduate and postgraduate levels between 1948–49 and 1964–65, paralleled by

Table 5.9 Subject group profiles: Comparison of undergraduates and postgraduates, 1969–70 (full-time students only)

	Oxford		Cambridge		UK	
	Undergraduates (%)	Postgraduates (%)	Undergraduates (%)	Postgraduates (%)	Undergraduates (%)	Postgraduates (%)
Arts	40.8	32.7	34.0	24.6	23.1	13.5
Social Studies	22.2	22.2	19.6	14.7	20.6	17.4
Science	25.5	25.8	24.1	29.7	24.5	26.6
Medicine/Dentistry	6.5	2.6	7.7	2.3	11.0	5.0
Technology	4.5	4.9	10.5	12.5	16.5	14.2
Agriculture/Forestry/Veterinary Science	0.5	2.4	1.6	3.0	1.9	2.3
Education	0.0	9.5	0.1	11.5	0.7	18.3
Professional Vocational Studies	0.0	0.0	2.3	1.8	1.7	2.8
Totals						
Percentages	100.0	100.1	99.9	100.1	100.0	100.1
Numbers	7801	3033	8246	2121	180 179	39 129

Sources: UGC (1970: 18–19, 28–9).

modest growths in both the pure and the applied sciences (University of Oxford 1966b: 17, 23). During much the same time period, the postgraduate students in the natural sciences at Cambridge declined in comparison to those reading for higher degrees in other scientific fields. While in the 1960s, the shift was away from the science postgraduates in general and towards those in arts and social studies (University of Cambridge 1965: App. I; 1976: 3, Table 2). Thus while there was an across-the-board expansion of student numbers, the relative changes varied from university to university which, with respect to Oxford and Cambridge, meant that by 1969–70 their overall academic profiles at both the undergraduate and postgraduate levels were converging steadily.

Because of the more refined presentation of its data, the Franks Commission is again the best single source on the changing balance within subject groups between undergraduates and postgraduates at Oxford. In Table 5.10 we have supplemented, for the year 1969–70, the Commission's data with returns from the UGC. Because of the limitations in the data, we have not presented comparisons over time with either Cambridge or the national picture but these are raised, wherever possible, in the subsequent text. It should be remembered that immediately prior to the Second World War, those few graduate students at Oxford were concentrated overwhelmingly in the arts, social studies and the natural sciences, constituting approximately 10 per cent of the total student numbers in arts/social studies and 20 per cent of those in the natural sciences.

The significantly higher percentage of postgraduate students in Oxford's total student population was repeated across all the subject groups by 1969–70. If those taking education courses are incorporated in the arts subject group, then the differences between the universities narrow sharply in this field: in 1969–70, 28.6 per cent of Oxford's students in such a category would have been postgraduates, compared to 21.4 per cent at Cambridge and 22.5 per cent nationally. The changes to the national figure are so staggering that they cannot pass without comment. In 1969–70, there were more students taking postgraduate courses in education (the PGCE) than in any other academic area except the natural sciences, and in a combined education–arts subject group category they contributed over half the student numbers. So far, the theme of this chapter has been that the academic maps of Oxford, Cambridge and British universities as a whole converged during the post-war expansionist years. As a broad generalization this holds good, but it is still possible to point to important distinctions by refining the knowledge areas. As with previous analysis, Cambridge is once again closer to the national picture as its postgraduate students in education have a much larger impact upon the university's academic character than is true of Oxford.

Although the earlier evidence suggested that the expansion of postgraduate studies at Oxford was led by the natural scientists, Table 5.10 shows how after the Second World War there was a general movement in this direction. Indeed, excluding the comparatively small field of agriculture/forestry, the

Table 5.10   Postgraduates as a percentage of each subject group's total student population (full-time students)

| | *1948–49* | *1964–65* | *1969–70* | | |
	Oxford (%)	*Oxford (%)*	*Oxford (%)*	*Cambridge (%)*	*UK (%)*
Arts	13.3	20.5	23.7	15.7	11.3
Social Studies	–	23.2	28.0	16.2	15.5
Natural Sciences	25.8	27.5	28.3	24.0	19.1
Applied Sciences	6.2	21.3	29.7	23.4	15.8
Agriculture/Forestry	15.5	44.8	65.5	32.3	20.1
Medicine/Dentistry	3.1	16.7	13.3	7.0	8.9
Postgraduates as % of total student numbers	14.8	22.9	28.0	20.5	17.8

Notes: (1) The Franks Commission failed to separate postgraduate student numbers in arts and social studies for the year 1948–49. (2) Education and Professional/Vocational Studies have been excluded from the calculations for individual subject groups but included in the calculations for total student numbers.
Sources: University of Oxford (1966b: 17, 23), UGC (1970: 18–19, 28–9).

dynamic growth of postgraduate studies at the university occurred in arts and social studies. The position of agriculture/forestry at Oxford is interesting, for while its powerful inter-war presence in the university declined after 1945, it also rapidly changed its academic character by becoming predominantly a knowledge area for postgraduates. The comparative data suggest that this was a general trend that affected this field. What is particularly remarkable about the expansion of postgraduate studies at Oxford during these years was not only the increased visibility of postgraduates within the general student population, but their even representation in the major knowledge areas of arts, social studies, natural sciences and applied sciences. At Cambridge and nationally, postgraduates were less visible and more likely to be concentrated in the natural and applied sciences. It is important, however, not to exaggerate the differences. The UGC's figures for 1969–70 suggest a somewhat smaller postgraduate presence at Cambridge rather than one that favoured particular subjects. Secondly, the trend at Cambridge appeared to be very much in the same direction as at Oxford, with the postgraduate numbers expanding in the arts, social studies and the applied sciences but not to any appreciable extent in the natural sciences. Again the universities were developing common intellectual maps. It is almost as if there were a master plan to iron out their idiosyncrasies as they moved inexorably towards *the model* of the university. Finally, although the major knowledge areas in universities have developed their own organizational characteristics, and need vastly different levels of resources to underwrite their research activities, the across-the-board increases in postgraduate numbers would suggest that there was a universal commitment to the expansion of research.

It is clear, therefore, that the years of expansion that occurred after the Second World War were associated with very definite trends that restructured in a comparatively consistent manner both the Universities of Oxford and Cambridge and the general British university system. First, there was expansion that was especially marked for the postgraduate students. Secondly, that expansion had a differential effect and, although it is possible to point to the faster growth of particular knowledge areas, the more interesting development was the general convergence of academic profiles at both the undergraduate and postgraduate levels. Convergence occurred precisely because the pattern of expansion was uneven from university to university. In specific terms, Oxford shed some of its image as an arts-based university as its science and technology expanded; conversely, at Cambridge, the representation of the arts declined more slowly as social studies expanded. Oxford experienced the greater changes precisely because it had been a more peculiar university and the comparative stability of the distribution of Cambridge's student numbers, going back to the inter-war years, suggested that the overall system was gravitating in its direction. Of course, a greatly expanded range of comparisons would probably reveal a stronger ideal type than Cambridge. Thirdly, the growth of postgraduate student numbers was dependent upon a solid undergraduate base. With the possible exception of agriculture and forestry, and then more especially at Oxford, that undergraduate base was never overwhelmed by the surge in postgraduate student numbers. Fourthly, although science and technology have tended to become more postgraduate-centred knowledge areas than the arts and social studies, one remarkable development has been the extent to which such differences were eroded in the 1960s at both Oxford and Cambridge. As university knowledge maps converged, so individual knowledge areas assumed a more common character.

Could it be said that this expansion of student numbers was planned? The answer to the question is entirely dependent upon what is understood by the concept of planning. In the sense that it was widely predicted that during these years the demand for higher education was going to increase rapidly, then there was planning. Undoubtedly, the most famous projection of student demand was found in the Robbins Report. Not only did the Report try to predict future demand but it also helped to create an ethos which urged a sympathetic response (Committee on Higher Education 1963: 48–54). In fact, what the Robbins Report did was reinforce a favourable political climate, the official commitment to the expansion of higher education was already present. The more interesting question is whether the particular pattern of expansion that actually occurred was planned? The Robbins Report, however, set itself against the principle of planned expansion through state sponsorship:

> In principle, the problem of estimating the number of places required can be approached in two ways: by considering what supply of different

kinds of educated persons will be required to meet the needs of the nation, or by considering what the demand for places in higher educa-- tion is likely to be. We have decided that the second approach presents the sounder basis for estimates.

We have found the first approach impracticable. For, while it is possible, for a number of professions over a short time, to calculate with a fair degree of precision what the national need for recruits will be, we have found no reliable basis for reckoning the totality of such needs over a long term (ibid.: 48).

But such sentiments run up against the UGC's new terms of reference which, it will be recalled, enabled it to prepare and execute plans for university developments that it felt were consistent with national needs. There is no indication that the UGC used its powers in anything other than its traditionally circumspect style during this period. However, it is clear that certain kinds of developments were favoured over others and, given that quinquennial applications for future grants were vetted by the UGC, it was in a position to shape the overall pattern of expansion. But the circumstances were more subtle than this, for individual universities were aware of the flavour of official thinking and it is reasonable to suspect that this influenced their planning. Although the UGC's overview of future student numbers was never more than crude, it did require by the 1960s the universities to submit projections divided by arts and sciences, undergraduates and postgraduates. Thus it is no surprise that the relative positions of the natural and applied sciences improved over these years while the social studies remained stable and arts declined. However, we have shown that the impact of these develop- ments was not universal; that is, they influenced individual universities in different ways and that, by and large, they operated in reverse directions at the undergraduate and postgraduate levels. The comparatively greater ex- pansion at the postgraduate level in arts and social studies suggests that the UGC was being driven by forces within particular disciplines which wanted to preserve their standing within the overall academic map. In other words, not to engage in research risked a loss of academic status, and as expansion at the postgraduate level in arts and social studies did not incur the costs of similar expansion in the sciences, then there was little reason not to let the universities have their way, and indeed the UGC could exercise little direct influence.

Perhaps the most important point to make is that there was little need for rigorous planning in an era of general expansion, that the softly softly approach of the UGC brought about a slow restructuring of the universities which satisfied the political authorities without offending the universities. This was soon to change as the pressures from state and society increased while the commitment of resources to higher education dwindled. So it became increasingly difficult to restructure without affecting not only the relative positions of knowledge areas but also the traditional size of their territories.

Student numbers: The steady-state model

By the late 1960s, the enthusiasm for university expansion was waning and earlier projected growth rates were revised downwards. This is not to say that student numbers were to decline in the 1970s, but that the growth would not be as great as previously anticipated. Moreover, the easing of expansionist pressures in the 1970s was replaced in the 1980s by projections of a smaller university student base. So much of the change was related to financial pressures: the failure of the British economy to grow consistently at a rate that would meet all the demands for increased social expenditure, the determination of governments to control public expenditure, and the unwillingness of universities to cut their unit costs. Moreover, the correlation between finance and student numbers was stark and simple: the cost of maintaining the student base was met overwhelmingly by the Exchequer; curtail the Exchequer's input, then either the student base shrinks or the universities maintain, or possibly expand, numbers with fewer resources. With few exceptions students themselves did not generate income, for their fees were met by a combination of grants from the LEAs and the UGC, both of course ultimately funded by the taxpayer.

Although in the past two decades the size of the student population has been strongly influenced by financial restrictions, the judgement as to whether from the 1970s student numbers have been planned more purposefully has to be equivocal. Superficially, the UGC's indirect control of university development (the reflections in its annual surveys upon developments in various subject areas, the possibility of refusing to sanction projects, and the new requirement that universities provide more detailed breakdowns of projected student numbers) was reinforced by issuing Memoranda of Guidance for the 1967–72 quinquennium which, in the words of the UGC, 'tried to set out the general background for the university system as a whole and the particular considerations for each university separately' (UGC 1972–73: 25). The memoranda, however, were issued at the time of the allocation of the grant, thus trying to close the stable door as the horse was being allowed to bolt, which is a perfect illustration of the UGC's attempt to balance the contradictory pressures to which it was increasingly subjected (see Chapter 1). Five years later, the UGC appeared to have got its act together and issued a Preliminary Memorandum of Guidance in advance of the universities' preparation of their submission for the 1972–77 quinquennium (ibid.). This preliminary memorandum 'indicated the scale of expansion of student numbers by 1977 which the Committee had in mind for each university and certain other broad considerations for the university system as a whole, such as the maximum proportion of postgraduate work for which it might be realistic to plan' (ibid.). The implication is that the UGC was moving in the direction of guiding the development of individual universities as well as the overall university system, rather than simply passing judgement on the universities' submissions after their formulation. The tone of the language is mild but it does suggest a measure of dirigisme that was absent in the past.

However, in the world of consensus politics that both the UGC and the universities were trying desperately to preserve, it would be ridiculous to think in terms of rigidly imposed UGC norms that the universities had to follow slavishly or face the threat of UGC imposed sanctions. The UGC informed the Public Accounts Committee that, although universities some- times failed to meet their student targets, 'no university had deliberately used its available resources to provide more lavishly for fewer students' (UGC 1980–81: 31). Moreover, universities sometimes exceeded their target num- bers, which meant that they obtained additional fee income from the LEAs and it was entirely at the discretion of the UGC whether or not they would be allowed to keep it (ibid.: 32). Clearly, this was a world of gentlemanly bargaining. But, as university development from the late 1970s onwards had to take place within the confines of cash limits, so there was less room for flexibility on student numbers. It made little sense to impose financial restrictions upon the universities by cutting the UGC's annual recurrent grant while allowing them to increase their fee income by accepting more students. The Public Accounts Committee had seen this potential loophole and recommended that fee income should also be cash-limited (ibid.). Of course it was easier to resolve the potential problem by cutting the UGC's recurrent grant to counter increased fee income, rather than to change the law on the mandatory obligation of the LEAs to pay the fees of students awarded a university place. None the less, there was never complete rigidity; even when the winds of retrenchment were shrillest, the Secretary of State was prepared to accept the need for:

> amendment of student number targets of the relatively modest kind the Committee [that is the UGC] have recently announced when, after consultation with a university, the Committee believe that there is a good case for such a change and resources permit it (UGC 1981–82: 33–4).

Negotiated flexibility was always possible.

Despite of the periodically repeated stress 'about the desired change of emphasis in favour of science-based subjects and to protect the capacity of the universities to undertake research and to provide teaching of high quali- ty' (the Secretary of State, Sir Keith Joseph, in a letter to the chairman of the UGC, ibid.: 33), it would still be an overstatement to interpret the UGC's firmer control of student numbers as a manifestation of a positive planning ethos. If the intention was to ensure that universities operated within defined cash limits, then it made sense to have firm projections of student numbers, for these were the major element in the determination of the UGC's recur- rent grant and clearly some subject groups generated more costs than others.

Furthermore, once targets had been agreed, it was more difficult for the universities to attempt to increase their fee income by revising them up- wards. Of course, the universities were caught in two minds, that is whether to increase fee income or to maintain unit costs by restricting growth. By

Table 5.11 Total full-time student numbers: 1969–70 to 1989–90

	1969–70	*1979–80*	*1989–90*
Cambridge	10 367	11 337	13 219
Oxford	10 834	11 829	13 079
Total (GB)	219 308	292 738	334 479

Sources: UGC (1970: 18–19, 28–9; 1980a: 16–17, 24–5), UFC (1990a: 46).

choosing the latter course in response to the decline in the value of the recurrent grant, it could be reasonably argued that their concern was to maintain their traditional privileges, and had little or nothing to do with planning. Up to its very demise, the UGC invariably resorted to a combination of exhortation and the promotion of special programmes (which had but a marginal effect on the overall academic character of the universities) in order to influence university development. The greater control of student numbers, in the shape of setting targets, has to be put, therefore, in the context of the political determination to limit public expenditure upon the universities. The purpose is to make cash limits stick rather than to determine the shape of the academic map.

The Second World War provided a realistic divide in the presentation of the previous statistics: there was a lull in university expansion during the war years and after the war the UGC was given new terms of reference. It is contentious, however, as to when the post-war expansion declined to the point when it was no longer meaningful to see the university system as expanding. In the presentation of the data, therefore, we have simply extended the time sequence from 1969–70 onwards and have included the distributions for that year in the following tables in order to make it easier to draw comparisons.

Although there has been a considerable easing of university expansion in the past 20 years, it is perhaps a misnomer to describe this as the era of the steady-state model. Of course the picture has been complicated by the creation of new universities and granting other higher education institutions (most notably the colleges of advanced technology) university status. University expansion, therefore, was partly a consequence of relabelling institutions, a development that occurred in particular in the 1960s. However, as Table 5.11 reveals, overall student numbers increased by 52.5 per cent in British universities from 1969–70 to 1989–90 compared to 27.5 per cent at Cambridge and 20.7 per cent at Oxford. The repeated projections about the retrenchment of British universities in the 1980s are reflected, however, in the national trend, with a 1970s growth rate of 33.5 per cent declining to 14.3 per cent in the 1980s. Not surprisingly, as national student numbers stabilized, so the representation of Oxbridge remained steady as opposed to declining. In 1969–70, Oxbridge students constituted 9.7 per cent of all

British students and, although this figure declined to 7.9 per cent in 1979–80, thereafter it stabilized, albeit (if future projections are fulfilled) only temporarily. We are not in a position to provide precise quantitative criteria on the relationship between the size of Oxbridge and the extent of its direct influence upon the university system, but probably what has been happening is a concentration of this influence as its relative size has diminished. Thus it is possible that different university networks have emerged within the overall system. Of course, if there is evidence to this effect, then it has to be squared with the fact that as expansion occurred then the trend in the subject group distribution of student numbers in fact suggested a convergence of the academic maps of the individual universities. But there is no reason to suppose that a general convergence in the academic character of individual universities cannot run parallel with the creation of particular networks within the overall system. If this is so, then the interesting questions are what criteria define the various networks and how are they sustained?

The distributions presented in Table 5.12 are complicated by the increasing importance of part-time students in the profiles. As far as undergraduate student numbers are concerned, the part-time students can be safely ignored – although they may constitute a significant input at some universities, their national impact has been slight, and to date entirely negligible at both the Universities of Oxford and Cambridge. For postgraduates, however, the situation is very different. Although, given the years that we have selected for comparison, part-time postgraduate student numbers were not recorded in the UGC returns at either Oxford or Cambridge until 1969–70, they have always figured prominently – as we have noted – in the national picture, so both reducing and creating a distinction between Oxbridge and the rest of the British university system. The apparent decline in postgraduate student numbers in the 1970s was not as sharp as Table 5.12 implies, for part-time postgraduate student numbers increased markedly in the 1970s (up from 697 to 986 at Cambridge, from 796 to 1676 at Oxford and from 19 483 to 27 658 nationally). Despite all of the equivocations that have been produced by a change in the presentation of the statistics (there were students registered for postgraduate degrees at Oxford and Cambridge who were not in full-time residence long before they started to show up in the UGC returns), it is fair to conclude that the 1970s were at best plateau years for the growth of postgraduate student numbers, and while in the 1980s the relative importance of postgraduates in the overall student population was again on the increase, the rapid shift in the balance between undergraduate teaching and postgraduate supervision within the British model of the university slowed down. These are conclusions which would also be supported by an analysis of internal university sources (University of Cambridge 1988c: table 1; University of Oxford 1971: table 1; 1981: table 1; 1987: table 1).

Throughout this time period, the UGC's statistical returns presented the subject group distributions for postgraduates and undergraduates separately, and so it is now possible for us to do likewise. Unfortunately for our purposes, the UGC employed more refined subject group categories over time.

Table 5.12 Undergraduates/postgraduates as a percentage of total full-time student numbers

| | 1969–70 | | | 1979–80 | | | 1989–90 | | |
	Undergraduates (%)	Postgraduates (%)	Total no.	Undergraduates (%)	Postgraduates (%)	Total no.	Undergraduates (%)	Postgraduates (%)	Total no.
Cambridge	79.5	20.5	10 367	83.0	17.0	11 337	77.5	22.5	13 219
Oxford	72.0	28.0	10 834	79.3	20.5	11 829	78.8	21.2	13 079
Total (GB)	82.2	17.8	219 308	83.7	16.3	292 738	82.3	17.7	334 479

Sources: See Table 5.11.

In order to aid comparison, with the exception of amalgamating veterinary sciences with agriculture/forestry, we have decided to stay with the subject groups used in Table 5.7 for the year 1969–70, which has meant restructuring some of the UGC's subsequent categories. Most problems were caused by the UGC's introduction of a 'multidisciplinary studies' category. In Tables 5.13 and 5.14 we have derived our 1988–89 student numbers from the presentation of data for university cost centres (thus relying on Volume 3, *Finance*, rather than Volume 1, *Students and Staff*, of the statistical returns for the universities). Although this has enabled us to bypass the multidisciplinary category and so maintain consistent subject groups, such a manoeuvre is not without its pitfalls. The student numbers for the cost centres were presented as full-time equivalent student loads, which is no problem as far as the undergraduates are concerned (nearly all of them were full-time students) but makes postgraduate comparisons over time more difficult because of the increasing proportion of part-time postgraduates. The complications caused by this variation in the statistical basis of the tables will be commented upon in the text.

Whereas we described the years between the end of the Second World War and 1970 as a time of convergence, since then the academic maps have remained relatively stable. By 1988–89, the only really significant difference between the Cambridge and the national student subject group profiles was the more pronounced representation of the arts at Cambridge, whereas at Oxford the over-representation of arts students was accompanied by their continuing under-representation in technology and medicine. There were few consistent trends and what few there were (e.g. the increased presence of science and technology at Oxford and of medicine at Cambridge) were small in size. It would be meaningless to construct a parallel diagram as we did for the time period 1949–50 to 1969–70 indicating the consistently declining and expanding areas, for overwhelmingly there were few clear trends but rather small shifts and minor fluctuations. The smaller subject group areas (agriculture/forestry and veterinary science, education, and professional and vocational studies) had no undergraduate presence at Oxford in 1988–89, again illustrating the university's academic distinctiveness. This is partly accounted for by the reorganization of faculties (so that agriculture and forestry are incorporated in a Department of Plant Sciences) and the UFC's construction of its subject groups (so that business and management studies – which have a small undergraduate presence at Oxford and to our way of thinking would be more sensibly recorded in the professional/vocational studies category – have been classified as social studies). The last point raises the question of the more general shift towards vocationally oriented studies. The UFC's statistics reveal their increasing presence (e.g. of nursing, accountancy and planning besides business and management studies) in British universities. Part of the history of British professions is the incorporation of at least part of their training programmes within the universities in order to upgrade their status and regulate their entry requirements. Although management and business studies has penetrated Oxford (and is

Table 5.13 Full-time undergraduate subject group profiles: 1969–70 to 1988–89

	1969–70			1979–80			1988–89		
	Oxford (%)	Cambridge (%)	GB (%)	Oxford (%)	Cambridge (%)	GB (%)	Oxford (%)	Cambridge (%)	GB (%)
Arts	40.8	34.0	23.1	39.9	28.9	22.4	41.3	29.3	22.3
Social Studies	22.2	19.6	20.6	22.4	19.4	23.8	20.3	21.2	26.2
Science	25.5	24.1	24.5	26.7	24.5	22.7	27.1	22.5	24.3
Medicine/Dentistry	6.5	7.7	11.0	5.4	8.9	11.3	6.3	9.8	10.9
Technology	4.5	10.5	16.5	4.7	10.3	14.6	5.0	11.8	12.3
Agriculture/Forestry/Veterinary Science	0.5	1.6	1.9	1.0	2.7	2.1	0.0	1.5	1.5
Education	0.0	0.1	0.7	0.0	2.8	1.5	0.0	2.0	1.5
Professional/Vocational Studies	0.0	2.3	1.7	0.0	2.5	1.7	0.0	1.9	1.1
Totals									
Percentages	100.0	99.9	100.0	100.1	100.0	100.1	100.0	100.0	100.0
Numbers	7801	8246	180179	9379	9409	245093	9752	10035	258661

Sources: UGC (1970: 18–19; 1980a: 16–17), UFC (1990b: 21–58).

Table 5.14 Full-time postgraduate subject group profiles: 1969–70 to 1988–89

	1969–70			1979–80			1988–89		
	Oxford (%)	Cambridge (%)	GB (%)	Oxford (%)	Cambridge (%)	GB (%)	Oxford (%)	Cambridge (%)	GB (%)
Arts	32.7	24.6	13.5	30.9	22.4	11.7	32.6	21.2	11.6
Social Studies	22.2	14.7	17.4	25.3	18.7	20.9	25.2	17.9	24.3
Science	25.8	29.7	26.6	22.4	32.1	23.3	26.4	29.7	22.5
Medicine/Dentistry	2.6	2.3	5.0	4.6	2.2	7.4	5.3	5.3	10.1
Technology	4.9	12.5	14.2	4.2	11.0	14.0	5.0	12.9	12.9
Agriculture/Forestry/Veterinary Science	2.4	3.0	2.3	2.4	0.7	2.3	0.0	0.6	2.0
Education	9.5	11.5	18.3	10.1	11.8	17.3	5.6	10.6	15.3
Professional/Vocational Studies	0.0	1.8	2.8	0.0	1.2	3.1	0.0	1.9	1.3
Totals									
Percentages	100.1	100.1	100.1	99.9	100.1	100.0	100.1	100.1	100.0
Numbers	3033	2121	39 129	2450	1928	47 645	3975	3376	72 487

Sources: UGC (1970: 28–9; 1980a: 24–5), UFC (1990b: 21–58).

penetrating Cambridge) – albeit not without considerable equivocation – the data suggest that as in the past the university has been cautious in its welcome to the latest wave of professional infiltration.

As with the undergraduate profiles, the most notable feature of Table 5.14 is the stability of the relative presence of the subject groups over time. If there could be said to be a significant growth area, then medicine/dentistry came closest to fitting that description, while the only sharp decline was in education at Oxford during the 1980s. A comparison of the undergraduate and postgraduate distributions confirms the close relationship that we noted previously. Education is the only significant exception to this generalization (it is essentially a postgraduate subject), while the arts subjects have a notably higher profile among the undergraduates. Again, it is Oxford that deviates most sharply from the national picture, with approximately 20 per cent more of its postgraduates studying an arts subject (compared to approximately 10 per cent more at Cambridge), countered by a lower percentage representation of its postgraduates in education, technology and medicine/dentistry. If a crude generalization can be made, it is that whereas the natural sciences and social studies have gained a very firm foothold in Oxford, the more directly vocationally biased disciplines (with the obvious exceptions of law and medicine) have remained more on the margins of the university in comparison to Cambridge.

Because the figures for 1988–89 are based on full-time equivalent student loads, whereas those for 1969–70 and 1979–80 exclude the part-time students, then the generalizations we have made about postgraduates need to be treated cautiously. Between 1979–80 and 1989–90 (the UGC did not make the information available in 1969–70 and breakdowns for individual universities are still unavailable in the UFC's statistics), the national subject group patterns of the *part-time* postgraduate students also remained stable over time (UGC 1980a: 34–35; UFC 1990a: 16–17). Moreover, for many years, the University of Cambridge has published its own statistics on student numbers as full-time equivalent student loads, and they also reinforce the same point with the important exception that the proportional representation of postgraduates in the natural sciences grew rapidly at Cambridge in the 1980s coupled with declines in the social studies and arts (University of Cambridge 1976: 4; 1980a: 4; 1989d: 3). What the inclusion of the part-time postgraduates tends to do is to push the overall postgraduate profiles towards education, the arts and social studies and away from the natural sciences and technology. In the case of education, this is almost certainly a consequence of the large number of teachers who registered for part-time master's degrees designed to fit into their work schedules. At the same time, those registered for higher degrees in science and technology complete them more quickly than the postgraduate students in arts and social studies. Although in quantitative terms the part-time postgraduate students modify academic profiles, it is more difficult to ascertain their impact upon the academic culture of the universities. Even if their part-time status goes with a presence on campus it may be marginal in its effect, and if there is no attendance the influence could be non-existent.

Table 5.15 illustrates that the decline in postgraduate studies in the 1970s cut across the complete disciplinary range, while particular subjects (most notably forestry and agriculture) were affected by restructuring within individual universities. Although there may be government edicts to the effect that science and technology need to be more vigorously pursued within the universities, they are not immune from the general pressures that shape university development. However, having made the point, it should be noted that invariably it is science and technology which have higher proportions of postgraduate students and that this is especially true of Cambridge. The interesting exception was the University of Oxford; in 1988–89, only education and social studies had a higher proportion of postgraduates than in the university's total student population. It is perhaps unwise, however, to concentrate too much upon internal differences, for what is more significant is the resumption of the steady encroachment of postgraduate studies. Excluding education because it has been essentially a postgraduate course in British universities, and agriculture/forestry because of the restructuring of courses at Oxford and Cambridge, we note a strong resurgence of postgraduate studies across the board in the 1980s.

The period since 1970 is best described, therefore, as one of stability, in which the rapid expansion of the 1950s and 1960s cooled, and the academic maps formed by the end of those years congealed. To some extent, our choice of comparative reference points has underestimated the upheavals that took place. The governmental emphasis, reflected in the UGC's annual reports, that university education would contract, was at its most pronounced in the early 1980s. By the late 1980s, the universities were emerging from the trough into what could well be a new era of high growth. Our tables, therefore, have not reflected fully the extent of the crisis in the early 1980s. Although there were some interesting developments within subject areas, most notably the infiltration of the universities by a number of professional groups that previously had shunned – or been shunned by – the universities, the overall impression is that the relative strength of the broad subject areas stabilized during these years. There was not a dramatic change in the knowledge maps, but clearly important new developments were set in motion and in future more refined analysis will be needed to measure their progress. The data of the late 1980s suggest that the overall university system is on the verge of changing its academic character dramatically. The 1990s will show whether seeds of potential change flourish or perish.

Conclusions

It is hardly surprising to find that the student profiles of the Universities of Oxford and Cambridge while changing have remained remarkably stable over time. As there has been no attempt in twentieth-century Britain to restructure systematically the purposes of higher education, relative continuity in their academic character was bound to prevail. Perhaps the most

Table 5.15 Postgraduates as a percentage of each subject group's total student population (full-time students only)

	1969–70			1979–80			1988–89		
	Oxford (%)	Cambridge (%)	GB (%)	Oxford (%)	Cambridge (%)	GB (%)	Oxford (%)	Cambridge (%)	GB (%)
Arts	23.7	15.7	11.3	16.8	13.7	9.2	24.3	19.6	14.6
Social Studies	28.0	16.2	15.5	22.8	16.4	14.6	33.5	22.1	20.6
Science	28.3	24.0	19.1	18.0	21.2	16.7	28.4	30.7	20.6
Medicine/Dentistry	13.3	7.0	8.9	18.2	4.8	11.2	25.8	15.3	20.7
Technology	29.7	23.4	15.8	19.0	18.0	15.7	28.7	26.9	22.7
Agriculture/Forestry/Veterinary Science	65.5	32.3	20.1	39.2	5.2	17.6	0.0	11.9	26.9
Education	100.0	98.0	84.4	100.0	46.6	69.0	100.0	64.3	74.2
Professional/Vocational Studies	0.0	16.6	26.3	0.0	8.9	26.7	0.0	24.9	24.5
Totals									
Postgraduates as % of total student numbers	28.0	20.5	17.8	20.7	17.0	16.3	25.0	25.2	21.9
Numbers	3033	2121	39129	2450	1928	47645	2975	3376	72487

Note: The statistics for 1969–70 and 1979–80 are for full-time postgraduates only, those for 1988–89 are full-time equivalent student loads and thus incorporate part-time postgraduates.

Sources: UGC (1970: 18–19, 28–9; 1980a: 16–17, 24–5), UFC (1990b: 21–58).

significant change has been in the sheer size of their student bodies. With a few exceptions – the years following the two wars, the early 1930s and early 1980s – the universities have grown steadily. And yet this growth must be placed within the context of the changing character of higher education, for some of the expansion resulted from the relabelling of institutions, most notably granting the CATs university status. Furthermore, although international comparisons raise the question of whether like is being compared with like, there is considerable evidence that, notwithstanding expansion, the age participation rate in Britain remains substantially lower than in many other industrialized nations. Growth at Oxford and Cambridge has been kept in check by the physical constraints of their locations in thriving cities, and almost certainly (although less is made of this) by their collegiate characters.

Although over the years official enthusiasm for the universities has waxed and waned, it has in this century generally encouraged their growth. Despite some support within the universities for the bilious slogan that 'more means worse', the universities themselves have also been persuaded of the need to expand and there is no foreseeable end to the process. For example, with reference to Oxford's plans for 1991–2 to 1994–5, the University's *Gazette* notes that:

> If the recent rate of growth (the equivalent of 2 per cent per annum over the past five years) were to continue to the end of the decade, the student population would have grown by the year 2000 by just over 3000 to around 17 000. Council and the General Board, however, do not think that the University should aim for growth on this scale. But some growth is essential, albeit at a substantially reduced rate (University of Oxford 1990d: 679).

Oxford's intention, therefore, is to aim for a growth rate of approximately 1 per cent a year until the end of the century, which is in line with Cambridge's proposed expansion in its own plan for 1991–2 to 1994–5 (Yarde 1990: 3). It could be reasonably argued that rather than the state forcing more students upon reluctant universities, the universities themselves have long accepted the need to increase their student numbers. Indeed, many within the universities have claimed that the nation's long-term interests are served by a thriving higher education sector; an argument that was expressed frequently in the lean years of the late 1970s and early 1980s. The intention in those difficult years was to reaffirm the post-1945 commitment to expansion *per se* as the best means of fulfilling national needs.

But in what direction should the universities develop? While within the universities the support for growth has become almost universal, this further question was potentially highly divisive. Again, although the UGC was prepared to issue the occasional caution, the official response was that the universities needed to embrace more wholeheartedly the sciences, and more especially the applied sciences. The key consideration, which was rarely addressed directly, is whether growth in the favoured knowledge areas would be at the expense of growth elsewhere, or whether all would flourish while the relative subject balance within the overall knowledge map slowly changed. What our review of student numbers has shown is that development followed the latter course. Over time, the balance between arts and science has drifted in favour of the latter, and in the post-1945 years even that bastion of the arts, Oxford, acquired a greatly augmented engineering base. It goes without saying that it was easier politically to achieve a gradual redrawing of the academic maps within a context of general growth. What was so threatening about the early 1980s was the government's intention to restructure within the context of overall retrenchment.

Despite the incremental shift towards science and technology, it is important not to lose sight of some very important constants – that Oxford remains to this day predominantly an arts-based university, that the relative size of engineering at Cambridge is scarcely larger today than it was in the years immediately preceding the Second World War, that regardless of its image to the contrary Cambridge has always had a higher proportion of its undergraduates reading for degrees in arts subjects than in the natural sciences and mathematics combined, and that for all the growth in engineering at Oxford it still remains very much a minority interest at the university in comparison to the national picture. The judgement, therefore, has to be equivocal as to whether the state has been successful in its drive to increase the presence of technology and science within British universities.

The move towards science and technology was partly countered by the rapid increase in the number of postgraduate students in the arts and social studies during the expansionist years of the 1950s and 1960s. This was particularly true of the University of Oxford and in a comparatively short space of time there was a substantial shift away from the essentially undergraduate character of the university, to parallel a trend that had occurred somewhat earlier at Cambridge. It is true that full-time postgraduates form a higher percentage of total full-time student numbers in science and technology, but not to the extent that we anticipated and the differences are eroded (except at Cambridge) if the part-time postgraduate students are taken into consideration. In other words, with the exception of the 1970s, postgraduate students have come to occupy a more prominent place within *all* knowledge areas.

If the expansion of postgraduate numbers is taken as an increased university commitment to research (as opposed to teaching), then there has been a general move in that direction. It is almost as if all knowledge areas have incorporated the expansion of postgraduate studies in order to sustain not only their own development but also their own academic standing within the university. As we will discuss in Chapter 7, research in the sciences is sharply differentiated from the arts by the level of its external funding, and thus the number of research workers it can sustain. There are indications, however, that other knowledge areas – most noticeably within the social studies – are being pulled in the same direction. The pressure to make the universities more research-oriented institutions has, like the push for expansion, been taken over by the universities. Occasionally, as in the case of its advocacy of university expansion, the state has found itself hoist with its own petard as it fought to contain the mounting costs to the Exchequer.

Our historical analysis of university student numbers was dominated by the converging trends that emerged in the post-1945 expansionist years. Expansion had a differential impact, so that the relative shift of student numbers in each subject group was such as to move both Oxford and Cambridge closer to the national pattern. Inasmuch as it had a more peculiar academic map, this entailed greater shifts at Oxford than at Cambridge. Within this overall convergence, we stressed the importance of seeking out the development of more specialized inter-university differences. Thus, although postgraduate numbers have expanded generally relative to undergraduate numbers, postgraduate students in education occupy a much more critical position in the national figures than is true either of Cambridge, or even more so, than of Oxford. Similarly, the character of the broad subject group categories has evolved so that more refined analysis could show that over time we are no longer comparing like with like. So a detailed breakdown of particular categories (and social studies needs special attention), may reveal significant inter-university differences that are disguised by the broad subject group comparisons. Cambridge has always had a stronger vocational bias in its academic map than Oxford (as seen in the presence of architecture, veterinary science and the large, long-established representation of engineering) and it will be interesting to see whether and in what form the two universities will incorporate, for example, nursing, planning, accountancy and management/business studies.

Although we commenced this chapter by noting the ways in which the state tried to influence the distribution of student numbers, our analysis has stressed its essentially indirect approach to achieving its goals. Given new terms of reference in 1946, the UGC could have acted in a more dirigiste fashion but chose not to. It was only in the 1960s that the idea of a planned system of higher education began to emerge as a serious possibility. But what form was that planning to take? Thinking in the 1960s could not ignore the Robbins Report, undoubtedly the most famous – although not necessarily the most influential – official analysis of higher education in Britain. The Robbins Report set itself firmly against the notion that universities could be instruments of manpower planning. For the Robbins Report, planning was understood as the need to relate opportunities for university education to the predicted demand for university places. In reality, despite much exhortation and small-scale incentives to the contrary, the idea of a planned university system has failed to transcend the Robbins formula.

There are two key reasons for the failure of the state to embrace a more positive understanding of planning. To have done so would have brought to an abrupt end the principle of university autonomy and until comparatively recently no government was prepared to go that far. Secondly, because of governmental pressure, the state's concern with the universities has been taken up increasingly by financial considerations; more particularly on how to limit the Exchequer's input while getting more out of the universities in return for that input. Thus when governments were prepared finally to challenge university autonomy, it was with the purpose of achieving financial rather than planning objectives. From approximately the mid-1970s, the primary consideration has been to force the universities to work within cash limits with no guarantee of adequate supplementation to compensate for the ravages of inflation. There are financial compensations, in the form of additional fees provided by the LEAs, for admitting more students, but without increases in the annual recurrent grant to underwrite those extra students the universities face the prospect of educating more students with a lower average income per student. This is not to deny that there have been special schemes to promote certain knowledge areas, but these have been insignificant in comparison to the main thrust of persuading the universities to educate more students while limiting the additional cost to the Exchequer.

Both Oxford and Cambridge have projected smaller growth rates in the future. Inevitably, this will lessen still further their direct influence upon the rest of the university system. As they have emphasized consistently the necessity to maintain academic standards, it is scarcely likely that they will purposely plan their future student numbers at substantially lower average costs. But in several academic areas, some universities will go for growth and lower their unit costs. As the system started to expand again in the late 1980s, this train of events was set in motion. Moreover, there is always the possibility that sooner or later both Oxford and Cambridge will cash in on their undoubted status by charging, as they are permitted, additional tuition fees. However, the present struggles may be merely an interim stage as we move onto a student voucher scheme, partly underwritten by the Exchequer, in which universities tailor their courses and their costs directly to meet consumer demand. In such circumstances, how much would the consumer, or indeed the state, be prepared to pay for Oxbridge's perceived excellence? It is just one of the interesting questions that may emerge in the near future.

6
Controlling Knowledge and Organizing the Community of Scholars

The domain of the academics

The evidence to the Asquith Commission reports the following reassurance of H.A.L. Fisher, President of the Board of Education, to the Universities of Oxford and Cambridge:

> The State is, in my opinion, not competent to direct the work of education and disinterested research which is carried on by Universities, and the responsibility for its conduct must rest solely with their Governing Bodies and Teachers (Royal Commission on Oxford and Cambridge Universities 1922b: App. 4).

In the nineteenth century, however, Parliament had demonstrated its willingness to prod the ancient universities into new academic directions, and the desire to expand their scientific activities underlay in part the Exchequer's willingness to make recurrent grants after the First World War. Although the state might promote new knowledge areas, there was no question that it would determine how the universities were to control their academic affairs. Above all else, the organization of knowledge was the special domain of the dons. The aims of this chapter are to describe, analyse and evaluate in some detail how the two universities have organized their intellectual activities, to examine some of the more important attempts to streamline the traditional organizational model, and to consider the consequences for academic structures given the decline in UGC funding and the concomitant demands for the more efficient management of resources.

Inasmuch as the state was responsible for the expansion of scientific activities at Oxford and Cambridge, it has exercised the most profound influence upon the organization of knowledge at the two universities by taking much of the responsibility for academic control out of the hands of the colleges and transferring it into the hands of the universities. In view of the infrastructure that science required – laboratories, equipment, materials and technicians – it was far from a foregone conclusion that the colleges had the necessary resources, and even if they did whether they had the incentive to make them available to the scientists. Until after the Second World War, the colleges were essentially undergraduate teaching institutions and their resources were used to maintain existing commitments rather than to underwrite new developments. It would be a historical travesty to claim that there was no college input into the growth of the sciences at the universities of Oxford and Cambridge, but it needs to be recognized that science developed in response to (1) a redirection by Parliament of resources from the colleges to the two universities and (2) the direct and recurrent infusion of Exchequer grants. The Asquith Commission revealed that by 1920 there were no college laboratories in Cambridge and that the supervision of science students was the responsibility of the university rather than of the colleges (University of Oxford 1966a: 34). College laboratories, although of declining significance, survived in Oxford until after the Second World War (Wilkinson 1986). However, excepting the professor and the reader, not a single Oxford college appointed either a fellow in engineering science or offered a scholarship to the department's undergraduates until after 1945 (Interview: Howatson, 20 July 1989).

The transmission and extension of scientific knowledge has certain requirements. Teaching is centred around the laboratory and the lecture hall, while research is invariably a team effort. But to be effective these activities have to be organized – lectures have to be scheduled, laboratories have to be run, equipment has to be ordered and set up, while the work of the team must be co-ordinated. It is not that the arts subjects require no management, but that the range and intensity of the organizational requirements are far less demanding. Traditionally, the key resources for the arts scholar, both undergraduate and don, have been a well-stocked library and time, and at both Oxford and Cambridge some of the specialized college libraries are first rate. How then should science be organized if it is to flourish? At the Universities of Oxford and Cambridge, science, unlike the arts, developed within departments. Up to the present this has been the key organizational unit for science at both universities. Does this represent an inevitable concession on the part of the two ancient universities to the necessities of science? If so, how is this organizational form to be reconciled with the fact that the other knowledge areas are organized mainly within faculties? As a consequence, are there two universities within one – one staffed by academics who make the token genuflection to their faculties while their first loyalties are to their colleges, the other staffed by departmentally based scientists who enjoy the status and perks of college life but whose loyalties to it are essentially instrumental?

The universities and their traditional organization of knowledge

In both Oxford and Cambridge, the academic business of each university is overseen by the General Board of the Faculties. At Oxford, following the recommendations of the Franks Inquiry, the General Board exercises its responsibilities under the auspices of the Hebdomadal Council and is 'responsible for the academic administration of the University' (University of Oxford 1989a: Title V, Sect. 1.1). Cambridge's General Board is required to 'advise the University as to educational policy' and, and more routinely, to 'perform such duties in connexion with the work of the Faculties as may be assigned to it by the Statutes and Ordinances' (University of Cambridge 1988d: Statute C, Ch. 1V.1). Such general statements tell us little about the weight of their respective inputs into the policy-making process, and one of the main criticisms of both General Boards has been of their alleged involvement in the minutiae of administration to the detriment of their policy-making role. It has never been easy, however, to isolate academic issues from the multifarious concerns of a university. Educational policy cannot, for example, be formulated – especially in today's context – without some consideration of pertinent financial variables. Moreover, both General Boards are entrapped in a complex institutional web. Oxford's Congregation and Cambridge's Regent House will be required constitutionally to approve important academic developments. Oxford's General Board is formally subject to the authority of the Hebdomadal Council, and following the approval of the recommendations of the Wass Syndicate, the Council of Senate is to assume the same relationship to Cambridge's General Board. There are also pressures, both for change and conservation, from the complex network of departments, faculties, syndicates, etc., that make up the overall academic structures of the two universities.

The comparatively similar functions of the respective General Boards are complemented by similar compositions. The Cambridge General Board is composed of:

a. The Vice-Chancellor or his deputy, who shall be Chairman
b. Elected members, so that there shall be two representing each Group of Faculties [note there are four such groups]
c. Four members appointed by the Council ... (ibid.: Statute C, Ch. 1V.8).

Thus there are a total of 13 members of Cambridge's General Board, about half the size of its Oxford equivalent which has the following make-up:

a. The Vice-Chancellor
b. The two Proctors
c. The Assessor
d. A representative of the Hebdomadal Council
e. Eight members of Congregation elected by Congregation from a list of designated Faculties
f. Eight members of Congregation elected by Congregation from an alternative list of designated Faculties
g. The General Board may also co-opt up to two members of Congregation each for a period of not more than four years (University of Oxford 1989a: Title V, Sect. 11.1 and 2).

It is potentially, therefore, a body of 23 members.

Although the vice-chancellor may sit on the General Board at both universities, he is not its key member. Oxford's General Board elects annually one of its members as vice-chairman (who now has the title of chairman) who, according to the statutes, can hold the office for up to 4 successive years but invariably serves for only 2 years. As the vice-chairman is a full-time post, and its holder chairs the meetings of the General Board, he or she is in a position to be the General Board's most influential voice. Following the vice-chancellor, this is the most important of the university's policy-making posts. Indeed, it could be claimed that the work of the General Board is generally more significant for the university than that of the Hebdomadal Council, and as the vice-chairman can exercise more control over the general board than the vice-chancellor does over the Hebdomadal Council, then this is the most critical policy-making role within the university. The situation is very different at Cambridge, where one suspects that its General Board is strongly influenced by the secretary general of the faculties who, as an official, is not formally even a member of the Board. At Cambridge, the vice-chancellor, or his deputy, will chair the Board for only 2 years and will have other heavy responsibilities. The secretary-general's influence is also enhanced by the fact that the role is not – as at Oxford – so clearly subordinate to the registrary (a situation that will change once the Wass recommendations are in place), that Cambridge usually appoints to the post long-serving academics, and that the reputation of past secretary-generals has helped to establish the legend of their dominance of the General Board.

Of greater importance than individual roles is the fact that both General Boards provide yet another example of that most characteristic form of university government, that is government by committee. The size of Oxford's General Board may suggest that it is a more unwieldy body than Cambridge's but, although the total memberships may ratify decisions that emerge from the General Boards, as is so often the case the groundwork is done in committee. In fact, the key committee at Oxford is the Resources Committee, which is a joint committee of the Hebdomadal Council and the General Board. At most, it consists of 10 members and controls both the annual budget as well as making recommendations about long-term financial planning (University of Oxford 1989a: Decrees and Regulations, Ch. 11, Sect. 11.1). At Cambridge, the crux of the General Board's work is undertaken by its Needs Committee, which in the past has been concerned essentially with the distribution of the University Education Fund, that is the largest component of the university's budget. Despite this immensely important function, there are those who have doubted whether many members of the university are even aware of its existence!

It is evident from the composition of both General Boards that they are representative bodies with faculties electing the largest block of members. Although the situation has changed somewhat in recent years, the faculties are the second tier in the academic structure of the Universities of Oxford and Cambridge. At Oxford, there are currently 16 faculties and at Cambridge there are 20, and it should come as no surprise to learn that as the twentieth century has progressed so the number of faculties has increased. New academic subjects have tended to argue that they would have a stronger sense of their own identity (and presumably better protect their interests!) if they were organized independently. Each faculty is governed by a faculty board which is composed mainly of *ex-officio* members (i.e. professors and heads of departments), elected members and a small number of co-opted members. The Oxford statutes make provision for the election of a chairman by the faculty board (University of Oxford 1989a: Title VI, Sect. 11.4), while the Cambridge statutes prescribe elections for both a chairman and a secretary, although the latter post may in fact be filled by a university official (University of Cambridge 1988d: Statute C, Ch. 111.5). At both universities, the elections are held annually and, although there is no statutory bar on continuous re-election, the tradition is of short-term service, that is 2 years at a maximum. At Oxford, a faculty may be divided into sub-faculties; the duties of the faculty board are then performed by the sub-faculties, although remaining subject to the approval of the former. The sub-faculties, usually meeting once a term, can conduct their business in meetings consisting of all members of the sub-faculty, although they will have an elected chairman and secretary. For example, the Faculty of Physical Sciences, as a consequence of its sheer size, has delegated its responsibilities to sub-faculties.

The tasks of the faculty boards will vary widely and many have delegated their functions, *de facto* if not *de jure*, to departments. The main responsibility of the faculty boards is to guide the academic affairs of their faculties (e.g. to draw up lecture lists, to approve the structure and content of their curricula and to sanction course syllabi) and, although they may submit reports on wider academic matters, they tend to stick to the particular rather than take up broader issues. On the science side of both universities, the key organizational unit is the department and, although their faculties are formally responsible for academic matters as just described, it is the departments which prepare estimates of expenditure, monitor how budgets are spent, draw up accounts, and appoint faculty. On the arts side of Oxford and Cambridge – including pure mathematics at Cambridge – the faculty boards retain control of financial matters, but as their budgets are composed primarily of faculty salaries, the financial discretion that faculty boards have exercised in the past has been negligible. As long as the key resource of academic staff cannot be changed without the approval of the General Board, this will remain the case. In recent years, the situation has been modified somewhat by the larger intrusion of equipment expenditure in the budgets of the arts faculties, but there is a long way to go before this matches the equivalent expenditure in science and medicine.

The second tier of the academic organization of the Universities of Oxford and Cambridge is shared, therefore, between the faculty boards and the departments. At Oxford, where with the agreement of the General Board the functions of a faculty board can be performed by a sub-faculty, the latter each encompasses one large subject, which in the case of engineering sciences means one department, while for physics and chemistry it covers several

departments. At Cambridge, a large department may have its own faculty
board (as is the case with engineering) or a faculty board may have responsibilities for several departments or even a combination of departments and
subjects that are organized solely in faculty boards. For us, the key question
in this seemingly unending labyrinth of possibilities (and note the exclusion
of academic subjects that are neither departmentally organized nor managed
by a faculty board!) is the relationship between departments, faculty boards
and the General Board of Faculties. Heads of departments are formally
responsible for the efficient management of their departments. In the first
instance, they hold their posts for 5 years but some can serve for more than
one term. The primary academic function of the departmental heads is to
enhance the reputation of their departments, which in concrete terms invariably means that there is a healthy inflow of research funds and an equally
healthy output of research publications. Administratively, the heads are
responsible for the financial management of their departments, which for all
matters at Oxford means that they negotiate directly with the General Board.
At Cambridge, the situation is somewhat more complex as departmental
estimates are agreed between the deputy treasurer of the Financial Board and
the head of department, and then require the approval of the General Board.
Another critical difference at Cambridge, and we have much more to say on
this below, is that the equipment grant – which is of vital concern to the
science departments – is agreed by another administrative level known as the
Council of the Schools.

Although in organizational terms the Universities of Oxford and Cambridge have incorporated science through the traditional department structure adopted by most British universities, and granted in similar fashion
the departmental heads considerable authority, they have also attempted to
fuse the departmental system into a system of faculties and faculty boards
in which authority is much more dispersed. For example, besides the sub-
faculties at Oxford, the University Decrees state that a number of departments (nearly all of them science departments) are required to have
departmental committees and these have the right 'to advise the head of the
department on all matters affecting the department, with particular reference
to a. annual estimates; b. allocation of resources and accommodation; c.
junior academic appointments' (University of Oxford 1989a: Decrees and
Regulations, Ch. 11, Sect. XIII 2.5). Although it may sound little more than
good management practice, perhaps no more than common sense, one head
of an Oxford department has told us that he would not instigate any major
initiative without first consulting the departmental committee (Interview:
Smith, 6 July 1989). The larger science departments at Cambridge may in
fact have more than one committee to assist the head in running its affairs.
For the Physics Department (that is the Cavendish Laboratory), there is
both a policy committee and a teaching committee (Interview: Pippard, 15
May 1989). These committees may have no statutory authority, but any
head would be foolish to act contrary to their direct wishes. Should the head
and committee appear to be parting company, it may be more advisable for

the head to engineer a stalemate and be delegated the authority to act! Apparently, this is not an uncommon occurrence.

In view of the powers that reside in departments, and the ability of departments to take over the formal functions of faculty boards (e.g. the science departments are in *de facto* control of their own appointments), the question arises as to whether faculty boards, or even sub-faculties at Oxford, are essentially marginal to the interests of most scientists. This is an especially pertinent consideration for those departments that are large enough to constitute in their own right a faculty with its own faculty board (e.g. Cambridge's Department of Engineering). An important constitutional point is at issue here. Departments are by statute managed by their heads and, although they have to work within the statutory framework, and presumably will have accumulated sufficient experience to act competently, they have the security that comes from being head of department. Those who feel obliged to challenge the head within the context of the department are on more insecure grounds than if they were to mount their challenge within the context of the faculty board (or sub-faculty at Oxford) on which the departmental head may be no more than an *ex-officio* member. Faculty boards are not institutions that approve of, and certainly do not encourage, strong leadership. They constitute a forum within which the rank-and-file members of the universities are able to make their voices heard on an equal footing with their colleagues on matters that can be central to their careers. Even so, a cost–benefit appraisal might still question the meaningfulness of the evident duplication of functions. Moreover, to carry the day at the faculty board may be of little significance if the department is the key organizational unit.

These organizational differences are – as is true of so much else of the present-day Oxford and Cambridge – a product of the way the two universities developed historically. The arts subjects developed within the colleges and their organizational framework evolved from the grass roots; it was the creation of mutually satisfactory arrangements made by college tutors. The science departments flowed out of a different tradition. They were created rather than evolved institutions, products of the universities rather than of the colleges. Moreover, departments are a reflection of the belief that if science is to flourish, it has to be organized departmentally. In managerial terms, this finds expression in the need to run laboratories and to employ materials and personnel effectively. In academic terms, science professors provide the intellectual leadership that is necessary if their departments are to have a sense of direction. It is interesting to think in terms of the cultural reinforcements of this model. Widely experienced Cambridge administrators have referred to the readiness of the scientists to accept authority more willingly than their arts colleagues. The disciplined teutonic origins of chemistry may still be shaping the behaviour of the contemporary chemistry faculty! The argument, however, can be couched in different terms: the arts faculty is not so much enthused with a democratic spirit as undisciplined, while the scientists, thanks to their very willingness to accept authority, are better prepared to act collegially. Undoubtedly, the experience that the science professors have gained in managing departments with sizeable budgets and a large staff have enabled some of them to adjust comfortably to the managerial ethos that is currently in vogue. The multi-million pound agreements between Oxford's Departments of Pharmacology and Clinical Pharmacology and different firms within the pharmaceutical industry have some of the hallmarks of high-powered business deals.

We have argued that the organization of the academic pursuits of the two universities reflects the attempt of Oxford and Cambridge to come to terms with two differing intellectual traditions. It is important, however, that the end result should not be seen as simply a complex organizational model. The complexity is not merely the response to the historical fact that differing intellectual traditions developed within the universities at different points in time, but also reflects the attempt to infuse both traditions with the same values. This is *not* complexity for complexity's sake, that is the mere accumulation of a series of pragmatic decisions. The colleges had to incorporate the scientists, but science needed to take cognizance of the values that had shaped the development of arts and mathematics. All had to adjust to the fact that the universities would be the major employers of faculty as the twentieth century progressed, and that the departments would be the primary focus of loyalty for many dons.

Undoubtedly, the central value associated with college teaching is that academic matters should be the responsibility of the individual tutors. The organization of teaching that emerged within the colleges developed in response to individual initiatives and the mutually agreeable arrangements remained under the control of the participating fellows. This legacy of grass-roots control is reflected in the character of faculty boards: they are not in the pocket of the professors or heads of departments, their chairmen serve for 1 or 2 years at the most, and they aim to create a consensus out of their constituent elements rather than to impose decisions upon faculties. If academic matters were the business of college tutors, then it follows that they were *not* the concern of university officials. Although we will need to modify this statement, the faculty boards have been loathe to acquire a secretariat. In the past, both the chairmen, which is not surprising, and the secretaries, which is surprising, have been academics, and in return have received some compensation, usually by a lightening of their teaching loads. The science departments have not been immune to these forces; for example, at Oxford there are statutory obligations upon departmental heads to set up departmental committees and those sub-faculties which follow departmental boundaries have meetings of all their members once a term.

Although the faculty boards and departments have incorporated some of the traditional values, inevitably their growth has meant that new values have had to be built into the system. As departments and faculties expanded, it became increasingly difficult to hold on to the idea that maximum grass-roots participation could be sustained while organization was to be shunned. Faculty boards are representative institutions on which the notables also have a right to sit and, although they may contain their mavericks, it is difficult to believe that they represent anything other than the weight of respectable opinion in the various faculties. Rose and Ziman, admittedly in a dated view, have been particularly scathing about the faculty boards in arts which allegedly have a 'long and dishonourable tradition of unopposed elections' and lead to the concentration of power 'in the junta of middle aged men' who, allegedly, are not unknown to act in a most undemocratic manner (Rose and Ziman 1964: 139). Clearly, this is not a judgement that necessarily applied to all the faculties of both Oxford and Cambridge, and not one that would be shared widely today. Even if the principle of representation has been abused, none the less it has been the means of sustaining the idea that control remains in the hands of the rank-and-file academics.

But if science departments were to be managed effectively by their heads, then how could this be reconciled with the rights of their members? What occurred at both Oxford and Cambridge was a separation of academic matters, especially those relating to teaching, from questions of finance. The heads of departments have special responsibilities for the financial management of their departments. The rights of the faculty at large are more potent in the areas of curricula and examinations, that is in those very areas where they were traditionally strong. Research, as opposed to teaching, poses some interesting problems. The colleges, of course, were noted for their teaching, whereas research is very much a twentieth-century development closely associated with the expansion of science. It is indisputable that the reputation of a department, especially a science department, is based upon its research record. If departmental heads are concerned with their departments' reputations, and it is difficult to imagine the reverse being true, then they have to be involved in research; that is encouraging and managing it if not actually doing it. Finally, the research effort of a department is heavily dependent upon its success at securing financial support. There is a constant pressure to obtain research grants, and the connections of the departmental head could make the difference between success and failure. Moreover, the heads need to fight within the university for a fair share of internal resources, for without equipment and space it is impossible to undertake research in many scientific fields.

The heads of departments therefore become managers of resources with special reference to the research efforts of their laboratories. Although research in science is invariably a cooperative venture under the direction of a team leader, it has come to share some of the values that embrace research in arts, which is perhaps better described as scholarship. Departments may be managed by their heads but their members decide for themselves what research they will undertake. It remains the property of the scientists, i.e. it is under their direction. So the bond between the arts-centred teaching tradition established in the colleges and the science-centred research tradition developed in the university laboratories is that both activities are producer-controlled. A key contemporary issue is whether this tradition can continue.

Inevitably, how the academic structures work in practice is to some extent dependent upon the administrative styles of the key actors – departmental heads, faculty board chairpersons, at Oxford the vice-chairman of the General Board, and the high-ranking officials. However, despite the significance of the individual input, it is possible to make some tentative generalizations about how the system has functioned. In certain respects, notwithstanding the strictures of Rose and Ziman, it is a model which has strong elements of both representative and participatory democracy built into it. Individuals may choose not to get involved, and faculty board membership may degenerate from elective posts to sinecures, but there are well-established participatory rights and formally representation is invariably based upon election. Democracy suggests that there is considerable latent authority at the grass roots of the system, but this is coupled with the fact that historically very few things, even quite minor things, could be accomplished without the formal approval of the General Boards. Moreover, even today, if major changes to the structure are contemplated, then it is very likely that a grace will have to be put to either the Regent House at Cambridge or Congregation at Oxford. This may be very democratic in the sense that the membership of the two universities has ultimate control of the academic structure, but this may be used – and indeed has been used – to thwart changes that may be felt to be highly desirable within particular parts of the system. Such a scenario may be exceptional, but the fact that it can happen has had a profound impact upon how the two universities control their academic affairs.

In a nutshell, these are systems of control that function effectively only by working consensually, and for many dons this is how it should be. There are, however, two main difficulties which can and do emerge: although it is possible for the system to change through a consensual *modus operandi*, it is invariably a slow process and, while this may be approved of within the universities, it may exasperate powerful external parties whose patience is more limited and whose priorities are different; and systems that work consensually tend not to encourage radical self-evaluation; so, although change may occur, it is likely to do so within the established structural parameters. There is nothing especially remarkable about these observations as most institutions, certainly British universities, have a powerful in-built desire to preserve themselves. What needs to be analysed is the impact of such processes upon the ability of Oxford and Cambridge to respond positively to the contemporary concerted pressures for change and their efforts to maintain themselves as world-class universities.

Changing the organization of knowledge: External pressures and the internal dynamic

If one were to describe diagrammatically the manner in which the Universities of Oxford and Cambridge have organized their knowledge maps, then the bicycle wheel represents the best model, with the General Boards constituting the hub and the faculty boards and departments the spokes. Over time, the wheel has acquired more spokes as the number of faculty boards and departments has increased. Although there has been considerable internal support for the values on which this model is based, there has also been both powerful scepticism as to whether the values are realized in practice (note that both Rose and Ziman were insiders) and whether, in any case, it is a structure that is appropriate for today's world. What comes as some surprise is the longevity of the dissatisfaction with the academic structures and the repetition of essentially the same critical points.

Evidence presented to the Asquith Commission by past and contemporary vice-chancellors revealed contradictory evaluations of the general boards. The Revd Blakiston of Oxford was scathing in his criticisms: 'Its members were often inclined to abstain from voting. It was too large a body to deal with finance, and its administration of the Faculty Fund of £7100 annually was haphazard and unsatisfactory' (Royal Commission on Oxford and Cambridge Universities 1922b: App. 1). Whereas Oxford's then current vice-chancellor (Dr L.R. Farnell) was laudatory, for he 'regarded the General Board as the most useful and efficient Body in the University'! (ibid.). The evidence from Cambridge supported Blakiston's negative view and this was the line taken by the Commission's report:

> Owing to its size and composition, [they are referring to Oxford's General Board] it must tend, almost inevitably, to develop the same characteristics as the General Board at Cambridge, and to become a collection of individuals representing special interests, rather than an organic Board with a corporate judgment and a common interest in the educational needs of the University as a whole' (Royal Commission on Oxford and Cambridge Universities 1922a: 76).

The Royal Commission was reiterating what has become the most persistent criticism of the two General Boards, that they are representative bodies which defend particular interests rather than devise policies for the good of their respective universities as a whole. In terms remarkably similar to those of the 1922 commissioners, Oxford's Franks Inquiry concluded that: 'The key point to get right, and it has been wrong in the past, is the General Board.' And a little later in the report we read that:

> We do not believe that the General Board can ever fulfil its proper duty if it is a battleground for conflicting interests. It must have initiative and be capable of planning ahead with the skill of men who understand the points of view of sectional groups but are not committed to them' (University of Oxford 1966a: 246–7).

The report proposed a smaller General Board for Oxford (which was not implemented) and a vice-chairman who would serve for 4 years and act as its *de facto* head (which was implemented).

For Cambridge's Grave Report, which like Oxford's Franks Inquiry was part of a general movement towards reform in the 1960s, the answer lay not so much in a smaller General Board but rather in the delegation of authority.

The General Boards at both universities were courts of appeal on academic issues large and small and, consequently, were grossly overloaded with matters of detail that should be resolved elsewhere. Although it may seem sensible to permit appeals from below to the General Board, it does result in both a crippling workload and a sense of grievance in those whose appeals are rejected. The Grave Report saw the delegation of authority as a means to ensure that issues are resolved as close to their source as possible and *not* passed up to the General Board to be fudged (University of Cambridge 1967b: 345). Although few proposals of the Grave Report were implemented, the delegation of responsibility and authority is also a central theme in the report of the Wass Syndicate and we can expect these recommendations to be acted upon.

Central to the concept of delegated authority is the understanding that only a small range of business should be referred to higher bodies, that the numerous appeals permitted by the present confusions should decline as the lines of authority become clearer and more definitive. The implications of this are two-fold: that the separation of financial from academic matters has to disappear, and that academic matters are the business of academic bodies and, consequently, there can be no ultimate appeal to the Regent House or to Congregation. It may be widely felt within both universities that to curtail the formal rights of Congregation or the Regent House in such a manner would be too great an infringement of the principle that in the last analysis authority must reside within the legislative bodies of the universities. However, to retain the legislatures as the final courts of appeal would inevitably extend the process of policy making, for there would always be the possibility of some parties refusing to negotiate seriously in the hope that they could carry the day elsewhere. Moreover, to continue at least the partial separation of academic planning from financial planning perpetuates the failure to co-ordinate responsibility for matters that are self-evidently related. At the very least, this is implicit in the arguments of those who would transcend the fudging that has so often emerged from the centralization of formal authority in bodies, that is the two General Boards, which traditionally have tried to reconcile deeply impregnated vested interests.

The varying criticisms of the academic structures have one overriding message: the General Boards have failed in what should be their main purpose, that of advising the universities on educational policy. They have been bogged down in the details of academic administration and have lacked the means to formulate the broad outlines of educational policy. These criticisms are dependent upon the acceptance of a particular view of both the functions of the General Boards and on how they should perform those functions. But these are by no means uncontentious issues. For many, the General Boards should be institutions that co-ordinate proposals from below rather than impose policy from above. In other words, according to this perspective, they are meant to be administrative rather than policy-making bodies.

Reformers have also argued that efficient administration is dependent upon the implementation of certain principles. In an amazing observation, the Franks Report claimed that:

> It is a generally accepted principle of administrative organization that a superior body cannot effectively supervise more than five to eight subordinate bodies. When their numbers go beyond this range, consultation and discussion become difficult or impossible, relations distant and formalized, and paperwork greatly increases (University of Oxford 1966a: 254).

It logically followed therefore that 'the academic activities of Oxford should be divided into five new faculties'! Although not so bold as to appeal to the science of administration for legitimation, the Grave Report wanted to increase the size of Cambridge's General Board from 13 to 20 members ('we do not believe that in a Board of, say, twenty members, the disadvantage of increased membership would outweigh the advantages . . .') but by way of compensation the new General Board would have two Needs Committees (University of Cambridge 1967b: *op.cit.* 346–8). As we move from Oxford to Cambridge we leap from science to faith. What is happening is patently obvious: these are partisan views on what the purposes of the General Boards should be, and how they should be structured to achieve those purposes; the rest is simply legitimating camouflage.

Although the academic structures have proved remarkably resilient in the twentieth century, a number of developments have taken place which have strengthened the hand of the reformers in both universities. What is less certain is the eventual outcome of this process of change, for while the old hub and spoke model is being transformed the new model is still taking shape. The external pressures fall into the two broad categories of financial stringency and academic planning. Financially, the most obvious change was the decline in real terms in the size of the UGC's recurrent grant in the early 1980s. As the UGC had to decide how to distribute the misery, so individual universities were forced to make their own retrenchments. In the final years of the UGC, the pressures for academic planning intensified. The UGC required universities to outline their future academic maps, which would include targets on more refined categories of student numbers, to be accompanied by the projected financial support. In other words, the academic and financial variables were correlated. Within the context of these two general pressures, various specific developments occurred – for example, the move to formula funding and the evaluation of the research performance of departments – that provided the advocates of change with additional powerful ammunition. While the UFC may not intensify the move towards centralized planning, what will not change is the increased stress upon the costing of academic development.

It would be wrong to suggest that there was no recognition of the close relationship of the academic and financial variables before the universities were sucked into the nation's economic crisis in the mid-1970s. In a very detailed statement to the Franks Commission of his 'personal views and comments', H.H. Keen, Secretary to the Curator of Oxford's University Chest from 1946 to 1964, reflected on the continuing failure of the university to match its academic plans to its current income. Allegedly, the university was continuously overstretched financially and ever hopeful of more generous settlements from the UGC in the following quinquennium (University of Oxford 1965: Pt 14). However, while the Franks Commission was very concerned that Oxford's General Board should be structured in a manner that enabled it to control the university's academic map, it never tackled the question of relating this control to the university's income or the problems posed by its increasing financial dependence upon a state that was ever more parsimonious. In fact, the most conspicuous weakness in the Franks Report is its failure to consider seriously the university's finances and how its income could be related to its academic plans. Clearly, the pressures had to be sharper before Keen's message would be taken seriously.

In its own evidence to the Franks Inquiry, Oxford's General Board exhibited a self-satisfied view of its past role. It perceived itself as co-ordinator of demands rather than as an initiator of policy and was clearly happy with its lot. That the Franks Inquiry viewed the role of the General Board differently is evident from its recommendations, and although its proposed structural changes were not implemented, it is widely agreed that the creation of a full-time vice-chairman to act as its *de facto* head has rejuvenated the Board. More recently, the arrival of formula funding has mitigated the onerous burden of negotiating spending estimates with departments and faculty boards, and compensated somewhat for its own lack of financial expertise. It is difficult not to build historical biases into formula funding – after all there is an established faculty in place and the FTE student load has been calculated in advance – but once in place it does lighten considerably the burden of resource distribution. Not surprisingly, the main problem is trying to resolve how best to redistribute resources should the formula reveal that current allocations are grossly inappropriate! No-one can be so naive as to believe that in a university speedy adjustments are possible. Relieved, however, of some of the minutiae of financial management, Oxford's General Board is in a position to raise interesting financial questions like, for example, asking departments to account for the comparatively high costs of their practical classes (Interview: Smith, 6 July 1989) or perhaps even to account for a comparatively weak research rating.

Although the science departments at Oxford have valued their direct links to the General Board because of the financial autonomy this has given them, in recent years the faculty boards have intruded more frequently into their affairs. This is particularly true of the Faculty Board for the Physical Sciences which, interestingly, even the Franks Inquiry had considered almost large enough to constitute one of its proposed five super-faculties. The intrusion has taken the form of using the principle of formula funding to redistribute resources among the varying departments within the Faculty of Physical Sciences. The advantage (and some would say the disadvantage of formula funding) is that resources can be redirected without making explicit judgements about the relative academic merits of different departments. It all depends on the criteria built into the formula. However, at both Oxford and Cambridge, the problem of allocating resources selectively is made more difficult by the fact that in the UGC/UFC research selectivity reviews, nearly all their cost centres were rated in the top two categories. If all are excellent, how is it possible to discriminate among them?

The increased role of Oxford's Faculty Board of Physical Sciences in resource allocation does suggest the tentative growth of an additional tier of academic management on the science side of the university, a view strongly reinforced by the creation of a Physics Management Committee. Thus it is possible to see large but interrelated areas of academic activity being co-ordinated by overarching management bodies with responsibilities for long-term academic planning. The Physics Management Committee has wide statutory authority: to undertake strategic planning for physics, to be attuned to major directions in future research and the associated funding possibilities, and to make decisions on the allocation of money, space and posts among the various physics departments (University of Oxford 1989a: Decrees and Regulations, Sect. XLV.1). Although the management committee only advises the chairman of physics, it is inevitably a body which, besides eroding his traditional authority, must restrict the freedom of the various individual physics departments. Moreover, as it is an administrative layer between the physics departments and the General Board, it is difficult to see how the latter can reach any decisions about the former without involving the management committee. In this sense, it also restricts the authority of the General Board.

In view of their considerable control over the way in which they spend their budgets, including freedom of virement, the science departments at Oxford have already been delegated authority. The problem with the premise that binding decisions should be made as far down the chain of formal command as possible is that the individual institutions may fulfil their own interests without enhancing the character of the whole. The answer of course is to delegate within agreed boundaries while reserving other matters for referral to higher levels in the chain of command. It comes as a great surprise to learn from Keen's personal evidence to the Franks Inquiry that in his day:

> ... actual expenditure is not required to correspond to the estimates except that, during the last few years of financial stringency the departments have been required to obtain the permission of the General Board or the Chest, as the case may be, before creating a new post (University of Oxford 1965).

This appears to be one of those rare cases in which authority was delegated but not responsibility! As the faculty boards have started to intrude upon departmental autonomy, so Oxford's General Board has rescinded its past willingness to delegate authority without the commensurate responsibility. This is not academic planning in the sense of drawing up a blueprint which the university then sets out to fulfil, but rather an inevitable response to protracted financial crisis. When one of the few certainties about the future is that the university can expect to receive a declining recurrent income from the state, then departments cannot be allowed to exceed their estimates other than in the most exceptional of circumstances, and they certainly cannot be allowed to accrue on their own authority commitments with long-term financial consequences for the university. In order to keep a rein on the departments and faculty boards, Oxford's General Board has improved its accounting procedures immeasurably, while some departments also have their own accounting systems which enable them to monitor closely their own balances. The lackadaisical world that shines through a great deal of the evidence presented to the Franks Inquiry appears to be very much a thing of the past.

The imposition of a greater measure of financial responsibility by the University of Oxford upon its constituent academic units has forced departments to think more carefully about their resources and priorities. They are required to obtain overhead costs on research projects and they share the income with the university. For projects which are not considered to constitute 'basic research', the pressure is on the departments 'to seek whatever the market will bear' (University of Oxford 1990f). Such income may well be vital to maintaining, for example, departmental subscriptions to journals or providing seed money to float other projects. Departmental heads have to decide how they will distribute university grants (such as the equipment grant) that support research among their faculty. Will the funds go disproportionately to those who bring in most external research income? And what does one do about those members of faculty who are pursuing important research avenues but in fields unlikely to obtain external funding? In order to avoid being bogged down in the details of administration, the departmental heads now have more assistance from full-time officials. The Oxford science departments, therefore, have become more entrepreneurial, more cost-conscious and more tightly managed – both within the departments and from the centre – and all this has been achieved without any fundamental changes in the way the university has organized knowledge. It remains a hub and spoke model, although the creation of more management committees (were chemistry and the biological sciences to follow the lead of physics) would alter the picture substantially.

In comparison to the incremental change at Oxford, the University of Cambridge has moved more boldly. It has modified quite significantly the traditional structure outlined above and will consolidate those changes if the recommendations of the Wass Report are implemented in full. Since approximately the mid-1960s, a very important organizational layer between the General Board at the centre and the faculty boards and departments on the periphery has been evolving. This layer consists of three Councils of the Schools and one Interfaculty Committee. Although the reasons for the different nomenclature are significant, in effect all four bodies perform roughly similar functions. Two of the councils, the Council of the School of Physical Sciences and the Council of the School of Biological Sciences, were created after the Asquith Commission, but even a cursory glance at their minutes would reveal that it was not until the 1960s that they started to perform important functions. In 1984, two parallel bodies were established: the Council of the School of the Humanities and Social Sciences and the Inter-faculty Committee for Arts and Humanities. The different nomenclature reflects the fact that the faculties comprising the Interfaculty Committee for Arts and Humanities saw their committee as providing a forum for the exchange of ideas between equal parties rather than as a body which pos-sessed executive authority (Interview: Allen and Horne, 11 July 1989). The members of the Interfaculty Committee for Arts and Humanities (the Facul-ties of Architecture and History of Art, Classics, Divinity, English, Modern and Medieval Languages, Music, Oriental Studies and Philosophy) appear to see themselves as the custodians of that tradition which firmly places control of knowledge in the hands of the individual scholar.

The Councils of the Schools and the Interfaculty Committee are represen-tative institutions but have not succumbed to the temptation of making decisions that simply divide the spoils. As is customary, they have each established their own committee structures and, not surprisingly, the desire of the interested parties that they should be represented on the crucial Needs Committees has led to the creation of very delicate electoral procedures (Interview: Payne, 13 June 1989). Their respective terms of reference are written in roughly the same language: 'The Council of the School shall advise on any matters that are referred to them by the General Board, and by the Faculty Boards and comparable authorities for other institutions included in the School. The Council of the School shall have such powers of reporting to the University as are assigned to Faculty Boards' (University of Cambridge 1988d: Ordinances, Ch. V: Schools, Councils of the Schools and Interfaculty Committees). One important difference between on the one hand the Schools of Physical Sciences and Biological Sciences and, on the other, the Interfaculty Committee for Arts and Humanities and the School of the Humanities and Social Sciences, is the provision within the ordinances for a secretary to each of the two former schools. Although the latter two bodies also each have secretaries, they are part-time posts and cannot be expected to have the same status and authority as a position that is estab-lished by ordinance. The secretaries of the Schools of the Physical Sciences and the Biological Sciences each act as secretary to the councils of their schools and to the councils' committees and in our opinion they are crucial roles in Cambridge's changing academic structure.

The emergence of the Councils of the Schools as important institutions in the academic structure at Cambridge owes much to the former Secretary General of the Faculties, Ian Nicol. In Nicol's time it was widely felt within the university that the General Board, and in particular its powerful Needs Committee, was overburdened by the statutory requirement to sanction so many comparatively minor recommendations reaching it from the vast array of institutions which were under its control. Although a widely expressed sentiment from the Asquith Commission to the Grave Report, there was still the problem of putting it into effect in a form that would be widely supported. Prior to becoming Secretary General of the Faculties, Nicol had had wide administrative experience in the science area of the university, including the post of secretary of the School of Physical Sciences. What the General Board required was bodies that would reduce the inflow of messages by co-ordinating them and ranking their importance. Since the science area of the university already had the councils of the schools with terms of reference that were wide enough to take on these functions, what better solution than to turn to them? With the encouragement of the General Board this started to happen and, as the innovation was successful, so the Council of the School of the Humanities and Social Sciences and the Interfaculty Committee for Arts and Humanities were created in 1984, and new terms of reference were drawn up for all four schools.

One key area of responsibility under the control of the Councils of the Schools, subject of course to the sanction of the General Board, is the distribution of the equipment grant. This has always been critical to the science subjects, but with the arrival of computers has assumed a wider importance. Secondly, the Councils of Schools have the task of prioritizing the varying demands for developments that emerge from the departments and faculty boards. The order of priorities is then sent to the General Board for its Needs Committee to decide what demands can be fulfilled. This forces the representatives of the various departments and faculty boards on the Councils of the Schools to have a clear idea of their own priorities, to work out at least preliminary costings, and to construct in detail the supportive case. Clearly, failure to act effectively can result in dire consequences. The assumption is that the Councils of the Schools, or more accurately their Needs Committees, can undertake these tasks more effectively than the General Board because the schools contain a depth of expertise that is unavailable to the General Board. With its 13 members, the range of academic expertise on the General Board is spread so thinly that it is rarely competent to make the necessary choices between apparently equally pressing cases.

As the ordinances make clear, the Councils of Schools are only advisory bodies and faculty boards and departments can make direct appeals to the General Board, but whether the General Board would be prepared to listen is another matter. Where such disputes have occurred, the General Board has invariably referred the matter back to the appropriate Council of the School. However, the problem remains that, because authority has not been clearly delegated to the Councils of the Schools, the parties to the negotiations within their Needs Committees may not be prepared to make the necessary compromises in the hope that they can extract more concessions from the General Board. Moreover, there still remains the possibility of an ultimate appeal to the Regent House where anything can happen and sometimes does! The second major weakness is that the equipment grant forms the only direct financial relationship between the Councils of the Schools and their faculties and departments. As matters stand, the departments and faculty boards negotiate their estimated expenditure with the deputy treasurer of the Financial Board and these estimates are then approved by the General Board. The draft estimates are sent to the Councils of Schools for comment, but that is the limit of their authority and if it were to be extended the estimates would need to reach the Councils of Schools sooner if they were to have an effective input (Interview: Franks, 13 June 1989). Finally, there are certain academic subjects which, although formally part of a school, have a direct relationship to the General Board for all financial matters, which inevitably weakens the ability of the Council of the School to fulfil its co-ordinating function. Examples of these semi-autonomous kingdoms are the Department of Chemical Engineering, which is in the School of Physical Sciences, and the Clinical Medical School and the Department of Clinical Veterinary Medicine, which are both in the School of Biological Sciences. There may be sound historical reasons for these aberrations, but it is hard not to draw the conclusion that piecemeal development has impeded rational organization.

One way of measuring the effectiveness of the organizational control of institutions is to evaluate the part they have played in bringing about change. Like all other British universities, the first response of Cambridge to the cut in its recurrent grant was to impose economies upon its expenditure. While it was possible to achieve this at the level of the individual department and faculty board through their annual negotiation of expenditure estimates with the deputy treasurer, the Councils of Schools still had to negotiate reductions in the equipment grants. In fact, the Councils of the Schools proved themselves adept at formulating models for the overall development of their respective departments and faculties, which were not based on the simple premise that misery should be equally distributed. The School of Biological Sciences has faced an especially severe financial crisis because not only was it subject to the more general stringency, but also the arrival of formula funding revealed that in comparison with the other Schools it had been overfunded. In a perverse sense, the crisis has been turned into a minor triumph. While disputing the alleged extent of the over-funding, the Council of the School has agreed with the General Board to a plan which would eradicate its apparent largesse over a 3 year period while still allowing the school to fill vacancies deemed critical to the long-term well-being of the school. Undoubtedly, the key figures in these attempts to manage rationally the recent cuts in UGC funding have been the secretaries of the schools. It is they who have collected the necessary statistics, collated and presented them, and offered the initial tentative proposals. Invariably, the secretaries of the schools will have a broader and deeper overview of the financial and administrative affairs of their Schools than the academic members of the Councils. Besides the chairmen of the Councils no-one else was in a position to perform such tasks and few chairmen – who, remember, invariably see themselves as full-time academics on temporary leave – are ever likely to immerse themselves in such detail. Of course, in the final analysis, the members of the Needs Committees, followed by the General Board, had to endorse the recommendations, but whose proposals were they in the first place?

The above examples of change represent responses to the recent protracted financial crisis. It is hard to imagine, however, that we are ever going to reach a situation in which financial support will be sufficient to meet all the demands for expenditure that are generated within the universities. Moreover, it is our contention that it will be difficult to stop the logic of the planning process that has been set in motion. Within the universities, there are an increasing number of persons who can see the sense of the efficient management of resources and have a vested interest in making a system work that attempts to secure that end. As the largest single provider of university income, the state retains the motivation to sustain the external pressure in favour of such changes.

Independently of the responses to the decline in the input of state resources, there have been several examples of educational change at Cambridge which owe much to the efforts of the Councils of the Schools. The School of Physical Sciences at one time incorporated a Department of Colloid Sciences. After a review by the General Board, it was decided that the department should be phased out, a decision that was not ratified by the Regent House. Subsequently, the Council of the School of Physical Sciences was invited by the General Board to review the department. It likewise reached the conclusion that the department did not have a viable future at Cambridge and the decision in favour of closing it was upheld. On this second occasion, it proved more difficult to oppose the winding-up proposals because they had been formulated within the department's own School, presumably the body best equipped to judge its future viability and most likely to defend it if it were a long-term asset. Although the School had less formal authority in this matter than the General Board, it in fact had the resources that made its decision more acceptable to the university at large.

In the above case, the school demonstrated its greater effectiveness than the General Board, whereas the decision to close the Department of Applied Biology (which took full effect in October 1989) illustrated their ability to work closely together in order to achieve the same goal. The Department of Applied Biology had been under pressure for some years, as reflected in the level of student demand, staff morale, research income and publications output. The final straw was the UGC's evaluation of its research record, for the Department of Applied Biology was the *only* department in Cambridge to receive a below-average rating. The Council of the School of Biological Sciences took the opportunity to review the department and came to the conclusion that when its professor retired it should be closed. Interestingly, the School's constitutional right to pursue this course of action was challenged. What the General Board did was to confirm the rights of the School in this matter and to issue under its own name the School's report.

The research evaluation exercise conducted by the UGC also prompted Oxford's General Board into action. Its one particularly weak spot, according to this exercise, was the Department of Educational Studies. The general board set up its own committee of enquiry and decided that the department was worth saving. To this end, more resources were to be committed to the department including the decision that the department should have its own chair (Interview: Butler, 20 July 1989). What is interesting to note are the differing levels at which Oxford and Cambridge took action and how in both cases the decisions were not dependent solely upon expertise located specifically in the General Boards. The School of Biological Sciences provided the key decision makers at Cambridge, while the General Board at Oxford created its committee of experts. Of course at both universities, the General Board had to ratify the decisions. Whereas these two examples of change had been stimulated by the UGC's research evaluation exercise, the immediate impetus for action over the Department of Colloid Sciences had been provided by the department's professor who, due to retire, wanted to know what was going to happen to his department. Presumably, he suspected the worst and rightly so given the eventual outcome.

External pressure for the universities to modify their academic structures does not inevitably carry the day. A case in point is the University of Cambridge's defence of its Department of Clinical Veterinary Medicine. There are six such departments in the country and it was proposed to close two of them, one at Glasgow and one at Cambridge. Both universities mounted a vigorous defence of their respective departments and the proposed closures, after being put on ice, have now been dropped. Whether the decision not to implement the recommendations of the Ryder Report was sound need not concern us here. What the fracas does illustrate, however, is that there are real political boundaries to academic planning. Some powerful figures within the University of Cambridge itself were not opposed to closure but the department was successful at swinging the weight of the university behind its defence and the department's critics decided not to stick their heads above the parapet. Again there is nothing surprising about this, but it does suggest that it is easier to act 'rationally' when the futures of the comparatively small or weak are at stake (aerial photography, applied biology and educational studies) rather than the large and/or politically powerful.

The examples of change we have presented were responses to fortuitous events rather than acts of rational academic planning. There were problems with Cambridge's Department of Applied Biology and Oxford's Department of Educational Studies long before the unfavourable UGC evaluations of their research records stimulated internal action. In similar fashion, a review of Cambridge's Department of Colloid Sciences was initiated by an impending professorial retirement. What needed to be built into the system was a process of continuous review. In its absence, it is easy to imagine that problems could accumulate steadily over time, waiting for some special event before any action would be taken. In fact, the General Board at Oxford has instigated a process of regular departmental reviews, incorporating outside expertise, so moving the university away from crisis management towards routine academic reviews if not academic planning. Cambridge has moved in the same direction, although there are mechanisms which first determine whether a full review is needed or not. Although this may conceal some shortcomings, it is presumably pointless to incur the expense of a full review if all the measures seem to suggest that it is unnecessary.

At Cambridge, the organization of the academic structure is currently being modified by the implementation of the Wass Report. The central proposals are: (1) '... that the General Board should be formally subordinated to the Council so as to be accountable to it for its management of the University's academic affairs'; (2) '... that the General Board in turn would delegate to Councils of the Schools a great deal of decision making in matters of detail', and like the Council of Senate, the General Board 'would concern itself with matters of policy'; and (3) '... that membership on the General Board would no longer be dependent upon the principle of Faculty representation with the current Faculty representatives replaced by members linked to the Councils of the Schools' (University of Cambridge 1989a: 627). It is important to note that, unlike the Financial Board, the General Board will not become a committee of the Council and, although it will be accountable to the Council for the management of its affairs, it remains at the apex of the academic policy-making process. None the less, once the proposals are in place, they will signify official recognition of both the informal process of change in recent years (in much the same way as Oxford's Franks Inquiry sought statutory change to match the contemporary realities of Oxford's system of government), and significantly extend those developments.

The Wass Report adds some flesh to its key proposals for academic devolution by suggesting the means for achieving them (ibid.: 629–34). These include providing the Councils of the Schools with increased administrative support, an enhanced role for the chairmen of the Councils of the Schools, the expectation that these chairmen would be members of the General Board, a 5-year term of office (with the possibility of reappointment) for heads of departments and chairmen of the faculty boards, and responsibilities for faculty board chairmen similar to those currently exercised by departmental heads (i.e. for those subject groups organized in faculties rather than departments). In one way, the Wass Report represents only another manifestation of the much expressed desire for a greater delegation of authority within the university, but from another perspective it offends the sensibilities of many elements within the university. Some faculties will take unkindly to the notion that the chairmen of their faculty boards need to be more positive leaders and that they should serve as such for at least 5 years. Also, the belief that the academic organization of the university requires further full-time administrative support if it is to function more effectively will raise the fear of bureaucratic intrusion into what some dons still believe is their exclusive domain. The main frame of the Wass Report has been accepted but it remains to be seen whether these critical details will also be sketched in.

What appears to be happening at both the Universities of Oxford and Cambridge, although with special reference to the latter, is that more authority is accruing to the middle levels of the academic structures – that is the faculty boards and the Management Committee for Physics at Oxford and the Councils of the Schools at Cambridge. In diagrammatical form, a simple hierarchical model is being structured, but for it to assume a more coherent shape at Oxford the number of faculty boards will have to be reduced drastically (as the Franks Inquiry proposed) or another administrative/policy level will have to be established, e.g. more management committees to act as filters between the present departments and the General Board. The alleged advantage of the hierarchical model is that the details of administration will be handled at the lower levels leaving the General Board, in the words of the Wass Report, '... more time to deal with major new academic developments and broad questions of policy in the context of the University's Academic or Institutional Plan' (ibid.: 631). The Wass Report has also suggested that the General Board should retain some resource allocation tasks (e.g. the distribution of the University Education Fund among the schools) and should conduct negotiations with outside bodies on matters that affect teaching and research. It is likely that, although within the hierarchical model *formal* authority will reside with the General Board, that the real authority will reside at the middle levels of the structure. It is a question of where the expertise is located. The middle levels of power have the range to transcend the multitude of interests represented by departments and faculties and yet the expertise remains sufficiently concentrated to have greater confidence in its decisions. On the General Board that expertise is too thinly spread for it to do other than accept recommendations from below or set up special enquiries – as it does now – that draw upon those in the middle levels of the structure.

At both the Universities of Oxford and Cambridge, it is possible to conceive of the General Boards as becoming essentially honorific bodies: their detailed functions are either standardized (as undoubtedly conditions of service must be) or are responses to decisions reached below (as budgetary allocations invariably are), while their policy function is both colonized or is expressed in such broad terms that it is little more than platitudes without the bite that decisions reached elsewhere can give it. The recasting of the academic structure proposed by the Wass Report could help to rescue the General Board from being overwhelmed by the details of academic administration only to consign it to a role in which it states the self-evident while acting as the servant of others.

Conclusion

Not surprisingly, the manner in which the two universities organized knowledge within the faculty system had built into it many of the values that developed from teaching within the colleges. The departments that encompassed science, although part of a different intellectual tradition, were readily integrated into the faculties. The separation of teaching and curriculum issues from research and finance enabled a compromise to be reached which blended the ethos of control by departmental heads with the idea of academic democracy. And both teaching and research were equally intent on defending the autonomy of the university, that academics knew best what should be taught and what should be researched. It would be unwise, however, to overstress the harmony of the faculty and departmental systems within the Universities of Oxford and Cambridge, just as the present integration of science within the colleges cannot disguise the previous history of mutual suspicion, but none the less in view of the potential for conflict the system seems to work surprisingly smoothly.

Just as the development of science forced the two universities to assume responsibilities for the organization of knowledge, so the science departments remain in the forefront of organizational innovation and they are pulling the more reluctant arts subjects along in their wake. What is under challenge at Cambridge in particular is the idea of departmental autonomy. Not only have the Councils of the Schools succeeded in closing departments, but also the Council of the School of Physical Sciences has succeeded in bringing about the amalgamation of smaller departments in the fields of chemistry and earth sciences. In parallel fashion at Oxford, the Physics Management Committee now oversees the multifarious interests of its several physics departments. It is our prediction that this process will be carried further with the main recommendations of the Wass Report being put into effect at Cambridge, matched at Oxford by a long overdue amalgamation of faculties.

If there is a change in both structure (a more hierarchical system with delegation of authority and clear lines of responsibility) and procedures (greater reliance upon formula funding, standardized communication channels and – perhaps somewhat contradictory – more departmental entrepreneurialism), then it is important to ask what will happen to the values on which the old model was based. So far, this is an issue which has received scant attention. The Franks Inquiry claimed that its proposed reforms would enable Oxford to have a better chance of maintaining itself as a university of international status while preserving its core values. In similar vein, the Wass Report has reiterated the need to reassert the democratic character of Cambridge while allowing it 'to respond more swiftly and decisively to current needs'. And like all reformers, Wass believed the circle could be squared:

> In spite of the difficulty of reconciling these two objectives, we believe that they are both important and that a way must be found of achieving both these aims if Cambridge is to retain its place as one of the leading universities in the world. In the paragraphs that follow proposals are set out for a system of government which we believe would satisfy these two requirements (University of Cambridge 1989a: *op.cit.* 619).

Undoubtedly, the belief may be there but, in our opinion, it is asserted rather than proven.

What we have been witnessing is the slow decline of the collegiate-inspired value system that formed the basis of the universities' organization of their academic interests. Whereas at one time there were doubts as to whether science could be incorporated in the collegiate model of the university, the question for the future may well be how easily the arts can accommodate themselves within university environments that are dominated increasingly by the interests of science. And where does the state stand in this debate? A consistent theme in the history of the UGC was its avowed intention to allow the universities to organize their own academic affairs, and the principle of the non-interference of government in these matters has been reiterated on numerous occasions, from Fisher to the present. However, the indirect influence of government and state has always been significant. It was Exchequer grants that made the expansion of science possible. Government policy imposed financial stringency which made it imperative for universities to manage the affairs of their departments more tightly. Formula funding was developed by the UGC as a mechanism to ensure the more equitable distribution of a declining Exchequer input into the universities. The UGC/ UFC research selectivity exercises, besides having financial implications for universities, also added fuel to internal university debates as to the relative merits of their departments. Universities still decide what their academic maps will be, but they are increasingly accountable for those decisions. In some cases, this may mean paying a high price by sustaining knowledge areas that are costly or poorly regarded, or by failing to develop academic fields that could prove financially rewarding. While the state's influence may remain essentially indirect, this does not lessen the severity of its impact upon how a university chooses to organize its academic affairs.

7

Oxford, Cambridge and the Research Tradition

The defence of excellence

In recent years, there has been considerable emphasis upon the need to distribute the state's funding of higher education more selectively. Because it has been easier, and certainly less politically contentious, to quantify the research records of universities, greater selectivity has occurred in the state's allocation of research, as opposed to teaching, resources. On the teaching front, the struggle to obtain greater returns for the state's financial input has taken the form of reducing the unit costs of students, a move encouraged by offering financial inducements. If in the future those considered to have the most outstanding research records are to be treated more favourably than other universities, then both Oxford and Cambridge are well placed to ensure their long-term beneficial treatment. Although traditionally undergraduate teaching universities, contemporarily Oxford and Cambridge are as much, if not more, concerned with the generation of new knowledge as with the transmission of established knowledge. While they may still claim to deliver a high-quality undergraduate education, given additional costs such as college fees, it is unlikely that their unit costs of teaching would compare favourably with many other British universities. Moreover, teaching quality is not easy to assess, and any claims to better first degree results must take into account the characteristics of the student populations. In other words, it may be difficult to substantiate the claim that an Oxbridge undergraduate education represents value for money. Currently, the battle on teaching costs is being fought and its outcome is uncertain, but the battle on research excellence has been fought, and clearly Oxbridge has triumphed.

There is a powerful tradition in British social science that interprets the advantages of our most prestigious educational institutions in structural terms. Central to this argument is the proposition that these institutions are part of an interlocking network of élite institutions that confer mutual benefits upon their members. Are the rewards that these members receive deserved, or are they the consequence of their ties to the magic circle? This is not an issue that we can resolve here, and perhaps in the sense that it creates a problem out of what is an inevitable social process it is not worth pursuing, but what we can demonstrate is that there is firm evidence to substantiate the elevated research reputations of both Oxford and Cambridge. Which is not to say that everyone would accept either the criteria on which those reputations are based or the means of assessing those criteria.

In 1986, the UGC published its assessment of the research efforts of the institutions that were in receipt of its annual recurrent grant. The UGC constructed a list of 37 cost centres, which at several universities consisted of more than one department, most notably the 3 cost centres labelled 'other social studies', 'language-based studies' and 'humanities'. A simple 4-point scale was established: outstanding, above average, average and below average. The UGC was hazy about the precise criteria that determined the individual rankings ('outstanding' allegedly indicating national pre-eminence), but as this was the Committee's first attempt to create a national perspective on the research records of British universities, such crudity was not altogether surprising. At least it was possible to compare the research performances of the same cost centres within different universities – that is according to the UGC's criteria – assuming that the measurements were accurate. The problem the critics faced was the paucity of alternative ranking lists. It may be legitimate to question how the UGC constructed its own rankings, or even to criticize the purpose of the exercise, but in the face of a policy push to direct research funding on a narrower range of targets what was required were alternative means of measuring research excellence and the construction of different ranking lists.

Table 7.1 records the UGC's assessment of the research rankings of the Oxford and Cambridge departments (not the correct label for all the subject groups). Perhaps the most surprising aspect of this ranking list is not the number of departments ranked 'outstanding' but the almost complete absence of a tail at either university. The individual colleges of the University of London produced as many 'outstanding' scores, but taken as a whole London had a sizeable tail and a much lower overall research rating. We have already commented upon the reaction of the Universities of Cambridge and Oxford to those subjects rated 'below average', i.e. applied biology at Cambridge and educational studies at Oxford. At Cambridge, the Department of Applied Biology had faced powerful internal critics for many years and the UGC's ranking was to prove the final nail in its coffin. At Oxford, an internal review recommended, not without some opposition, the strengthening of educational studies, although it may be some time before this pays dividends.

Even if all the UGC's exercise did was to confirm what we already all suspected, none the less it would have been very difficult to have moved towards a more selective allocation of the UGC's input into university research without first attempting to assess the relative merits of departments. The internal reactions at both Oxford and Cambridge reaffirmed their commitment to making sure that they remained in the forefront of research. Indeed, a former vice-chairman of Oxford's General Board has argued that

Table 7.1 UGC's research ranking of departments at Oxford and Cambridge, 1986

	Outstanding	Above average	Average	Below average
Oxford	32	4	2	1
Cambridge	35	11	6	1

Source: Crequer (1986: 4–5).

the university should raise questions of any of its departments that failed to receive a top rating (Interview: Smith, 15 September 1989). However, as the Oxford strategy reveals, it did not automatically follow that an unfavourable UGC ranking would lead to a department receiving less support from its university. But if the Oxford and Cambridge examples are typical, it would suggest that universities are now more purposeful in how they allocate their resources. But more purposeful or not, there is some limited evidence to the effect that the research evaluation exercises have had only a marginal impact in actually changing established resource allocation patterns (Griffiths 1991: 1).

In 1989, the UFC, using modified cost centre categories and a different rating scale, repeated the previous exercise. With the new 5-point scale, the highest score of 5 was intended to indicate 'research quality which equates to attainable levels of international excellence in some sub-areas of activity and to attainable levels of national excellence in virtually all others' (UFC, as quoted by Turney 1989: 1). In theory, the rankings across subject categories can be compared because of the measuring standard of international excellence, although one wonders whether the various panels were in a position to give much consideration as to what precisely constituted the benchmark of 'international excellence'. Again we have extracted the individual 'departments' from within the 37 cost centres to produce Table 7.2.

Because of the different ranking scale, and the use of additional criteria, it is unsafe to compare in detail the findings of 1986 and 1989, but not surprisingly the general picture appears to have altered little. Educational studies and management studies rated only a '2' at Oxford, the same as Dutch studies at Cambridge. Again the divide between Oxford, Cambridge and some of the colleges of the University of London on the one hand, and the remaining British universities on the other, was confirmed. So much so that Turney (1989) boldly proclaimed the findings confirmed 'the pre-eminence of the Cambridge–Oxford–London triangle'.

Although the UGC/UFC undertook the evaluation of the research competence of universities essentially for its own purposes (which have important funding implications), it does not take much imagination to realize its wider ramifications. Obviously, the individual universities, even if they fail to act on the information, can scarcely ignore the message. There is also the

Table 7.2 UFC's ranking of the research records of Oxford and Cambridge departments, 1989

	Score				
	5	4	3	2	1
Oxford	27	7	3	2	0
Cambridge	31	10	6	1	0

Source: Richards (1989: 2–4).

possibility that those who fund research will be influenced by the findings, which would turn the rankings into a self-fulfilling prophecy. Interestingly, some of those universities hit hardest by the 1981 cuts in recurrent grant responded by increasing their research income and yet few of their departments (note, for example, the University of Salford) were ranked favourably in the evaluation exercises. What appears to be happening is the emergence of different kinds of research traditions within the universities. While one finds favour with the UGC/UFC panels, the other is attractive to those who want concrete answers to precise problems. While this may enable departmental research to flourish despite adverse ratings, it intensifies the fragmentation of the university system. Within itself this is not necessarily undesirable, but it is important that the criteria which determine funding decisions should either be less discriminatory or more explicit about the research tradition they favour.

The Universities of Oxford and Cambridge, with the ranking lists working very much in their favour, are at the other end of the continuum from universities like Salford, and it is difficult to see how this pre-eminence can be shaken. Even if nepotism and conspiracy are ruled out of the equation (and we realize that not everyone would want to do so), both universities have so many advantages in establishing research excellence that it would be surprising if they were not dominant. As Halsey and Trow's (1971: 230) research has shown, there is an aura to Oxbridge which attracts both faculty and students. Secondly, their comparatively large size – that is by British standards – works to their advantage. A small department, perhaps heavily dependent upon the input of one or two stars, is always vulnerable to rapid fluctuations in its reputation, for if the star leaves so may the whole research team and the department's standing evaporates. In science, research is dependent upon a steady flow of high-quality graduate students and as the science departments at Oxford and Cambridge are both large and prestigious the supply is guaranteed. On the output side, they train numerous graduate students who sooner or later end up in positions of responsibility in laboratories. But now we are approaching the positive advantages of their belonging to, perhaps even creating, the most favourable sociocultural networks. On the debit side, it has been pointed out to us that Oxbridge suffers from a measure of perverse discrimination from academics at other universities who, presumably motivated by envy, will do their best to prevent resources going to either Oxford or Cambridge. Although this probably does occur, it is no easier to substantiate than the reverse proposition that Oxbridge's advantages accrue from nepotism as opposed to merit. Presumably, there may even be some who genuinely believe – contra contemporary developments – that it is better for the long-term development of British research to spread the jam thinly rather than thickly.

Historically, the Universities of Oxford and Cambridge have been associated with the development of their science departments, while their colleges have supported the arts faculties. In recent years, with the more or less complete incorporation of the science faculty into the college system, more colleges have been prepared to support science research through the appointment of research fellows. It is difficult to pin down the precise numbers, and they are certainly nowhere near as large as the very substantial body of research workers paid for directly out of departmental research grants, but they do provide another potential input into the science departments, and when times are hard it may make the difference between mounting a project and leaving it in cold storage.

A range of variables interrelate, therefore, to ensure that the Universities of Oxford and Cambridge continue to maintain their established reputations for research excellence. The structural characteristics (diversity in depth) encourage the necessary external support for research (reinforced at the margins by wealthy colleges) which is so vital if the laboratories are to undertake the work that creates international reputations. Once that has been established, it becomes almost a self-fulfilling prophecy, or at the very least it forms a mould that is difficult to break. What the research selectivity exercises of the UGC/UFC will result in is the reinforcement of this process, and the UFC, despite a more *laisser-faire* approach than the UGC, is committed to another review exercise. Given the intention to target the support for research more precisely, perhaps no alternative was possible, and it is even conceivable that next time around the universities will be required to act more decisively upon the findings.

The proof is in the pudding: Analysing research expenditure patterns

This section of the chapter will examine the relative success of the individual departments at Oxford and Cambridge in obtaining research grants and will make some tentative comparisons between the Oxbridge statistics and those for all British universities. The intention is to show the ever-increasing importance of research income in the budgets of the science departments and to examine the changing balance of university research. Do the data require us to think of universities as institutions which incorporate different areas

Table 7.3   University of Oxford: Expenditure of academic areas met from research grants (£000s)

	1965–66	1969–70	1979–80	1989–90
Arts	3	1	93	1 351
Social Studies	45	94	259	2 638
Education	12	36	14	196
Physical Sciences	776	894	3 346	8 026
Biological Sciences	187	373	906	10 117
Applied Sciences	109	293	1 264	4 431
Pre-clinical Medicine	190	365	1 706	5 265
Clinical Medicine	92	156	2 623	15 442
Mathematics/Computing	6	47	219	1 409
Total All areas	1420	2259	10 834	48 875

Sources: University of Oxford (1966c, 1970b, 1980b, 1990a).

of academic endeavour whose boundaries are defined by the broad subject areas, or as integrated institutions in pursuit of common goals?

Annually the Universities of Oxford and Cambridge publish an account of the expenditure of their academic departments but they have grouped their courses differently over time, and their categories differ. We will examine, therefore, the trends for each university individually and then make our comparisons. The reader should consult the Appendix to learn how we have constructed our subject group categories for Tables 7.3–7.6.

The most striking feature of Table 7.3 is the very large percentage increases in the research grants of all knowledge areas. Not surprisingly, those subjects with low starting points have made the largest gains over the total period, but even the physical sciences with their comparatively high initial input increased their research funding more than ten-fold. The second point to note is the vast increase in the research funds of the biological sciences and of both pre-clinical and clinical medicine. Medical research is now clearly established as the leading research area in the University of Oxford, dwarfing both the applied and physical sciences. The success of both the Departments of Pharmacology and Clinical Pharmacology in signing lucrative research deals with pharmaceutical companies illustrates the potential that industrial sponsorship has to alter the university's research map. The magnitude of this change should not be underestimated, for the expenditure of the Faculty of Physical Sciences from research grants in 1965–66 totalled more than *all* the other faculties combined. A far cry from the situation that now prevails.

The changes within these broad knowledge areas disguise some significant shifts within particular departments. For example, in 1965–66, the Department of Biochemistry's expenditure from research grants was just under £45 000; by 1989–90 it was over £4.5 million. In 1965–66, the Department of Experimental Psychology's research grant expenditure was under £17 500, while by 1989–90 it had risen to almost £900 000. The general picture also hides some important changes in the balance of research income for departments within the same faculty. The domination of research grant expenditure by the Faculty of Physical Sciences in the mid-1960s was heavily dependent upon the input of the Department of Nuclear Physics. Out of the £776 000 total for the Faculty of Physical Sciences in 1965–66, the Department of Nuclear Physics contributed £444 000 or 57.2 per cent. In the 1980s, research expenditure in nuclear physics levelled off and the Department of Atmospheric Physics has assumed the lead in research expenditure within the Faculty of Physical Sciences. Historically, the Department of Zoology – excluding the rather special case of the Department of Biochemistry – has been the clear leader in research expenditure within the Faculty of Biological Sciences only to be matched in recent years by the newly constituted Department of Plant Sciences.

Despite the differentiation in the research expenditure of the medical and science departments, they all have to be described – at least in expenditure terms – as research-oriented departments. Obviously, some departments are larger than others, and some are less favourably placed to compete for research grants, but they are all travelling inexorably down that road. The one exception to this generalization is the field of mathematics, for most of the income from research grants has been generated not by the mathematicians but by the computer personnel. Disregarding this important exception, there is a clear differentiation in these terms between the science/medical departments and the university's other academic areas, although Table 7.3 may not give this initial impression. In the arts and social studies, there are a few specialized departments or research units (e.g. the Department of Social and Administrative Studies, the Criminological Research Unit, and the Wellcome Unit for the History of Medicine) that obtain sizeable research grants, whereas many large faculties are almost bereft of research income. For example, the core faculties of English, Medieval and Modern Languages, Literae Humaniores, Law and Modern History between them covered little more than £100 000 of their total expenditure from research grants in the late 1980s, which puts them in a different league from the science departments, and, moreover, in the arts and social studies the research grants are awarded disproportionately to specialist research outfits rather than to the university's mainstream academic institutions. Although the development of narrow research institutes has also occurred in science and medicine, the major departments have also been fully incorporated within the research explosion. The data lend themselves, therefore, to the proposition that the intellectual activities of the University of Oxford are sharply divided along the 'arts'/'science' boundary. Although research may be a common activity (the arts and social studies at Oxford were – like the sciences – rated very highly in the UGC/UFC research selectivity exercises), clearly it is an activity which assumes contrasting forms. The different knowledge areas involve radically different resources to tackle their core problems and pose the university with their own unique organizational challenges.

Table 7.4   University of Oxford: Expenditure met from research grants as a percentage of all other expenditure

	1965–66	*1969–70*	*1979–80*	*1989–90*
Arts	0.4	0.1	2.1	14.4
Social Studies	10.7	17.1	10.6	37.3
Education	19.4	45.0	4.0	26.8
Physical Sciences	75.7	66.0	71.7	77.3
Biological Sciences	36.2	55.4	54.0	153.5
Applied Sciences	61.6	97.7	86.9	105.1
Pre-clinical Medicine	31.1	45.5	71.7	139.7
Clinical Medicine	26.0	30.0	89.0	198.6
Mathematics/Computing	6.2	30.7	32.7	54.7
Total	35.2	40.5	49.7	93.1

Sources: See Table 7.3.

Perhaps the best way of demonstrating the gap between the science departments and the university's other academic areas is to look at expenditure from research grants in relation to expenditure from all other sources (see Table 7.4). The increased importance of expenditure met from research grants in the accounts of the arts and social studies areas of the university are heavily dependent upon innovations such as the creation of the Wellcome Unit for the History of Medicine and the full incorporation of Queen Elizabeth House into the university. Without their inputs, the amount of expenditure covered by research grants in the arts and social studies would decline substantially. It would be unwise, however, to place too much emphasis on the special nature of such factors, for universities are supposed to evolve and these can be seen as natural developments within the context of a changing university environment. Much the same has occurred within science, for example the creation of departments without undergraduates and specialized research units, but the distinction is that research expenditure is a very big element in the budgets of all the medical and science departments including those – such as engineering sciences, pharmacology, organic chemistry and the Clarendon – with large numbers of undergraduate students. This cannot be said of the full range of subjects in either the arts or social studies.

If any further proof were needed, Table 7.4 demonstrates yet again the extent to which the University of Oxford has become a research-oriented university. This is not to say that undergraduate teaching is no longer taken seriously, even in those parts of the university so heavily involved in seeking research funds, but rather it is a statement about the changing academic character of the institution, that is the shifting balance between its central commitments. In this respect, there does appear to be an important distinction between the various academic areas within the university. The trend commenced with the physical and applied sciences, but the relationship between their funding inputs appears to have stabilized. By way of contrast, the departments in the biological sciences and both clinical and pre-clinical medicine were slower to enter the search for research funding, but this input into these knowledge areas had yet to peak. The expenditure of mathematics/computing has shown a steady if less dramatic increase; it is not the steady-state model of the physical or applied sciences, neither is it the runaway 'success' of biology and the medical fields. Finally, as already noted, none of the other knowledge areas – whether it be arts, social studies or education – seem to be in a position to compete in these terms.

One further important consideration that has to be taken into account is the decline in the value of the UGC's recurrent grant to the University of Oxford. In other words, the financial significance of the research grants has been heightened by the fact that the university has had less to offer its departments. It would be unwise to assume that the departments tried to increase their research funding simply in order to compensate for the loss of university resources, for the surge in research income clearly commenced before the 1981 cut-backs or even the mid-1970s crisis. Moreover, it would be simplistic to hypothesize such a relationship even if the fit were better. However, if research contracts do have a sizeable overheads costing built into them, and departments share this with the university, then it could become increasingly necessary for departments to maintain their research income if they are to sustain a whole range of their activities. Some may fear such long-term reliance on the benevolence of the marketplace, but the alternative, given the entrenched parsimony of the state, of a rapidly fading gentility, must seem even less attractive. It will be interesting to see, therefore, the extent to which departments are capable of sustaining the funding of their own activities and what repercussions this has on both the quantity and quality of their research activities.

For much of its recent history, the University of Cambridge has presented the accounts of its departments and faculties according to four groups of faculties with an additional category for 'other institutions'. The four groups correspond roughly to different knowledge areas: (1) humanities; (2) social studies; (3) applied and physical sciences including mathematics; and (4) the biological sciences including pre-clinical, clinical and veterinary medicine. However, they were created as roughly four equal groups to secure the broad representation of faculty interests on the university's General Board. Therefore, we have reconstructed the groups by subdividing them into more refined categories and rearranging some of the individual placements (see Appendix). The accounts for 1989–90 were not constructed on the basis of the above four groups, but we have re-ordered the information to fit the subject categories listed in Tables 7.5 and 7.6. We believe this results in a more coherent set of academic categories and makes for easier comparisons with the University of Oxford. We have not, however, attempted to create categories that are strictly identical in meaning to the Oxford constructions. This would have involved too great a re-ordering of the subject groups to

Table 7.5   University of Cambridge: Expenditure of academic areas met from research grants (£000s)[a]

	1965–66	1969–70	1979–80	1989–90
Arts	9	17	32	300
Education	9	16	35	112
Social Studies	95	212	558	1 888
Physical Sciences	362	536	2 025	10 336
Applied Sciences	191	417	1 297	4 792
Mathematics/Computing	50	38	334	2 176
Astronomy	17	44	247	834
Biological Sciences	139	181	741	3 945
Pre-clinical Medicine	157	220	1521	8 241
Clinical Medicine	40	80	472	4 404
Veterinary Medicine	39	65	92	442
Totals	1 108	1 827	7 354	37 470

[a] The rounding up of numbers, plus a few exclusions of small academic units, has produced slightly different totals from those listed in the university's *Abstract of Accounts*.
Sources: University of Cambridge (1966, 1971b, 1981, 1990).

very little effect. The most important inter-university differences will be discussed in the text.

The University of Cambridge has been somewhat less successful than the University of Oxford in securing research grants, and the gap between the two universities has widened over the past 25 years. The areas where Cambridge has held a consistent advantage are the physical sciences, the applied sciences and mathematics/computing. The overall widening gap between the universities is very much a consequence of the massive growth in the value of research grants in the biological sciences and clinical pre-clinical medicine at Oxford. Although Cambridge has expanded rapidly its activities in these areas, Oxford had a firmer base on which to build (Cambridge did not establish its School of Clinical Medicine until the 1960s). The relative position of the physical sciences is also different at the two universities. In the mid-1960s, the physical science departments at Oxford dominated by a very large margin all the other knowledge areas in terms of their ability to attract research grants. By the late 1980s, this advantage had disappeared to such an extent that the physical sciences were only in third place, behind the biological sciences and clinical medicine. By way of contrast, although the 1965–66 data show the physical sciences at Cambridge as the leading research area in these terms, its advantage over other knowledge areas was much smaller than at Oxford, but it is an advantage that it has continued to maintain, albeit by a shrinking margin.

At Cambridge, as at Oxford, there is the same significant internal distinction between arts on the one side of the university and the medical and

Table 7.6 University of Cambridge: Expenditure met from research grants as a percentage of all other expenditure

	1965–66	*1969–70*	*1979–80*	*1989–90*
Arts	1.6	2.9	1.4	3.8
Education	13.0	20.8	13.6	11.0
Social Studies	16.5	20.8	22.3	21.8
Physical Sciences	28.6	50.6	72.7	94.9
Applied Sciences	21.3	45.2	49.3	45.0
Mathematics/Computing	16.3	18.6	41.3	54.6
Astronomy	30.9	107.3	142.0	125.4
Biological Sciences	21.5	29.1	45.4	83.0
Pre-clinical Medicine	21.9	27.0	56.0	96.4
Clinical Medicine	12.5	26.4	45.9	64.3
Veterinary Medicine	16.7	27.4	15.7	19.3
Totals	18.7	31.0	42.3	56.6

Sources: See Table 7.5.

science departments on the other side of the university, and – as at Oxford – social studies closer to the arts than to the sciences and medicine. The big increase in arts research expenditure in the 1980s was attributable almost entirely to linguistics, although it should be pointed out that the Department of Oriental Studies has also contributed consistently to the research income of the arts. In the social studies, the inputs have been more widely dispersed than at Oxford, but none the less the markedly heavier contributions have come from the Department of Applied Economics, the Institute of Criminology (Faculty Group 11), Archaeology and Anthropology (Faculty Group 1V), and Land Economy, Social and Political Studies, and the History of Medicine (all listed under Other Institutions). The social studies form, therefore, a somewhat broader bridge between the arts area and the scientific and medical departments than is the case at Oxford, although again much of the research income has accrued to rather specialized institutions rather than to the main faculties.

In view of the University of Oxford's greater success at attracting income from research grants, it was to be expected that expenditure met from research grants would form a lower percentage of total expenditure at Cambridge. By 1989–90, only the physical sciences at Cambridge met a higher percentage of its total expenditure from research grants than at Oxford. It would be unwise, however, to make too much of the inter-university comparisons, as the presentation of the data (for example, the location of the equipment grant) has changed over time and departments have other means of generating income besides obtaining research. None the less, despite these equivocations, Oxford has by and large marginally outperformed Cambridge on this front. Only astronomy at Cambridge (like pre-clinical and clinical

Table 7.7   University of Cambridge: Sources of grants and contracts for research

	Research councils		Government bodies[a]		Other sources		Total
	£000s	%	£000s	%	£000s	%	£000s
1955–56	94	30.7	113	36.9	99	32.4	307
1965–66	522	45.8	218	19.1	400	35.1	1 139
1969–70	1 157	58.3	302	15.2	525	26.5	1 984
1979–80	6 547	63.7	1 040	10.1	2 692	26.2	10 279
1989–90	19 226	50.9	2 810	7.4	15 751	41.7	37 787

[a] Government bodies include UK local authorities and UK health and hospital authorities in addition to UK central government bodies.
Sources: University of Cambridge (1957, 1967a, 1971c, 1980b and 1991d).

medicine, the biological and applied sciences at Oxford) meets over half of its expenditure from research income. But Cambridge's Institute of Astronomy is a comparatively small outfit given over entirely to research activities, so this development is none too surprising. It does come as something of a surprise, however, to learn that the applied sciences at Oxford have as strong a research focus as at Cambridge where they took a much firmer root at an earlier date. All of the scientific and medical subjects, with the small exception of veterinary medicine at Cambridge, have seen a consistently steady increase in the significance of research income in their departmental accounts. None of these equivocations, however, can deny the truth of this simple generalization – contemporarily science and medicine in general are centred as much, or even more, around their research activities as their teaching duties.

From the mid-1950s to the present, the University of Cambridge has published annually in its *Reporter* a comprehensive record of the sources of its research income ('Research Wholly or Partly Supported by Funds from Outside Bodies'), which makes it possible to examine how the university's sources of research income have diversified over time. The same issue of the *Reporter* also recorded until the mid-1970s the origins of each department's research monies, so facilitating the same analysis for the departments.

Table 7.7 shows the heavy dependence of the research effort at the University of Cambridge between 1955 and 1970 upon an expanding financial input from the research councils. However, the growth in research income from other sources matched the expansion of the research councils' investment in the 1970s (not too difficult given its comparatively low starting point) and more than outstripped it in the 1980s. As a consequence, Table 7.7 points to three financial phases: an initial balance between the input of the funding bodies; a period in which the research councils grew more dominant while the input from government departments declined in percentage terms quite rapidly; and, more recently, the decline in the paramount position of the research councils coupled with a rapid growth in the importance of funding from non-state sources. It should be pointed out that only a fraction of the latter resources has consisted of money from British industry, with the largest share contributed by UK-based charitable organizations.

Should the balance of inputs from the research councils and from 'the market' (note a small portion of overseas grants are in fact financed by foreign governments) continue to move in favour of the latter, then the research character of Cambridge would be influenced increasingly by what the market is prepared to finance. However, what is more striking is the sheer concentration of the resources from the research councils in comparison to the inputs from other sources. In the financial year 1989–90, the handful of research councils were recorded as awarding contracts and grants worth over £19 million, compared to the some 300 individual sources for the almost £16 million that were made available by 'other' institutions (University of Cambridge 1991d: 599–606). For those disparate institutions to shift significantly the research balance within the university, either they must be disproportionately interested in research in particular fields (e.g. medicine as opposed to the applied sciences) or prepared to sponsor research of only a particular kind (e.g. applied as opposed to basic research). In fact, over half the income from 'the other institutions' came from what the *Reporter* has described as 'UK-Based Charitable Bodies' and almost all of these were medical in character (The Wellcome Trust, Cancer Research Campaign and British Heart Foundation are good examples).

It does appear, however, that the financial input of 'the market' and 'the state' into research has been moving broadly in the same direction. For example, as a percentage of the total resources donated to Cambridge by the research councils, the input of the Medical Research Council (MRC) rose more sharply than the inputs of the other research councils. The rapid expansion of Cambridge's research effort was underwritten mainly by the research councils between 1965 and 1980, so as the largest dispenser of largesse, it is the Science and Engineering Research Council (SERC) for which the university should be especially grateful. Between 1965 and 1980, over 60 per cent of research council monies came from the SERC (the comparable figure for 1955–56 was 37.4 per cent when the source was the Department for Scientific and Industrial Research), while over the past 10 years it has declined to approximately 50 per cent. This poses a potential problem for those departments that have been especially dependent upon the SERC for research funding, for should the input of the SERC continue to decline in relative terms, they have no choice but to seek alternative sources of funding if they intend to maintain their high visibility in the university's overall research profile.

As Table 7.8 illustrates, the relative success of the individual Cambridge departments at obtaining research grants and contracts has shown remarkable stability over time, which would suggest a measure of flexibility on their part in relating to the funding agencies. The emergence of the Department of

Table 7.8 Cambridge departments: Ranking by research grant income

	1955–56	1965–66	1969–70	1979–80	1989–90
1st	Physics	Physics	Engineering	Physics	Physics
2nd	Agriculture	Engineering	Physics	Engineering	Pathology
3rd	Engineering	Chemistry	Chemistry	Pathology	Chemistry
4th	Physical Chemistry	Metallury	Applied Economics	Zoology	Engineering
5th	Colloid Science	Agriculture	Metallurgy	Physical Chemistry	Metallurgy
6th	Metallurgy	Applied Economics	Computer Laboratory	Metallurgy	Zoology

Note: The School of Clinical Medicine and the Super-conductivity Interdisciplinary Research Centre have been excluded from the calculations
Sources: As for Table 7.7.

Pathology as a major research earner reflects the general enhancement of the research base of Cambridge's pre-clinical medicine departments. The three departments of Physics, Engineering and Metallurgy (now known as Material Sciences and Metallurgy) have been among the top three earners of research income throughout this time period, and it seems appropriate, therefore, to examine – as far as the data permit – the sources that have financed their research. In 1955–56, neither Engineering nor Metallurgy had much research council income (engineering recorded two grants from the then Department of Scientific and Industrial Research, while Metallurgy listed no such grants). The research of both departments was heavily dependent upon finance from government ministries, especially the Ministry of Supply. Whereas the input from industrial resources into Metallurgy was evident, the almost total absence of a similar input into the Department of Engineering was surprising. In an expected contrast, the Department of Physics had several research council grants, a smaller income from government departments but as much indus-trial money as Engineering. By 1974, the picture had changed markedly. All three departments, that is Engineering, Metallurgy and Physics, had become major recipients of grants from the SERC (especially, as previously, Physics); the input from government departments – notably the Ministry of Defence – also made a large contribution to all three departments; while Engineering had increased substantially its industrial funding, with Rolls Royce Limited as one of its major benefactors. It would be incorrect to describe the varying inputs as of equal importance to all three departments, but the range of funding within each department meant that there was no over-reliance upon any one source. Whatever changes have occurred since the mid-1970s, they have not – as yet – been sufficient to challenge the traditional research dominance of physics at Cambridge, but the rapid rise of pathology would suggest that it could be only a matter of time before – as at Oxford – both pre-clinical and clinical medicine replace the physical and applied sciences as Cambridge's largest centres of research activity. Clearly, the position of engineering is already waning. The question is whether the physical and applied sciences can show their previous aptitude for tapping into new sources of funding, so decreasing their reliance on the projected declining input from the state.

Research funding: A comparative perspective

UGC statistics provide the best comparative record of the research activities of British universities and they show British universities in general earning a higher percentage of their income from research grants and contracts. In 1988–89, the Universities of Oxford and Cambridge, with the rather special exception of the University of Wales' College of Medicine, filled the top two places (see Table 7.9).

In the sense that at both the Universities of Oxford and Cambridge there has been a smooth upward curve in the percentage of recurrent income met

Table 7.9   Research income as a percentage of total income

	1967–68			*1979–80*			*1988–89*		
	£000s	*%*	*Rank*	*£000s*	*%*	*Rank*	*£000s*	*%*	*Rank*
Cambridge	1 583	15.4	4th=	10 279	22.0	1st	30 245	25.5	3rd
Oxford	1 849	17.3	2nd	10 779	21.0	2nd	40 746	30.9	2nd
UK	24 068	10.9		174 257	13.4		638 680	20.0	

Sources: UGC (1968b: 89–90; 1980b: 106–7; UFC 1990b: 10–11).

from research grants and contracts, the two universities have been moving consistently in the same direction, although the pace has been faster at Oxford over the past 10 years. What clearly happened within the university system as a whole was a growing dependence on the UGC's annual recurrent grant until the late 1970s, which was been followed in the past 10 years by the lessening of that dependence through the generation of mainly research income. In the sense that both Oxford and Cambridge have moved along that path over a much longer time period, they could be said to have provided a model for other universities to follow (obviously along with those institutions which have also followed in the same direction). The 1988–89 UFC statistics reveal that several institutions now receive over 22 per cent of their recurrent income from research grants and contracts. Besides Oxford and Cambridge, these include London, Loughborough, UMIST, Southampton, Surrey, the University of Wales' College of Medicine, Dundee, Edinburgh and Heriot-Watt. These are institutions of contrasting characters and, although individual universities may be more sharply differentiated from each other in the future, this general pull in the direction of research complicates the picture. Inevitably, research has figured more highly in the profile of the academic activities of many departments and the UFC's decision to distribute more selectively the research support element in its annual grant can only reinforce the process.

A breakdown by cost centres of the UGC's statistics has revealed no special idiosyncrasies; that is by 1988–89, the Oxford departments and faculties in general consistently met a higher percentage of their recurrent costs out of research income than the equivalent institutions at Cambridge and elsewhere. The differences are particularly noticeable in the medical and associated fields, but far less pronounced in science and mathematics. In the latter areas, both Oxford and Cambridge out-perform by a clear margin nearly all other British universities, a pattern that is repeated in social studies. The national figures in the various arts areas confirm what we have already observed about the Universities of Oxford and Cambridge, that these are not in general knowledge fields that depend upon the maintenance of their research income in order to expand their scholarship.

Conclusions

It has become customary in recent years for the universities to stress the extent to which their recurrent income is less dependent upon the UGC's annual grant. What this chapter has shown is the steady growth of the input from the research councils (which one should not forget is also taxpayers' money), coupled in the past 10 years with a greatly enlarged infusion of financial resources from the marketplace. This trend looks set to continue and, although it has not affected all universities equally, they have all to some extent moved down that road. Moreover, the clearer distinction between support for teaching as opposed to support for research will inevitably encourage a greater differentiation within and between universities in terms of the balance between their research and teaching activities. Given the UFC's greater emphasis upon the research component in its recurrent grant, and its intention to distribute it more selectively than hitherto, plus the research councils' current attraction for the concentration of their resources upon particular targets, it is evident that such differentiation is already well under way (Phillips 1989).

Within the above context, the Universities of Oxford and Cambridge have established themselves as among the market leaders. Indeed, it would be difficult to deny that Oxford is *the* market leader. The science departments at both Oxford and Cambridge have been increasing their dependence upon research income for many years now and, although this has been followed by selected departments in the social studies, the humanities have scarcely begun to move along this track. In relation to the overall academic character of British universities, the outcome of this process may not be the further rationalization of departments that was encouraged by the UGC (in the name of enhancing academic excellence and promoting cost-effectiveness), but rather a recognition of the need to preserve a range of departments in order that they can perform different functions. The UFC's more *laisser-faire* stance may reflect not so much an ideological commitment but rather a recognition of contemporary necessities. What is fascinating is that just as the ancient universities created a model of the university whose central tenets the UGC was prepared to sustain for the greater part of its existence, so the UFC may come to look upon Oxford and Cambridge as constituting ideal types for a critical segment of the new system of higher education. What is impossible to deny is that the state's increasing support for research, and the gradual move towards greater selectivity in the provision of those resources, has had the profoundest impact upon the model of the university.

In our previous research on public schools, we argued that their changing character (curriculum content, methods of pupil control, management styles and sociocultural goals) were shaped not so much by market forces, which affected the less prestigious independent schools more acutely, but more by their institutional links, especially their ties to the Universities of Oxford and Cambridge (Salter and Tapper 1985: 66–9). The main reason why the public schools changed was straightforward: to sustain their image as schools which either greatly improved the life chances of their pupils or which continued to occupy a critical place in cementing links between the leading institutions in this country (there are some who have no need to improve their life chances). In parallel fashion to the public schools, the central interest of both the Universities of Oxford and Cambridge is to perpetuate the idea that they are the leading universities in this country. Their development – both imposed and internally generated – of an alternative model of the university is a consequence of their need to sustain their pre-eminence. Moreover, like the public schools, given their connections both to the state and most of society's élite institutions, their leading academics were well placed to see what path they had to follow, although this was no guarantee that their universities would make the necessary adjustments. However, while the promotion of scholarship (in the arts) and of research (in the sciences) may have led to the retention of their academic dominance, it may have undermined both Oxford and Cambridge as institutions where future leaders go to learn the correct sociocultural values and form the right social ties. Clearly, this will not bother the overwhelming majority of dons who measure the worth of their universities according to the values of homo academicus, but undoubtedly it will disturb those who retain a wider view of the purpose of Oxbridge.

At the more concrete level of what has happened to the science departments of the Universities of Oxford and Cambridge, it would be niggardly to conclude other than with the observation that their respective histories represent two essentially outstanding success stories. Both have had to grapple with the protracted problems posed by the historically weaker areas of 'agriculture and forestry' and the lack of state support for their continued presence at either university. Cambridge has decided to terminate the Department of Applied Biology which housed these interests, while at Oxford their encapsulation in the recently formed Department of Plant Sciences has provided at least temporary respite (although there were some raised eyebrows within Oxford when the UFC's research selectivity exercise failed to award the department its highest ranking). The real success stories at Oxford are the fields of clinical and pre-clinical medicine and the Department of Engineering Science. Until recently, the SERC's longstanding support for nuclear physics research benefited Oxford, but the move away from 'big science' has forced the university to rethink its priorities. At Cambridge, the traditionally powerful research tradition of the natural sciences, and physics in particular, continues to hold sway. In the 1960s, it seemed as if engineering would assume the dominant research position, but rather surprisingly its challenge has faltered and the medical sciences lack as yet the base they have established at Oxford. If the need to augment research income continues apace, then it is possible that the applied sciences at Cambridge (of which the most critical departments are engineering, chemical engineering, and material sciences and metallurgy) may consider that it is in their best long-term interests to form their own school of studies. At present, located within the School of Physical Sciences, they appear to be rather overshadowed by some of their more illustrious neighbours. Finally, it should be noted that although astronomy, like nuclear physics, has suffered from its membership of the now unfashionable 'big science' club, its relative research position has been strengthened at both Oxford and Cambridge. Which only goes to prove the old adage that as the weak grow weaker so the strong grow stronger.

To increase research income is no guarantee of enhanced research excellence. However, it comes as no surprise to learn that those Oxbridge science departments which have done well in the two research selectivity exercises, have also an enviable record for attracting research income. As this will influence the UFC's distribution of its recurrent grant, a self-fulfilling prophecy may well be established, and it is hard to imagine that it will not also affect the thinking of the research councils. The challenge that this poses other universities is very menacing. If they are to compete in these terms, they face the problem of obtaining the necessary resources. However, if they decide to accept the role of teaching institutions, they are both acquiescing in a lower status for themselves and denying themselves a role in the central dynamic of science, that is the expansion of its knowledge boundaries. Alternatively, if they wish to formulate different goals, for example the development of alternative research avenues, not only do they have to determine what these will be, but also they have to convince their academic colleagues – as well as themselves – that they are worthy of pursuit. As always, for the less elevated to redefine what is to count as excellence is never an easy task. As much as it may be regretted, in a more variegated university system it would be naive to imagine that its different components will have equal value. The situation is complicated by the desire of universities to recover the overhead costs of research. If this is less possible to achieve with basic research projects, we may find a radical rethink as to the relative merits of different kinds of research or even a swift re-evaluation of what is to count as basic research. If this should occur once again pressure from the state (it was the UGC that prodded the universities into recovering overhead costs) will have demonstrated the potency of its indirect influence upon the organization of knowledge.

8

Controlling Admissions Procedures: Colleges, Universities and the Political Context

What are the issues?

Over the years, the admissions procedures of the Universities of Oxford and Cambridge have been exposed to a great deal of public debate. As Oxbridge entry affects the interests of an articulate middle class such concern is understandable. The frustrated ambitions of would-be Oxbridge undergraduates help to generate an apparently endless stream of articles that reveal the alleged Oxbridge entrance lottery. This popular concern has been reinforced by powerful interlocking political and intellectual forces. In its brief history, British educational sociology has expended much energy exploring access to educational opportunities. Oxford and Cambridge have been favourite targets; the social biases in their student populations seem to demonstrate the continuing inequality of educational opportunities in Britain. Furthermore, the sociologists have had a significant political input, especially into the Labour Party, but it is generally accepted that access to publicly funded institutions should be socially equitable, although how that is to be understood is quite another matter.

The traditional interest in undergraduate admissions has concentrated almost exclusively upon the question of who gains entry. Inasmuch as the perceived bias in the social composition of Oxbridge students has constituted a major pressure for change, this is also one of our concerns. However, we have wider interests and this chapter analyses in some detail the reforms of the 1980s. The intention is to use this case study in internally controlled educational reform to examine the character of the admissions procedures *per se* and to analyse the interaction of college, intercollegiate and university interests within the change process. Naturally, we relate the internal change dynamic to external pressures, both administrative and political. Perhaps the most significant development in the control and management of the admissions procedures at both universities was the creation of their admissions offices. Much of the administration is conducted centrally within these offices, and control of the process (albeit a fragile control) is in the hands of the intercollegiate bodies that are formally responsible for the admissions offices. This crucial development was a consequence of the creation of the Universities Central Council for Admissions (UCCA) and the necessity that Oxford and Cambridge centralize the administration of their own admissions procedures before they joined UCCA. As we will argue, this was a vital stage in shifting the control of the admissions process from the individual colleges to intercollegiate bodies. Thus, as was the case with college fees, external pressures played a critical part in developing the system of college government.

In this chapter, we examine access to that highly valued commodity, an Oxbridge education. If institutions control valued resources then, assuming the authority is in their hands, one of their most important functions is to decide how they will determine access to those resources. The means of entry has to be seen as legitimate, and the recruitment patterns have to be explained and defended with reference to the principles that guide the selection process. The admissions process is important not only for the way in which it relates the colleges and universities to their social context, but also because it influences how they conduct their daily business. The character of an Oxbridge education is based upon assumptions about the nature of Oxbridge undergraduates. Should these assumptions prove incorrect then, put simply, the system will fail. Either the recruitment process or the nature of an Oxbridge education has to change. The key, therefore, to changing the character of university education is to modify the qualities of the student intake.

Old and new biases: The pressures for change

In terms of the laws of supply and demand, admission to the Universities of Oxford and Cambridge did not pose serious problems before 1945. As a university degree came to be seen as an essential prerequisite for obtaining respectable employment, so the Oxbridge colleges faced the not altogether unwelcome embarrassment of an over-supply of good candidates. In an interesting personal communication, a former admissions tutor has reflected:

> I was in charge of the entry to Corpus [Corpus Christi College, Cambridge] from 1935 onwards. In those days the old ordinary degree still existed and few if any of the colleges held entrance exams. Corpus did because we did not admit candidates for the ordinary degree and wanted to be sure that those admitted were capable of reading honours. And in those days it was a question of getting enough candidates than of cutting down too long a list. The Colleges Entrance Exam is a post-war reaction to increased pressure (personal communication, 16 April 1987).

In fact, the increased demand changed the focus of concern. Prior to 1945, the social exclusiveness of Oxford and Cambridge was seen as essentially a financial problem, that is poor students could not afford the fees. After 1945, it became an admissions problem, that is it was unfair procedures that caused the social exclusiveness.

Asquith's Commission, as well as the nineteenth-century royal commissions, raised the question of the exclusion of potentially good scholars of humble social origins while the idle rich (although presumably not all the rich were idle and not all the idle were rich!) were readily admitted. In fact, by widening the competition for college scholarships, the royal commissions had benefited the bourgeoisie at the expense of the poorer ranks of society. The extent of later official concern was reflected in Parliament's charge to those statutory commissioners chosen to implement the Asquith Report:

> In making any statutes or regulations under this Act, the Commission-
> ers shall have regard to the need of facilitating the admission of poorer
> students to the Universities and colleges (Universities of Oxford and
> Cambridge Act, 13 and 14 Geo. V, 1923: Ch. 33, Sect. 6(2)).

In part, Parliament was picking up on evidence presented to the Royal Commission by parties both external to the universities (most vigorously by the Labour Party, the Workers' Educational Association and the Cooperative Union) as well as internal reform groups (notably the Oxford Reform Committee and the Committee of Younger Cambridge Graduates) (Royal Commission on Oxford and Cambridge Universities 1922b: 10–13, 53–7, 60–72).

The nineteenth-century response to the exclusion of the poor was to reduce the costs of an Oxbridge education. Mark Pattison, the legendary nineteenth-century Oxford scholar, advocated that compulsory college residence should be ended (Pattison 1868: 79). Early in the twentieth century, Lord Curzon, as Chancellor of the University of Oxford, had suggested ways in which the system of college scholarships and exhibitions could be reformed so as to encourage a wider social intake (Curzon 1909: Ch. 111). Later, the Asquith Commission devoted an extraordinary amount of time to investigating whether college costs could be reduced and urged colleges to consider purchasing supplies in common. The Commission also took up the question of whether more scholarships could be provided specifically for poorer scholars (Royal Commission on Oxford and Cambridge Universities 1922a: 133).

The Asquith Commission had spent much time reviewing the position of women at Oxford and Cambridge. The main issue was whether women should be admitted, as they already were at Oxford, to full membership of the University of Cambridge. Despite the Commission's complete support, the statutory commissioners were not directed by Parliament to implement the recommendation and women did not achieve equal formal status with men at Cambridge until after the Second World War. The general welfare of the women's college was also central to the Asquith Commission's Report and to further their interests the Royal Commission had 'no hesitation in recommending the payment of an annual grant from Public Funds for the benefit of the women's colleges at both universities' (ibid.: 171).

The reformist approach of the Asquith Commission can be contrasted with

Pattison's radicalism. Defenders of the colleges, while prepared to consider ways of expanding the number of able poor students, wanted colleges to remain at the centre of university life. The Report of the 1922 Royal Commission endorsed this and accepted the financial implication that 'college life must in our opinion always be comparatively dear' (ibid.: 165). The desire to retain the collegiate model of the university has been a cardinal principle in all the major internal reviews of Oxford and Cambridge, integral to which is the understanding that undergraduates, and indeed postgraduates, will be admitted to a college and that the colleges will remain in formal control of admissions policy. If you were to ask Oxbridge dons what characteristics of their universities they considered most sacrosanct, the retention of their collegiate identity would probably rank first.

Whatever the official encouragement may have been, it is evident that the demand from poor candidates and women did not upset the laws of supply and demand before 1945. Whereas expense kept out the poor, women were excluded by the paucity of places in women's colleges, reinforced by the operation of quotas. Since 1945, the situation has been changed dramatically by demographic trends, the greater market value of a university education, the state's assumption of the responsibility for paying fees, and – in the 1970s – the rapid move to co-educational colleges. The rising demand for places has meant that the colleges have more and more able candidates to choose from (which they have generally welcomed), but their choices have been subject to closer public scrutiny (which has caused considerable anxiety).

Formally, the solution to the dilemma has been relatively straightforward. Although a reforming Chancellor, Lord Curzon had argued that Oxford should continue to provide an education for the sons of the gentry:

> ... it appears to me to be a part of the function of Oxford to educate the Passman, and that, if it is to continue to deserve the name of a University, it has few more important duties to perform than to give a good general education to the man of birth and means (Curzon 1909: 117).

And even the 1922 Royal Commission (1922a: 166) had no wish to exclude entirely those who sought an Oxbridge education for primarily social reasons and left either without a degree or took a pass degree. In the more competitive post-1945 climate, there has been little room for such sentiments. Places are perceived as awards to individuals on the basis of their personal merit, and there would be scant support for Curzon's notion that the universities were obliged to educate a class of persons. The crucial problem has been how to define the concept of merit and then how to identify those who possess it. Put simply, the intention has been to identify those individuals who possess the intellectual potential to make the best use of an Oxbridge education. Ideally, the colleges would admit those who were best equipped to benefit from the courses on offer and exclude those who had less of the desired qualities.

In some interesting responses to our suggestion that the reform of Oxbridge admissions procedures in the 1980s had been motivated by the perceived political need to increase the social diversity of the student populations, several admissions tutors reiterated versions of meritocratic ideology. Compare the following personal communications from three individuals who in the past were closely involved in these matters:

> There are indeed social consequences of the actions we have taken but the object was to recruit strictly on the basis of merit as well as we could measure or judge. We would not accept a candidate because of his or her underprivileged social background and equally we would not reject an able person because that person had enjoyed educational and/or social advantage (personal communication: 14 April 1987).

> The whole point is that we try to *individualize* the admissions process, i.e. we recognize the obvious truth that this is a handicap race (getting the handicaps right is the difficult bit) (personal communication: 16 April 1988).

> We have not been making this our major priority (i.e. to widen the social base of Cambridge's undergraduate intake). As ever our major priority is to offer a superb national resource as widely as possible *to those whose academic talents merit it* (personal communication: 7 July 1987).

As the second quotation recognizes, personal qualities like merit and academic talent are at least partially determined by the sociocultural backgrounds of potential undergraduates. What is required, therefore, are procedures that will make allowances for the handicaps and admit those with the highest potential to make the fullest use of an Oxbridge education. But surely the problem is not that simple? Potential ability, in the form that it is required by the universities, is more likely to be concentrated in certain social groups. If those who are responsible for defining the goals of the university are also those who select the undergraduate intake, it is inevitable that without imposed affirmative action programmes they will engage in a measure of social selection. In the alternative scenario, they select individuals who are more likely to fail over those who are more likely to succeed. This is not to suggest that the personal qualities universities desire are determined only by social factors, but that universities are *not* neutral institutions in sociocultural terms and it is impossible to see how they could be. University selection, therefore, is inevitably a handicap race. However, we may want to change the admission procedures in order to vary handicaps.

None the less, a wealth of evidence shows that in comparison to other British universities, Oxford and Cambridge do have socially distinctive undergraduate populations with respect to class, gender and schooling, and that with respect to the overall population recruitment into higher education is in general socially distinctive. Obviously, such biases are not simply a consequence of the formalities of admissions procedures, but have developed out of the continuous interaction between British universities and their social context. It would have been foolish to have expected admissions procedures that did not discriminate socially in a context where the very ends and means of the universities were shaped, and inevitably so, by the social order. For most of the post-war years, there has been political pressure to expand and equalize educational opportunities and, as the universities with the most exclusive social intakes, Oxford and Cambridge in particular have felt the pressure to change.

The boldest course of action would have been a re-evaluation of the purposes of the university but few, if any, within the universities wanted that. And, as the above quotes have suggested, the suspicion of social engineering would not have permitted positive discrimination in favour of socially disadvantaged groups. The only viable option, therefore, was to tackle the admissions procedures which consequently have been reformed in piecemeal fashion over a long period of time, culminating in major revisions at both Oxford and Cambridge in the 1980s. As we shall see, the purpose of these reforms has been 'to equalize the handicaps'; if the procedures were meant to select solely on the basis of individual merit, in particular the potential to make maximum use of an Oxbridge education, then it was essential that they could be defended accordingly.

The case for procedural reform was overwelming. As the colleges formally controlled admissions, they had the authority to act and, as they were directing the reform process, inevitably the outcomes would be acceptable to them generally. Many of the problems were tied up with interests that had developed over decades; to most outsiders it seemed a byzantine system which could only be unravelled internally. Moreover, for the colleges to act boldly countered the threat of external political intervention. Why intervene if the colleges were putting their own house in order? Finally, it promised comparatively speedy action on precise difficulties while allowing the universities to bypass the larger issues. But whether it would deflect the more hardened political opponents of the Oxbridge colleges is another matter. Technical changes in admissions procedures will placate them only if they produce what are considered to be the desired results, i.e. student bodies shorn of their traditional social exclusivity. In other words, the external (and indeed some of the internal) critics have been more interested in goals than in means. Should the changes fail to deliver the goods, then the radicals have their own solutions – the imposition of quotas and/or financial penalties. But to date the radicals have been kept at bay, while the reformers have struggled to implement changes that would both maximize meritocratic values and secure the political high ground.

Getting the handicaps right: Fairness, simplicity and the reforms of the 1980s

In what follows we consider in broad terms the most distinctive features of the traditional admissions procedures at both Oxford and Cambridge and why in the 1980s it was felt necessary to overhaul them. The focus is upon the internal critique, more especially the charges levelled at the old order by the reports that brought about the new procedures. It would be quite mistaken to give the impression that the changes of the 1980s overhauled systems that, having stagnated for decades, were reformed only in the full-ness of time after considered reflection. In fact, the stability of the established procedures prior to the reforms of the 1980s were constantly under threat and the agreed changes can be seen, at least in part, as political responses designed to head off growing internal conflict. The admissions changes – and this is particularly true of Oxford – were an intercollegiate response to the various initiatives of individual colleges. Some colleges had instigated their own reforms, and it was the threat that these posed to the interests of other colleges, that provided the immediate stimulus for the broad reform packages of the 1980s.

The most distinctive feature of admissions to Oxford and Cambridge is that the process is controlled by the colleges rather than the universities. If the two universities are to retain their collegiate character, many would argue that the colleges must continue to control the recruitment of their students – to remove this function from the colleges would be a significant step towards turning them into mere halls of residence. However, following the strictures of the 1922 Asquith Commission – 'It is essential in our opinion that the two Universities should make themselves responsible for uniform rejection of unqualified students before they come into residence ...' (1922a: 166) – candidates have to meet minimum academic standards laid down by the universities before they can take up college residence. The main require-ment is that candidates receive two passes, that is at least E grades, at A level GCE. Furthermore, medicine at Oxford and medicine and veterinary medicine at Cambridge impose particular course requirements. Such unde-manding university barriers mean that the colleges have enormous latitude with the consequence that the admission of undergraduates has remained their domain.

Traditionally, Oxford and Cambridge colleges, in common with other British universities, had relied upon interviews and references to select their undergraduates. As demand outstripped supply, so the significance of the college entrance examinations, which had always been integral to the award-ing of college scholarships and exhibitions, increased. While over time the Cambridge colleges showed themselves more willing to award places con-ditionally on the basis of A and/or S GCE grades, there had always been a powerful body of opinion within the Oxbridge colleges against such a move. It was argued that the GCE examinations were better at measuring how well an agreed syllabus had been covered rather than discerning academic poten-tial. Indeed, this claim received some support in the influential Crowther Report: 'The second need is a recognition that the main purpose of the Advanced level of the General Certificate of Education is to be a school examination, and its use for university admission should be only as a pre-liminary measure of matriculation requirements – that is, it should be used for qualification only, not for selection' (Central Advisory Council for Education (England) 1959: 297). It was also reassuring to the dons that they both marked, and could reflect upon, the scripts of their candidates. Not only were the GCE scripts unavailable for scrutiny, but they had also been marked overwhelmingly by outsiders.

And what was allegedly good for the colleges was also allegedly good for the schools, for the college examinations provided their ablest sixth-form pupils with a more demanding intellectual exercise, or so the argument ran, than the standard public examinations. The incentives for ambitious sixth-formers were high because invariably the best performances in the college examinations were followed by offers of prestigious scholarships and exhibitions. Again the Crowther Report had offered its official support.

However, the mere fact that the admissions procedures for entry to Oxford and Cambridge were different to those of other universities raised some hostility as well as considerable suspicion. In particular, the fairness of the college entrance examination, regardless of its assumed pedagogical merits, had been questioned widely. The examination was meant to have a predictive value, that is it identified those candidates best able to benefit from an Oxbridge education. However, it imposed uniformity upon individuals who were different in ways that could interfere with the examination's supposed predictive powers. In other words, it treated equally those who were in fact different, and claims to the effect that this was known and compensated for were met with scepticism. There were two main doubts cast on the fairness of the procedures. College entrance examinations were sat by candidates in either the fourth or the seventh terms of their sixth-form careers. Was it really possible to evaluate on equal terms individuals who were at different points in their academic development? The statistics suggested not, for seventh-term candidates were disproportionately successful in obtaining Oxbridge places. Secondly, and in terms of the political pressure for change more significantly, seventh-term candidates were more likely to be pupils from independent schools, while candidates from the maintained schools were more likely to sit the examination in the fourth term. The independent schools, it was often claimed – and with considerable justification – were training their pupils for the college examinations and the prized scholarships. The private schools had many pupils who could afford to stay on at school beyond the second year of the sixth form, and they were equipped for the examinations in the sense that they knew what was expected of candidates and had the resources to ensure that their pupils acquired the necessary credentials to succeed. While the college examinations may have provided incentives for able pupils, they also led to the formation of annual scholarship league tables which some felt said more about the pecking order of schools than anything else.

It was possible to produce statistics to demonstrate, in the words of the Franks Inquiry, that the college entrance examinations were 'a searching test of promise' (University of Oxford 1966a: 70). The proof was the correlation between the degree performances of undergraduates and their status as entrants, that is as scholars, exhibitioners or commoners. Sir Desmond Lee subsequently produced statistics for both Oxford and Cambridge which showed similar trends and concluded that there was '... no general desire at either University to discontinue the college examinations or to abolish entrance awards' (Lee 1972: 41). However, the Franks statistics, although demonstrating the expected conclusion that exhibitioners obtained better degrees than commoners and scholars better degrees than exhibitioners, also showed that large minorities of both scholars and exhibitioners obtained third-class degrees or worse (University of Oxford 1966a: 179). But this was not a matter that was going to be resolved by statistics. Regardless of the predictive value of college examinations, it was their fairness or otherwise that was the focus of attention and as such they seemed fundamentally flawed. Probably more telling than the charge that they treated very different candidates equally, was the growing perception that they limited the field of would-be Oxbridge students. Potential undergraduates, so the argument went, decided not to apply for an Oxbridge place either because of the apparent complexity of the admissions process or, more subtly, because its very uniqueness suggested a desire to exclude those who did not already belong to the magic circle. If this were so, then scholars were not the best potential undergraduates but the best potential undergraduates of fields shorn of much talent.

Already it has been impossible to separate arguments about the fairness of the admissions procedures from questions about their complexity, or if not their complexity, then their uniqueness. Oxford and Cambridge required you to apply to their colleges, which then subjected you to special procedures. In the early 1960s, an initiative by the CVCP had led to the co-ordination of applications to British universities through UCCA. The distinctiveness of Oxford and Cambridge was reinforced by their initial reluctance to join UCCA, although by 1965 both universities were members. The creation of an overarching admissions system for British universities was accompanied by various reforms that reduced the complexity of Oxbridge procedures without removing their distinctiveness. The early 1960s saw the creation of the Oxford Colleges Admissions Office (OCAO) and the Cambridge Intercollegiate Applications Office (CIAO). Besides centralizing the administration of admissions, invariably the offices were the main channels of communication between candidates and colleges. Whereas college examinations had been set on a group wide basis, and the dates of each group's examinations were rotated from year to year, in time college examinations were standardized across the three groups and, in cooperation with UCCA, it was agreed that the Oxbridge colleges would complete their selection procedures by 31 January each year. By the mid-1960s, therefore, a much tighter admissions schedule had emerged.

But these were far from over-regulated marketplaces, as events, particularly at Oxford, were soon to prove. Although the 1960s had seen the emergence of tighter procedures, the colleges remained – and indeed still remain – in competition with one another for the best candidates. There was always the temptation therefore to stretch agreed practices in the hope of, if not scooping the jackpot, then of stealing a march on other colleges. At Oxford, college rivalry was reinforced by the use of college awards as 'trumps', that is a college could trump the offer of a commoner's place at another college by 'the bribe' of a scholarship or exhibition which the candidate was then obliged to accept. The Franks Inquiry recorded that the proportion of awards for men had increased from one-quarter of the undergraduate entry in 1923–34 to over one-third in 1964–65. Did the growth reflect more intense competition among colleges as they sought to attract better qualified candidates? Franks recommended that all closed awards should be abolished and that: 'The number of open scholarships held by undergraduates in a college should not exceed 10 per cent of the total number of undergraduates in that college' (ibid.: 413). In fact, during the troubled decade of the 1970s, the number of awards actually increased (from 748 in 1970 to 838 in 1980), although those holding awards as a percentage of total entrants remained fairly steady at 30 per cent (University of Oxford 1970a, 1980a). The 10 per cent target recommended by the Franks Inquiry remained as remote as ever.

The argument in favour of using college awards as 'trumps' was that it encouraged a more even spread of the most talented candidates among the Oxford colleges; that the less eminent colleges could use their awards to compete on more favourable terms. It was also true that entrance awards were very appealing to candidates, for even when the rules were changed to permit candidates to reject awards offered as trumps we discover that in 1982–83 102 out of 625 award winners received their awards from colleges not of their first choice (Committee on Undergraduate Admissions 1983: 22). It was possible, therefore, to consider entrance awards as a mechanism for regulating the flow of talented candidates into the colleges. Of course, the colleges who lost likely undergraduates perhaps felt that their candidates were being poached, and in some cases candidates who lost a place at the college of their first choice must have felt aggrieved. The dividing line between rules that sensibly regulated the market and sharp practice appears very fine.

The potential disputes at Oxford, stemming from the use of college awards as 'trumps', paled into insignificance compared to the heat generated by the various special admissions schemes launched by individual colleges. The scheme that attracted the most publicity was introduced at Hertford College, Oxford, by the college's admissions tutor, Dr Neil Tanner. A guaranteed percentage of the college's places were to be filled by matriculation, that is the only requirement that these candidates had to fulfil were the university's minimum entrance qualifications. They did not have to sit the college entrance examination or obtain high grades at either A or S level, although it was expected that many would do both. This seemingly high-risk strategy was rendered less precarious by in-depth interviews and close liaison with the schools. At least in the short-run, Hertford did indeed appear to have scooped the jackpot as its applications soared (inevitably resulting in a high rejection rate) and its standing in the Norrington Table (which ranked Oxford colleges by the performance of their undergraduates in finals) rose sharply. Inevitably, other colleges jumped on the bandwagon and in the process introduced their own refinements. One innovation was for colleges to form links with particular schools, guaranteeing them a few places again subject to matriculation requirements. It was not long before charges and counter-charges reverberated. For example, were colleges sticking rigidly to their published quotas of matriculation offers or varying the offers to suit their changing circumstances? The semblance of order that had emerged in the 1960s was disappearing fast and many feared the intense intercollegiate rivalry that was developing.

A somewhat different, but equally important, development at Cambridge was the steady increase in the number of conditional offers that colleges were prepared to make. Such offers invariably required candidates to make very high grades at A or even S level. Cambridge's greater willingness to move in this direction was related to the fact that it was a more science-based university, and accordingly many felt that the closer intellectual relationship of the A level science subjects provided an adequate measure of the students' potential. Although the Oxford colleges were prepared to travel some way down the same path, dominant sentiment in the University remained hostile to conditional offers. Between 1970 and 1985, the number of conditional, unconditional and matriculation offers – that is offers which did not require the candidate to follow the college examination route – for Oxford under-graduate candidates expanded from 0 to 11 per cent (University of Oxford 1970a: 1411, 1416; 1985: 30). By 1985 the Cambridge colleges were accepting almost half of their undergraduates without requiring them to sit college examinations (University of Cambridge 1985a: 6).

It is evident that the two Universities had evolved different admissions procedures prior to the changes of the 1980s. Oxford remained firmly com-mitted to college entrance examination, while increasingly the Cambridge colleges were less reliant upon them. There were many candidates at both Oxford and Cambridge who, having been made an unconditional offer, sat the college entrance examination with the incentive of winning an entrance award. As individual colleges started to make their awards on the basis of undergraduate work, rather than entrance examinations, then this incentive declined. It was to be expected, therefore, that the appeal of the college entrance examination would dwindle for Oxford as well as Cambridge candi-dates. However, the continuing sway of the college examinations at Oxford is illustrated by the fact that while between 1980 and 1985 the percentage of post-A level candidates who entered the university via the college entrance examination route declined from 63 to 34 per cent, the pre-A level candidates entering via college examinations grew from 30 to 56 per cent.

Undoubtedly, the various changes that emerged in the 1970s were moti-vated by the desire of individual colleges to broaden their appeal to a wider range of candidates. They were trying to draw more schools into the Ox-bridge orbit. The traditional admissions systems, with their heavy reliance on college entrance examinations, had been seen as unfair because the procedures were allegedly both esoteric and discriminated in favour of cer-tain candidates. But the reformers, while trying to broaden the appeal of

Oxbridge, were also making the general picture more complex. The question is whether the apparent advantage of a wider appeal was worth the greater procedural fragmentation and intense intercollegiate rivalry that was being generated. The tension was especially high at Oxford because of the more deeply entrenched belief in college entrance examinations and the stronger commitment to intercollegiate consensus. At Oxford, conditional and matriculation offers were on the increase, the move to co-educational colleges had stimulated considerable conflict in the 1970s, some colleges were threatening not to consider candidates if they had put certain other colleges as their first choice, and there was a real possibility that at least one college would withdraw from the Oxford Colleges Admissions Office. The potential outcome was chaos rather than fruitful competition.

The final straw at Oxford, as the Committee on Undergraduate Admissions (1983: 1) revealed, was Keble College's proposal 'to introduce a scheme in which applicants for Conditional Offers at Keble would be interviewed at the time of the Entrance Examination', so undermining the current admissions schedule. The Management Committee of the Admissions Office passed a motion, approved by 26 votes to nil with 2 abstentions, that no further changes would be permitted 'until the Colleges collectively have undertaken a review of the total University admissions procedures' (ibid.). Keble agreed to delay the implementation of its proposed scheme 'until the Colleges had decided on the recommendations of the review body', but kept up the pressure by requiring a decision to be reached before October 1983 (ibid.). Although the changes that had taken place at Cambridge caused some internal problems, the Cambridge colleges have always been relaxed about their more fissiparous character and, to some extent, their action on admissions was a response to the Oxford moves. Cambridge's tutorial representatives agreed on 17 February 1984 to set up a working party on admissions that would be composed of one representative from each college and chaired by the vice-chancellor.

Oxford's Report of the Committee on Undergraduate Admissions (referred to hereafter as the Dover Report after its chairman, Sir Kenneth Dover, then Master of Corpus Christi College), although not prepared to state categorically that Oxford's existing admissions procedures were unfair, argued that they should be changed because they were perceived as such. For the Committee a fair admissions procedure would be:

> ... one which neutralizes to the greatest practical extent all variables except the intellectual and temperamental suitability of an applicant for a degree course at Oxford; that is to say, which ensures that applicants have equal opportunity to provide evidence of their academic potential irrespective of age, social class, economic status and educational background (ibid.: 8).

In sharp contrast, the Report of Cambridge's Working Party was far less reflective about established procedures and devoted nearly all its space to describing how its proposed new practices would work. On the admittedly slender evidence of these two reports, the Cambridge colleges come across as more self-confident institutions and less guilt-ridden about past admissions procedures. However, Cambridge's advocacy of more simplified procedures was very explicit:

> In recent years, dissatisfaction with the procedures for admission to Cambridge and Oxford has grown both within the Universities and outside. At Cambridge, Colleges in general have come to depend more on public examination results, though the precise balance between the use of CCE [Cambridge College Examination] results and public examinations has varied from College to College and even by subject within Colleges, giving rise to complaints from schools and candidates for admission that application is a complex and forbidding process and chances of success may depend on a candidate's random selection of a College (Cambridge Tutorial Representatives 1984: 2).

As at Oxford, the intention was to end this muddle by making 'the admissions procedures more uniform and to appear simpler and closer to those used by other universities'. As their problems were similar, and they had a long history of sharing their experiences of admissions procedures, it may seem surprising that the respective working parties arrived at different solutions.

Oxford's Committee on Undergraduate Admissions reported in June 1983 and recommended that its proposals should come into effect in 1985–86. It was proposed that the Oxford colleges should have two modes of entry. The first, mode E, would be centred around a written examination which was similar to the traditional college entrance examinations. It could be sat only by candidates in the fourth term of the sixth form, so abolishing the competition between fourth- and seventh-term candidates. Successful candidates could be offered places subject to meeting the university's matriculation regulations. The other method of entry, mode N, would be for candidates seeking entry on the basis of conditional and unconditional offers, that is candidates who already knew their A and/or S level grades or had yet to sit them. For both modes of entry, interviews and references would continue to play their part, and colleges could require mode N candidates to submit written work or take an oral test, although the Committee discouraged the setting of written tests. The Committee hoped that this central plank of its reform package would be applied as widely as possible in order to standardize entry procedures across faculties and colleges. For example, while all candidates who wished to study medicine were required to sit the college entrance examination, the Dover Report urged the medical faculty to consider mode N candidates. Furthermore, it was argued that there should be no quotas for the differing categories of applicants and that colleges should *not* state preferences as to which mode of entry they preferred.

Besides trying to standardize the modes of entry, the Dover Report also made a number of important additional recommendations: college awards should be disassociated from entrance examinations, a college was not to make an offer to a candidate who already held an offer from a college higher on his or her preference list (in other words no trumping), candidates could make open applications rather than apply to named colleges, and subject tutors were encouraged to organize their applicants on a university-wide basis if this was felt to be advantageous. Inasmuch as the Dover Report reaffirmed the commitment to college examinations, it cannot be described as a radical document, but none the less the adoption of its recommendations meant that the admissions process was reformed very significantly.

In the sense that Cambridge's Working Party on Admissions (Cambridge Tutorial Representatives 1985) recommended the abolition of college entrance examinations, it can claim to be a more radical document. In place of the college examinations, the working party put forward the Sixth Term Examination Papers (STEP) which could be used 'entirely at the discretion of an individual college', although colleges could not require candidates to sit more than two papers (ibid.: 4). STEP was to be a public, rather than a college or university, examination and it was possible that non-Cambridge candidates would sit the papers. Since the dependence of the Cambridge colleges on the CCE had been declining steadily, the decision to jettison it was not as dramatic as may have first appeared. Certainly, its implications for the Cambridge colleges were no more far-reaching than the recommendations of the Dover Report were for the Oxford colleges. In a sense, the colleges of both universities sought to reaffirm the past: Oxford by refurbishing its college examinations and Cambridge by accepting the inevitability of the dwindling importance of the CCE.

Besides changing the examination system, Cambridge's Working Party also wanted to standardize various features of the admissions process: to put in place a detailed timetable, to control strictly any written tests that candidates could be asked to take when called for interview, and to introduce a standard interview form. Clearly, within the new admissions procedures, interviews would occupy a crucial position. Unless the candidate had already sat public examinations, then the interview provided the most telling evidence on which to make a judgement. Of course, bets could be hedged by requiring high grades in A or S levels, and there was also the STEP option. However, as comparatively small institutions, the Cambridge colleges had to avoid the risk of being too heavily over- or under-subscribed, which making conditional offers entailed. It is not too surprising, therefore, that the working party wanted interviewers to record an interview score; both the competition for places and the need to match closely supply and demand necessitated precise judgements. Since Cambridge had already disassociated college awards from admissions, there was no need for the working party to push the colleges in this direction. As at Oxford, candidates were to be permitted to apply without listing their preferred colleges. Finally, except for the distribution of medical candidates (note universities are awarded quotas of medical students), the old college groupings were to disappear.

Probably quite wisely the report did not delve too deeply into the question of whether it had constructed a fairer admissions system. But it was felt to be simpler, closer in practice to that operating in other universities, and yet still giving tutors the opportunity to see the examination work of candidates. While eroding the differences between Cambridge and other British universities, it also confirmed the university's exceptional nature. None the less, it was possible to argue that in certain cases the colleges were justified in using the STEP examination because of the fierce competition among very able candidates for a limited number of places. The STEP examination could be most usefully employed in helping to resolve marginal cases.

Excluding some minor but interesting reservations, the two reports were accepted by the colleges of their respective universities, but the fact that the Oxford and Cambridge colleges had chosen to take different paths caused both surprise and concern. The surprise was a reflection of the popularly held, and not altogether inaccurate view, that the two universities shared a common heritage which they would want to preserve. Schools, or rather those submitting large numbers of Oxbridge candidates, showed some concern. Obviously, it caused complications for them if the universities were to operate radically different systems and there were even absurd murmurings that either one or the other (although never both!) of the universities could expect to be boycotted. The concern may still be there, but there is no evidence to suggest that the schools which supply candidates have failed to cope with the changes and the alleged added complications.

The divergence of procedures was obviously purposeful. There have long been scheduled meetings between Oxford and Cambridge admissions tutors and Oxford's Committee on Undergraduate Admissions claimed to have discussed its interim report with the Executive Committee of the Cambridge Tutorial Representatives. Oxford could have waited until Cambridge had completed its own deliberations (Cambridge referred to Oxford's 'unilateral action'), but it was under pressure from colleges that were determined to go their own way unless the Committee acted speedily. Of course, the Cambridge colleges could have followed the Oxford lead but argued that the internal opposition to fourth-term examinations was considerable and produced evidence from the schools to show that if there had to be a choice between a fourth- or sixth-term examination, then a clear majority preferred the latter (ibid.: App. C). The simplest explanation of the divergence is that the two universities and their colleges, for all their shared heritage, reached the conclusion that their interests in the future would be best served by following different admissions procedures.

It could be argued that both Oxford and Cambridge are in such a commanding position within the university hierarchy that no matter what paths they had chosen to follow candidates would have been compelled to have adapted themselves accordingly. Both universities have reviewed their reforms and decided to continue with them substantially intact. One suspects that as long as the two universities continue to receive a more than adequate supply of good candidates, then they will persist with present practices. If there is political, as opposed to market, pressure again the colleges will adjust accordingly. For example, not everyone in Oxford accepted the view that seventh-term candidates should be barred from college examinations, and it is difficult not to draw the conclusion that the majority for the Dover proposals was guided as much by the public perception of the established procedures as by its own convictions. In the last analysis, therefore, the colleges are driven by highly practical considerations and it is these, rather than the high ground of what is most desirable educationally, that will determine what is changed and how.

Although the divergence of outcomes can be best explained by the evolution of the admissions procedures at the two universities, coupled with college perceptions on how best to secure their own long-term interests, this is not to deny that the two reforming committees interpreted their tasks in different ways. Oxford's committee saw fairness as the creation of procedures that treated equal candidates equally. While Cambridge's Working Party made no attempt to define fairness explicitly, it advocated proposals that would bring the Cambridge colleges closer into line with the practices of other universities while making available to tutors a mechanism that would enable them 'to discriminate more finely amongst candidates' (ibid.: 3). If Cambridge's admissions procedures were to be different, it was because they needed to be; this was not distinctiveness for the sake of being different. In both universities there was the expectation that the changes would broaden their social appeal, but neither advocated this (at least publicly) as one of their goals. The Oxbridge colleges have tried to widen their social networks in a variety of ways: producing more and better information and distributing it more widely, making visits to schools that rarely submit candidates, holding open days for sixth-formers at the colleges, and offering short-term schoolmaster/mistress fellowships. It is these additional efforts, rather than changes to admissions procedures, that are designed to broaden their social intake.

The admissions procedures are perceived, therefore, as neutral mechanisms for enabling the colleges to select the most suitable candidates. There is no reason not to describe them as fair in relation to the goals that they are designed to achieve. The Oxford colleges can now publicize their procedures as offering candidates a choice of entry modes (Pearson 1989: 11), while Cambridge can argue that their system is not so very different from that operated by other universities – it has the appeal of familiarity. But whether in the long run the critics will be satisfied remains to be seen, for their definition of fairness is about results rather than means. As long as Oxford and Cambridge have undergraduate populations that are socially distinctive from those of other British universities, then they remain more vulnerable to political intervention.

Although the Cambridge Tutorial Representatives had been worried by the increasing diversity of routes by which candidates could enter the university, this concern did not figure prominently in the report of their working party. The working party did close some of the options, for example by abolishing the CCE and urging that special arrangements for particular schools should be ended (Interview: Bowkett and Mitchell, 15 June 1987), but the emphasis was upon the standardization of procedures. As a consequence, the colleges could use one of a number of options within an agreed overall package all of which, with the exception of those colleges which wanted to make use of STEP, were in line with practice elsewhere. As we have noted, one of the pressures for change at Oxford was the increasing unease at the fragmentation of the admissions process. Oxford was more bothered than Cambridge by the proliferation of special schemes and there were powerful forces that wanted to limit the options available to colleges; it was as much a question of restricting procedures as of regulating them. In the summary of its recommendations, the Dover Report stated categorically that there should be only two selection procedures (Committee on Undergraduate Admissions 1983: 25). The Dover Report also urged a 5-year moratorium on change – and as if in fear that it would not last, argued that: 'All colleges should agree to adopt the same procedures and agree that those procedures should not be changed in the future *except by the proper machinery*' (ibid.: 25, our emphasis). The implication is that the process of change needs to be controlled at the intercollegiate level and that individual colleges should not act unilaterally. It could be argued that Cambridge was proposing variations on only one procedure, but significantly its working party chose not to emphasize that point and in its report paid no attention to potential mavericks.

If fairness was to be reinforced by simplicity, it was critical that the individual colleges at Oxford and Cambridge had to accept the spirit of the reform packages. This meant accepting constraints upon their freedom of action. The Dover Report had proposed that all the Oxford colleges and faculties should accept the two modes of entry and, consequently, there should be no specification in the Oxford prospectus of preferences for one entry mode over the other. In fact, this proposal was rejected by the colleges and the prospectus records preferred entry modes by faculty and college (see, for example, University of Oxford 1990c: 247). This gives rise to a situation in which simplicity evaporates rapidly. While candidates entering to study medicine 'must enter by mode E' (ibid.) – which at least has the virtue of consistency even if it contravenes one of the Dover Report's recommendations – for several subjects some colleges express a preference for one particular mode of entry while other colleges express no preference. Even more bizarre is that New College prefers mode N for its jurisprudence candidates, Queen's College and Mansfield College prefer mode E, and none of the other colleges express a preference! For modern languages, St Edmund Hall has a preference for mode N candidates, whereas six other colleges prefer mode E candidates. Medicine excepted, it appears that tutors within the colleges are responsible for these variations, that the faculties either have no view or they lack the authority to impose it. There may be excellent reasons for these differences, but they make it more difficult to substantiate the claim that Oxford has established simple admissions procedures. The two modes of entry may be intelligible and fair but how the colleges operate them introduces real complexities for prospective candidates. How are they to interpret the differences in college preferences? Having worked that out, how rigidly do they adhere to the listed preferences? What bearing do the differences have upon their choice of college? What image does this create in the eyes of candidates and their schools? Or is the pulling power of Oxford so great that this is an irrelevant consideration?

In fact, a more important issue than the character of the admissions procedures appears to be at stake. In Oxford's 1991–92 undergraduate prospectus of those colleges expressing a preferred entry mode for candidates (17 colleges are listed as expressing preferences), there were only 0 in favour of mode N compared to 72 in favour of mode E (ibid.). This may reflect the wish to avoid the uncertainty of matching candidates to the number of college places generated by a system of conditional offers, but a more likely reason is that Oxford tutors are inclined to believe that the mode E entry route will reveal more fully the kind of qualities they are seeking in candidates. In other words, the predictive qualities of A and S levels remain suspect. The risk, therefore, of admitting more candidates through the mode N entry route is that it could change the character of Oxford, and the intention of college tutors is to resist this. Cambridge, by way of comparison, has accepted that risk, for its colleges have made large-scale conditional offers for many years and have lived with the consequences. Even STEP is not seen as an examination that will bring out different qualities in candidates; it is essentially a means of providing further information to enable tutors to make up their minds in difficult cases.

Cambridge's Working Party wanted more information to be made available to candidates about the admissions practices of individual colleges and, therefore, recommended that college preferences for modes of entry should be published in the University prospectus (Cambridge Tutorial Representatives 1984: 4). The consequence was the publication of a complex table which summarizes college entrance policies (Cambridge Tutorial Representatives 1990: 124–5). Although some colleges have the same preferred entry mode regardless of the candidate's intended course, not one course has a preferred mode of entry regardless of college. The differentiation between STEP, S and A levels may not be that great (although whether candidates would agree is another matter), but again it raises the question of how to account for the variations and how candidates should respond to them if they wish to maximize their chances of entry. For colleges to state preferred entry modes, and this applies equally to the Oxford colleges, implies that the tutors are not so much matching candidates and entry modes (and note the report of Cambridge's Working Party stated explicitly that STEP would be a particular help with marginal candidates) but fitting candidates into a mode which either they prefer personally or best suits the colleges' interests. They are circumscribing the choice that the Dover Report wanted to give Oxford's candidates. In 1984, the Cambridge Tutorial Representatives had referred to the complaint that the admissions process was such that candidates sometimes felt that success could depend upon the random selection of a college. It is difficult to see how the situation has changed. At Cambridge, this is further reinforced by the fact that some colleges (for example, Christ's,

Fitzwilliam and Girton) are still prepared to offer places to pre-A level candidates subject only to their satisfying the university's matriculation requirements. Special entry modes, therefore, are still flourishing at Cambridge.

Cambridge can defend itself on more substantial grounds than the marginality of the differences between the preferred entry modes. It can claim fairly that it was not the intention of the working party to impose a straitjacket upon the colleges, but rather to standardize the modes and let the colleges impose those that they felt were most appropriate. But the continuation of the special entry schemes suggests that the modes have not been standardized and, while the variety may appear to insiders to be a colourful mosaic, to outsiders it is more likely to conjure up chaos. At both Oxford and Cambridge, the colleges have therefore shown their commitment to maintaining their individuality on questions of admissions. The significance of the changes brought about by the reforms of the 1980s cannot be doubted. Cambridge's abolition of the CCE coupled with the introduction of STEP, and Oxford's restriction of its college entrance examinations to only fourth-term candidates, were decisions that reverberated through the universities. To their credit the colleges endorsed them, but it is equally clear that not only do the colleges retain formal control of the admissions process but also they impose upon it an interpretation which they feel best accommodates their own special circumstances. The procedures now may be fairer, more akin – especially at Cambridge – to what prevails elsewhere, but it is still pertinent to ponder whether there is indeed one admissions system for each university or a number of systems shaped by a range of separate college interests.

Controlling the admissions process

Although the important changes of the 1980s were instigated by intercollegiate bodies at both Oxford and Cambridge, the formal control of the admissions process still rests with the individual colleges. The colleges have interpreted the packages that their reforming committees produced in a manner that best suited their own interests and in the process, if not exactly thwarted, then at least mitigated the drive for simpler procedures. Moreover, some would argue that the conflicting recommendations to candidates intending to pursue the same course at different colleges not only suggests a confused model but also one that is inherently unfair. To treat similar candidates differently implies that the process is geared to the interests of the colleges rather than to the needs of the candidates.

However, to say that the colleges have ultimate formal control of the admissions process at the Universities of Oxford and Cambridge does not take the analysis very far. The overall structure of control is composed of several layers and the purpose of this section of the chapter is to describe and interpret their interrelationship. There are the colleges themselves and all college fellows have some interest in admissions. Secondly, there are the intercollegiate bodies which have been developed to co-ordinate and, more arguably, to simplify procedures. Thirdly, there are the universities whose faculties and departments require an adequate flow of suitably qualified undergraduates. Finally, there are those bodies – such as the Standing Conference on University Entrance (SCUE) – which have both general administrative and supervisory responsibilities.

In the evidence that Oxford's Franks Inquiry took from the colleges, they reaffirmed their claim to admit their own undergraduates. While some colleges made the point more vigorously than others, it was a common thread in the evidence of all of them (University of Oxford 1965: Pt 13). At one time the right was based on the common college residence of most undergraduates and fellows, and the fact that college fellows taught their own students. Academic and social changes have weakened both arguments: for many undergraduates, teaching revolves around university laboratories rather than college tutorials, and family and faculty duties have drawn many teaching fellows away from the demands and pleasures of college life. It is important to stress, however, that although these changes have weakened the case for colleges selecting their own students, they have not destroyed it. Even science students will receive some tutorial instruction in their own college supervised by a college fellow, and most fellows continue to take a keen interest in the welfare of their college. For example, although it is customary to scorn publicly the ranking of colleges by the final examination results (of which Oxford's Norrington Table is the best known, and perhaps soon to disappear, example), in private they are taken seriously by many fellows. Perhaps the most critical defence of college control of admissions is that this is part of the definition of a college. If they lost control of admissions, they would forfeit the right to define their membership. In other words, controlling the admissions process, like managing their endowments, gives them the potential to shape their own character. In this context, it is hard to imagine that the open entry applications permitted by the present rules of both universities are ever likely to be very popular. The admissions process is partly about making a personal commitment to a college and an open application appears an unwise gambit for a candidate.

Since 1945, admissions tutors have become more powerful figures within the colleges. This is especially true at Cambridge where they can be full-time appointees (combining the admissions post with other administrative responsibilities) and may, on occasions, interview all candidates. Although the formal decisions on whom to admit are made by course tutors, the admissions tutors are well-placed both to influence decisions at the margins (resolving conflicts over particular candidates and the precise balance between subject groups) and to initiate broader changes (for example, to stimulate applications from schools that have not submitted candidates in the past). Although practice varied, it is evident that the masters of many colleges at both universities were very influential in the admissions process up to the 1950s. Although there are some exceptions, their influence has waned. The Franks Inquiry asked the college masters how many places they still had the power to fill. They suggested that at best it was three or four places, and more often than not, none (ibid.: Pt 7). Many were nostalgic about their relinquished rights. As the admissions process has become more structured, demanding and professional, it is not surprising that the admissions tutors have increased their authority. Some tutors may feel that they have more important things on which to spend their time, perceiving a heavy involvement in the admissions process as imposing onerous burdens while bringing few professional rewards. In such circumstances, it is the professionals – in this case the admissions tutors – to whom authority has gravitated, including, so one tutor told us, the ability to work the procedures, albeit only at the margins, contrary to college statutes, so great was his autonomy.

The most significant development in the control of the admissions procedures has been the growth of intercollegiate responsibility. From the 1920s, the colleges at both Oxford and Cambridge were organized in groups for the purposes of conducting entrance examinations and sharing out candidates. But major changes have occurred since the 1960s with a combination of variables intensifying the pressures for reform: the sheer increase in the number of candidates generating the need for more administrative support and smoother procedures, the more exposed political position of Oxbridge admissions demanding a response to the challenge, and the creation of UCCA raising the question of how the Oxbridge colleges were to relate to it. To be effective all three pressures demanded an intercollegiate response. One consequence was an increase in the authority of the admissions tutors, for they were the persons who invariably represented their colleges on the intercollegiate bodies that recommended policy. They also had the task of selling intercollegiate policies to their colleges. Increased institutionalization helped therefore to create a new class of professionals out of full-time academics.

In 1964, Noel Annan had chaired, on behalf of Cambridge's General Board, a Committee on Teaching. His committee produced a report which recommended the creation of an intercollegiate body to assist the rational planning of teaching by enabling the colleges and the university to co-ordinate their respective requirements (University of Cambridge 1964). The outcome was the Cambridge Tutorial Representatives Committee, which until recently has supervised admissions procedures on behalf of the colleges. The committee is composed of representatives of all the colleges with the vice-chancellor in the chair and the senior tutor of the vice-chancellor's college acting as the committee's secretary, so symbolizing the Committee's role in co-ordinating university and college business. Although the Tutorial Representatives Committee lacks the executive authority that Annan wanted it to have (how reformers love powerful committees), it has proven a very influential body on a whole range of issues, including admissions. For example, it was this committee that set up the 1984 Working Party on Admissions and which steered the reform proposals through the individual colleges.

Since the Lent Term of 1985–86, the Tutorial Representatives Committee has ceded supervision of the admissions procedures to the Admissions

Forum. As a comparatively self-contained area of business, one specific committee can deal conveniently with admissions issues, a move which helped to alleviate the burdens of the tutorial representatives. The Admissions Forum has a representative from each college, the admissions tutor, and has an inner sanctum known as the Executive Committee. This change in control was in fact one of the recommendations of the working party's final report on admission to Cambridge (1985: 5). For the most part, the Admissions Forum is autonomous of the Tutorial Representatives Committee, for the latter are not expected to discuss the business of the Admissions Forum again, and only 'in exceptional cases' would either the Admissions Forum or a college be expected to raise a particular item for discussion at the Tutorial Representatives Committee (ibid.: 3). At the intercollegiate level, therefore, the Tutorial Representatives Committee remains a rarely used final court of appeal on admissions issues.

In the early 1960s, the Oxford colleges were engaged in one of their periodic reviews of admissions procedures. According to evidence presented to the Franks Inquiry, the working party that reported in 1962 also argued that 'it would be advisable to set up a permanent body representing colleges to watch over the working of the Scheme' (University of Oxford 1965: Pt 14), but it opposed the idea of placing it under the jurisdiction of the Senior Tutors' Committee, Oxford's equivalent to Cambridge's Tutorial Representatives Committee. A Management Committee, composed mainly of college representatives (invariably admissions tutors), was established as the controlling body and met for the first time in December 1962. The final authority of the Management Committee is exercised at its termly meetings with representatives of all the colleges. Items can be referred back to the colleges, but when a substantive motion is finally put it constitutes 'a formal decision of the Associated Colleges if it is carried by a majority of two-thirds of the colleges present and voting' (Oxford Colleges Admissions Office 1969). In other words, there is majority voting, but there is every reason to believe that, like university government, intercollegiate government operates consensually. But, as we have seen, this is not to say that consensus always prevails!

At both universities, therefore, the intercollegiate control of admissions has been placed in the hands of one body, Cambridge's Admissions Forum and Oxford's Management Committee. In parallel fashion, the administration of the admissions process has become much more centralized over time. The administrative arm at Oxford is the Oxford Colleges Admissions Office (OCAO), while the Cambridge equivalent is the Cambridge Inter-Collegiate Applications Office (CIAO). It is hard not to form the impression that the Oxford office is a more potent body, although this may simply be a reflection of its location in Wellington Square alongside the university's central administrative bodies. The Cambridge bureaucratic apparatus is geographically more dispersed and seedier in appearance, and the admissions office (which, of course, is a college body) is no exception. Obviously, the respective offices perform similar functions: publicity, the processing of applications, and the co-ordination of the admissions schedule. However, the Oxford office has been operating somewhat longer (founded in 1962 as opposed to 1966) and it has administered college entrance examinations, something the Cambridge office never did. Although in formal terms the OCAO is an intercollegiate body – it was established as a separate company, its 12 directors are the management committee members and it has its own seal (Baskerville 1986) – to enter its premises in Wellington Square is, at least to the outsider, to feel the embrace of the university. The point is reinforced by the prominent part that the university played in the creation of the OCAO. The Working Party on Admissions that had recommended the office's creation had in fact been set up on the initiative of the vice-chancellor, and its secretary was A.J. Dorey who is the university's current registrar. In order to achieve a smooth launch, the university lent the office temporary administrative staff and made an interest-free loan. Clearly, the university authorities wanted this office very badly, to the extent of backing it with their own resources.

Despite its location and the university's support for its establishment, the OCAO, like the ICAO, has always been an administrative arm of the Oxford colleges and as long as admissions is their responsibility will remain so. The only significant intrusion of the universities has been to lay down matriculation requirements that candidates have to meet before they can become undergraduates. Over the years, as the faculties have relaxed their own requirements, so the universities' matriculation demands have eased.

It should not be assumed that this comparative absence of a university presence has meant that the college control of admissions has not caused the universities any problems. In a biting passage, Annan's Committee on Teaching observed:

> The fact that there has been almost no liaison between the University and the Colleges over admissions of undergraduates and their distribution among subjects has led to two difficulties. First, Faculties and Departments have not known until the beginning of the Michelmas Term how many undergraduates they would have to teach. Secondly, predictions of numbers based on study of long-term trends have sometimes proved totally inadequate because of unexpected fluctuations (University of Cambridge 1964: 1614).

In a follow-up that is so self-evident that it must be intended to be read ironically, the report comments:

> It is obviously important both that the staff and facilities of Faculties and Departments and the numbers of undergraduates reading their subjects should bear a satisfactory relationship to each other, and that Faculties and Departments should have sufficient warning of the numbers they will have to teach to be able to make adequate preparation (ibid.).

Remember Annan is not describing the unreformed Cambridge of the nineteenth century but rather the university in the very throes of expanding rapidly. This was a time which either accepted inefficiency more nonchalantly than is general in contemporary universities or had a sufficient reserve of resources to resolve the last minute tensions that it generated.

Interestingly, the Franks Inquiry had described Oxford as a world in which university and college co-ordination was equally unlikely but which, at least according to the Inquiry, had caused few planning difficulties. Thus we read:

> No great effort has so far been necessary; natural forces of supply and demand have produced an undergraduate population the distribution of which has not seemed unreasonable.... But apart from the development of Engineering Science, neither the increase in total numbers nor the great swing towards scientific subjects owes much, if anything, to conscious forward planning by the University or the colleges; it has been the result of pressure of good candidates for admission and of a host of decisions made in the colleges about their own individual policies, often without reference to the University or to each other (University of Oxford 1966a: 57–8).

If this was an accurate perspective, then, in view of Cambridge's apparent difficulties, Oxford seems to have been incredibly fortunate. However, one of the central messages of the Franks Report was that if Oxford were to prosper in the future, then it had to engage in more forward planning in which the voices of the university and the colleges were harmonized. On admissions policy the proposals of the Franks Inquiry were draconian. Despite the fact that the Hebdomadal Council in its evidence to the Inquiry had expressed itself as satisfied with the situation following the reforms of the early 1960s, the Franks Report recommended that the Hebdomadal Council should have overall responsibility for admissions policy, that the admissions office should be incorporated into the university's administration, and that its Management Committee should be reconstituted as a joint committee of the Hebdomadal Council, the General Board and the proposed Council of Colleges (ibid.: 82–3). For the Oxford colleges, this was far too high a price to pay for better university–college liaison and the recommendations were rejected.

The key variables involved in university–college liaison on admissions are the overall size of each year's entry and its distribution by subject. The universities have been constrained in these matters by the state but not to the extent that the targets have become a straitjacket. For a few subjects, there are imposed quotas of students (e.g. architecture, dentistry, medicine, veterinary science and PGCE students). The numbers are known in advance and the colleges decide how to distribute them among themselves. Universities have been required by the UGC, and now the UFC, to produce plans in which they project their student numbers by subject. However, the projected numbers are not carved in stone and in the present context where there is considerable political pressure to expand the overall size of the university undergraduate population, then the very idea of detailed forward planning is problematic to say the least. The best that can be expected, and perhaps no more is necessary, is a clear idea of overall student numbers and their division by major academic areas (arts, science, social studies and education) and level of study (undergraduates and postgraduates) coupled with more flexible subject breakdowns excepting those few cases where the numbers are determined centrally.

However, the fact that all universities, including Oxford and Cambridge, have been required in recent years to produce university plans which contain projections on student numbers by subject has required the colleges and universities to cooperate more closely. At both Oxford and Cambridge, much of the responsibility for this cooperation rests with the senior tutors who work through the Tutorial Representatives Committee at Cambridge and the Senior Tutors' Committee at Oxford. As there are separate college admissions bodies at both universities (Cambridge's Admissions Forum and Oxford's Management Committee), inevitably the questions on students numbers, their subject make-up and distribution amongst the colleges have tended to devolve to these bodies. Cambridge's Wass Report (while wishing to reconstitute the Tutorial Representatives Committee) has praised the work of the Executive Committee of the Admissions Forum which has met with the Needs Committee of the General Board to resolve the question of student target numbers by subject. At Cambridge this matter, plus other admissions issues that affect both the colleges and the university, will be dealt with in future by a Joint Consultative Committee on Admissions, containing representatives of the General Board, the Council, the Tutorial Representatives Committee and the Admissions Forum. The need for further college–university co-ordination at Cambridge was stimulated by the university's agreement to admit more home-based undergraduates to engineering courses (under the auspices of one of the special programmes launched in the 1980s) and the subsequent failure of the colleges to reach the student target numbers. One can take the view that such shortcomings are inevitable from time to time within collegiate universities, but presumably they cannot be allowed to occur too often, thus the recent institutional commitment to closer future liaison.

The comparative evidence on entry modes suggests that at Cambridge the colleges are much more likely than at Oxford to impose their own preferred modes. Several of the Oxford colleges record a dominant preferred entry mode for certain subjects: mode E for modern languages, mathematics and modern history, and to lesser extent, mode N for geology (University of Oxford: 1990c: 247). It would be too strong to say that these faculties are imposing their views upon the colleges, but it would be fair to suggest that a widely held faculty view is being reflected in the colleges. These observations should be treated cautiously as Cambridge has more alternative entry modes than Oxford, and thus there is more opportunity to appear fissiparous. What may be occurring is a convergence of interests so that all the parties are increasingly involved in making sure that they have the right number of high-quality undergraduates, an acceptable balance of subject numbers and the appropriate means of ensuring that these goals can be met. None the less, it remains true that while academic potential is a key variable for both the colleges and faculties/departments, the former are likely to be interested in a wider range of individual qualities.

Despite the potency of the internal forces that shape the admissions process at both Oxford and Cambridge, it is impossible to understand developments in the pattern of control without considering the external pressures. Just as it is evident that changes to the procedures – that is to make them fairer and simpler – were influenced by outside political forces, so the control of those procedures has been reshaped partly in response to external administrative demands. Indeed, it could be argued that the administrative pressure for change has been more effective than the political pressure. We have already discussed the planning demands of the DES (to contain the costs of college fees and thus by implication placing controls on student numbers) and of the UGC/UFC (to require universities to submit projected student numbers by subject, coupled with the imposition of some quotas) and how these necessitated further college–university policy co-ordination. Of earlier, and greater, significance were the external pressures that led to the creation of the admissions offices and the concomitant increase in intercollegiate control of the admissions process.

Although the Crowther Report had expressed its approval of college entrance examinations, including the system of scholarships, it had been less than impressed with the administrative efficiency of the Oxbridge admissions process; indeed, it was highly critical of university admissions in general. The pressure for change was obvious: the increase in the number of candidates and the impending creation of new universities demanded a more rational admissions system, one which would co-ordinate efficiently the demands of candidates and the courses that the universities offered. The Committee of Vice-Chancellors and Principals (CVCP) was persuaded that the universities needed to put their own house in order, otherwise changes would be imposed upon them. The outcome was the creation in 1958 of 'an *ad hoc* committee under the chairmanship of Sir Philip Morris, Vice-Chancellor of the University of Bristol, to consider what could be done to reduce the difficulties of the candidates and the schools caused by the increasing competition for entry to universities' (UCCA 1961–63: 1). The outcome was the creation of the Universities Central Council for Admissions (UCCA), which since 1962 has been the central clearing house for candidates applying to British universities.

Initially, neither Oxford nor Cambridge joined UCCA, and until they had established effective admissions offices it is difficult to see how they could have done so. It is likely that the increase in applications to the Oxbridge colleges, coupled with the internal pressures for reform, would have been sufficient to have brought about new structures and procedures, but the creation of UCCA undoubtedly speeded up the changes. Certainly, this view was confirmed by Lord Annan in his evidence to the Franks Inquiry:

Oxford and Cambridge are at present purring over the splendid co-operation between colleges concerning the vexed question of admissions. But does anyone believe that the present satisfactory agreement would have been reached unless the Committee of Vice-Chancellors had announced the setting up of UCCA and asked Oxbridge to finish their admissions for the year by 31 January? (University of Oxford 1965: Pt 11).

Interestingly, UCCA offered the Oxbridge colleges a carrot for joining the system. The Oxbridge colleges agreed to complete their admissions cycle by 31 January (invariably the Cambridge colleges had completed it by that date) and in return they were given 'a cast iron guarantee' by John Fulton, the chairman of UCCA, that until that date they would have first choice of the available candidates (University of Oxford 1962: 2). The 1962 Oxford Working Party on Admissions reflected that 'The concession of our "clear run" to the end of January is generous and should not be endangered' (ibid.: 11). What 'the clear run' amounted to is that other universities would not require a candidate to reach a decision on any offer that he or she had been made until the end of January.

Although UCCA was no more than a postbox, it required the Oxford and Cambridge colleges both to firm up their admissions schedules and to present a unified administrative front on admissions issues. There was no way that UCCA could have dealt with the colleges individually; if Oxford and Cambridge colleges were to become part of the general university infrastructure, they required both a central administrative apparatus through which the parties could liaise, and a policy-making machinery that could resolve the problems that such liaison might incur. For all the tension between colleges that may be generated by their barely disguised competition for good candidates, it is important not to forget this critical unifying force.

As the Oxbridge colleges were comparatively small institutions that wished to teach the undergraduates they admitted, they always had a concern for their student numbers and the subjects they were studying. Over time, as the state saw the need for higher education to engage in forward planning, so the colleges have been forced to share this interest with their universities. Even without this explicit external pressure, it was obvious that the universities and the colleges would need to liaise more closely if student and faculty numbers were to be interdependent during periods of rapid change. Although it is plausible to argue that the liaison was too long in the making, and even now fails to work as smoothly as it might, none the less it has arrived and gives the universities a much larger say in the admissions process. Where the colleges appear to remain supreme is in their continuing defining of the admissions procedures. However, although the individual colleges formally control these matters, they are increasingly regulated by intercollegiate bodies. In theory, the individual colleges can choose to establish their own procedures; in practice, they exhibit their individuality within parameters determined at the intercollegiate level. This is not to say that there is no tension between individual colleges and the intercollegiate decision makers. At both Oxford and Cambridge, the determination of the individual colleges to prescribe preferred modes of entry has weakened the push for simpler and more uniform admissions procedures. However, despite these manifestations of college independence, the intercollegiate level of government and administration is now so strong, coupled with the enhanced inter-penetration of college and university structures, that both Oxford and Cambridge can be described more accurately as intercollegiate universities, as federal rather than confederal institutions. The implication is that, although in statutory terms the intercollegiate bodies are subject to the control of the individual colleges, in reality they have acquired considerable legitimacy along with the autonomy and discretion which accompany it. Finally, it should not be forgotten that the creation of UCCA played a significant part in hastening these developments. The state's drive for administrative efficiency can sometimes have profound political repercussions beyond its own shores.

Conclusions

The colleges of the Universities of Oxford and Cambridge believe that they now have fairer and simpler admissions procedures and in the past few years there has been only muted criticism of the so-called Oxbridge admissions lottery. However, should there be a Labour government in the near future, this could change rapidly and it will be interesting to see whether the critics will be mollified by procedural change alone. We think not, and the colleges will have to demonstrate that the reforms of the 1980s have modified the social composition of their undergraduate populations. However, attention in recent years has moved away from the social class composition of student populations to the representation of women and mature students. In terms of these wider social variables, it should prove easier for Oxbridge to withstand its critics.

The changes of the 1980s confirmed the already diverging admissions policies of the two universities. Oxford is irrevocably wedded to college entrance examinations, whereas Cambridge is prepared to make offers on the basis of the candidate's performance in public examinations. Whether this makes Oxford more of a collegiate university than Cambridge is debatable, but it does mean that the Oxford and Cambridge colleges view their functions differently. The initial negative reaction in certain quarters to the contradictory paths taken by the two universities has all but disappeared. Given the prestige of Oxbridge, and the simple fact that the colleges at neither university were not to be pressured into premature change, then there was no alternative but to accommodate the differences.

Although the procedures may now be both fairer and simpler, this does not preclude the possibility of further rationalization. But rationalization can run up against college obduracy, an obstacle of which the Dover Report was only too well aware:

> It would not be hard for a small group of like-minded people to devise an admissions system of dazzling simplicity which would be abhorrent to most Colleges. It would, however, be pointless.... Our task has been to construct a 'package' which will be more acceptable to more people

than the present system (Committee on Undergraduate Admissions 1983: 3).

The problem is where to strike the balance between 'dazzling simplicity' and what the colleges are prepared to accept. Obviously, the Dover Report believed that the Oxford colleges would apply the proposed twin entry modes across all subjects. Their failure to do so may, however, only be temporary, and it is conceivable that over time the recommendations of the Dover Report will be adopted in full. In Oxford's 1987–88 undergraduate prospectus, 14 colleges expressed 83 preferences for one entry mode or the other; for entry in 1991–92, 17 colleges have recorded 80 preferences. The support for the college examination route is especially strong among tutors in modern languages, mathematics and to a lesser extent modern history. Outside these subjects, and indeed even for these subjects, the twin entry mode is the norm. Is it too much to expect that the Oxford colleges will standardize their entry requirements, so that candidates applying to different colleges to read the same subject can expect to be faced with identical preconditions? Or are we to believe that such 'dazzling simplicity' is so abhorrent to a minority of college tutors that the rationalizers shall not pass?

The clear advantage of the STEP examination is that Cambridge's tutors can see the papers of individual candidates. It is open to question, however, as to how useful the STEP examination is in helping tutors to make up their minds about candidates. Of the 3117 candidates accepted for entry in 1990, 60 per cent (1874) were offered places without being required to take a STEP examination (University of Cambridge 1991b: 5). If one of the objectives of the reforms of the 1980s was to bring the Cambridge system of admissions into closer line with practice elsewhere, then why retain an examination that so many tutors appear to have no need of? It could be argued that for Cambridge to have moved to a system that relied completely upon established public examinations would have been too bold a step. In other words, the STEP examination can be seen as a bridging device. The college entrance examination has been abolished but something is needed to smooth the ruffles of those tutors who doubt that A or S levels are good measures of academic potential and/or who need the reassurance that comes from seeing candidates' papers. If in the interests of simpler admissions procedures college diversity needs to be curtailed, then the abolition of the STEP examination seems a good place to start. It was too much to have expected that the Cambridge colleges would have abolished it at the very first review of their recent reforms but it can be expected, like the old entrance examination that it replaced, to wither slowly on the vine.

The key considerations for the admissions procedures are the number and the quality of the applicants who are prepared to expose themselves to their demands. It is difficult to answer the question of what is the ideal number of applicants for each available place without also knowing something about the academic potential of those applicants. Although both Oxford and Cambridge have increased their number of applicants in recent years, they receive fewer applicants per place than other British universities (*The Sunday Correspondent*, 29 October 1989). But, probably because of the social and academic images of the two universities, the Oxbridge candidates are highly self-selective. Approximately three applicants per place may be considered an acceptable ratio as long as their academic quality remains high and, unless this is eroded significantly, then it is unlikely that the colleges will broaden unduly their admissions criteria. Certainly, there would be considerable resistance to a perceived lowering of standards in response to an influx of a different kind of student. The Oxbridge experience has been seen as a high-quality product that needed to be made more widely available, not that it should be changed. There are already some who have raised the possibility of extending certain undergraduate courses in response to – among other pressures – the alleged dilution of pre-university educational standards. It is possible, therefore, that the future undergraduates of Oxford and Cambridge will be distinguished as much by the traditional nature of their pre-university qualifications as they were in the past by their social backgrounds. If the future model of British higher education is to encourage diversity, then this would seem to be an acceptable development. But, inevitably, educational variables are linked to social variables and some may feel, both within and outside the two universities, that Oxbridge's differentiation would be too costly.

It will be interesting to see if the comparatively orderly world of admissions that the Oxbridge colleges have created for themselves will survive if the market becomes more competitive and politically charged. Why should other British universities give Oxford and Cambridge 'a clear run' until the end of January? Why should candidates be precluded from applying to both Oxford and Cambridge? Are the other British universities prepared to pick up the Oxbridge 'conditional offer' failures in the summer in the expectation that they are none the less likely to be acceptable undergraduates? If there is a Labour government threatening economic sanctions because of the alleged social biases of Oxbridge's student body, will the individual colleges at Oxford (note the Cambridge colleges are not so constrained) wait for an intercollegiate response or will they break ranks and disinter their previous admissions initiatives?

The most notable development since the Second World War in the control of the admissions process has been the growth of the intercollegiate institutions. When the Tutorial Representatives Committee handed over its responsibilities for admissions policy to the Admissions Forum, Cambridge's form of intercollegiate control converged with Oxford's model. It is difficult to imagine that this will change substantially in the future. Even if the pressures to which we have referred should materialize, it is almost certain that they will be handled by the appropriate intercollegiate bodies. However, there is considerable room for the rationalization of the administration and government of the colleges at both universities, but this awaits developments which fall outside the narrow scope of admissions. The various intercollegiate bodies need to be linked in a more coherent fashion and their liaison with their respective universities needs to be formalized in greater detail. Admissions issues have already created a measure of university–college liaison (Cambridge's Wass Report has made further suggestions) which may serve as a model for other areas. Although in legal terms they may have separate identities, the interests of the colleges and of their universities are now in practice so closely entwined that they either sink or swim together. It is our conclusion, therefore, that despite its past fragility, the intercollegiate cooperation on admissions issues has stood the test of time and is now sufficiently well-developed to meet future challenges.

Part 4

Understanding the Process of
Educational Change

9

The Decline of Donnish Domination?

Unique institutions?

In a revealing 'behind-the-scenes view' of what is now commonly referred to as the Jarratt Committee, one of its members has claimed that the Committee was constrained by the necessity 'to function on the basis of a sample of universities and a selection of topics to be studied in depth', and apparently 'it was quickly agreed that Cambridge and Oxford should be excluded from the sample' of selected universities (Lockwood 1986: 15). With reference to the topics that the Committee wanted to study (financial management, purchasing, and the use and maintenance of capital resources), this may have been a defensible decision, but it helped to reinforce a widely held opinion that Cambridge and Oxford are unique universities. Although on this occasion their uniqueness may have saved them from public scrutiny, it has not meant that they are exempt from the strictures of the Jarratt Report. The UGC used the report to pressurize all the universities, including Oxford and Cambridge, into a re-evaluation of their methods of government and administration, and it was the dissatisfaction with Cambridge's response that helped to persuade the university authorities to set up the Wass Syndicate 'to consider the government of the University'.

The only viable conclusion to be drawn from the saga of the Jarratt Report is that while Oxford and Cambridge were sufficiently different universities to be excluded from in-depth studies intended to reveal an overall picture of university management, in future they would be required to conform to the principles established by the Committee. The view of the two universities suggested by this book is very different from that implied by the Jarratt Committee. It is our contention that Oxford and Cambridge represent the most complete examples of what we have termed the traditional ideal of the English university. Although as a consequence of this they must be considered to be exceptional institutions, they have had a profound influence upon the character of British higher education in general. They have been crucial in forming the values of the English model of university to which much of the rest of the system of higher education has aspired and, even more certainly, against which it has been judged. The form that the model has taken at

Oxford and Cambridge may be unique, but the values on which the two universities are founded have echoed loudly and persistently throughout the twentieth-century history of higher education in Britain.

In particular, Oxford and Cambridge have been most influential in establishing the idea that universities are autonomous institutions that are governed by their scholars. In fact, it may well be the case that most British universities are *not* self-governing institutions inasmuch as ultimate formal executive authority is located in their councils with a layperson in the chair and laypersons comprising the largest single element of the membership (Moodie and Eustace 1974: 97–123). At least since 1945, however, the influence of councils *vis-à-vis* senates within universities had waned, and central to the argument of the Jarratt Report was that this trend should be reversed. The primary purpose of senate, according to the Jarratt Report, was to co-ordinate and endorse the detailed academic functions of the university, while council should have the stronger input into university planning and resource allocation (Committee of Vice-Chancellors and Principals 1985: para. 3.50). It is realistic, therefore, to interpret the Jarratt Report as both a re-assertion of the formal constitutional position as to where executive authority in many universities resides, and as an appeal to an alternative tradition of university government, one less dependent upon the values of autonomy and donnish domination.

The purpose of this book has been to examine the changing character of the Universities of Oxford and Cambridge within the context of the more general pressures for change that British universities have experienced. This broad task has given rise to four main problems. There is the initial problem of understanding the nature of the pressures. This has not always been as straightforward as it may seem. For example, the Jarratt Report may be seen as either a forceful statement of the need for the universities to adopt a new managerial model of government or as a plea for a return to an alternative tradition of university government which has equal or even stronger constitutional legitimacy. On the specific question of university autonomy, the Jarratt Report could be interpreted as favouring its reinforcement rather than sounding its death knell. As Lockwood (1986) has written: 'The Jarratt Report came down heavily in favour of universities as individual corporate bodies managing their own affairs and futures.' But the key considerations, upon which Lockwood did not reflect, are who will exercise this corporate autonomy and how.

The second problem has been to examine the impact of these pressures upon the Universities of Oxford and Cambridge. A central assumption of our book is that the pressures for change have not borne down upon all institutions with the same degree of rigour. Do Oxford and Cambridge not only occupy the most prestigious position in British higher education, but do they also have a privileged position, one that has enabled them to resist the pressures for change and/or respond to them in a manner that has reinforced their pre-eminence? The third problem has been to analyse the implications of these developments (i.e. the nature of the pressures and of Oxbridge's responses to them) for the general character of higher education in Britain, or more especially for the English universities. If our opening assumption is correct – that is, Oxford and Cambridge have represented for the English universities the model of the university – then we need to know what happens to the idea of the university if its ideal representation changes, or alternatively if it fails to change while the values, structures and practices of other institutions do change. Indeed, the ultimate justification for concentrating upon the Universities of Oxford and Cambridge is the hypothesis that it is impossible to understand how the university system as a whole is developing without appreciating what is happening to those two ancient centres of learning.

The fourth problem, to which we have returned repeatedly, is our understanding of the dynamic for educational change. We have argued that the concept of autonomy was central to what we have termed the traditional idea of the university. While the universities accepted the obligation to respond to national needs, their autonomy allowed them to dictate the terms on which they would fulfil that expectation. The universities had no wish to be incorporated in the Board of Education's responsibilities. They feared the pressures that they would be subjected to if they were perceived as an integral part of a national system of education under the formal auspices of a bureaucracy which was responsive to its political masters and, through them, to society. The special arrangements that enabled the universities to receive recurrent grants from the Exchequer, without the accountability that invariably accompanies the receipt of state resources, were soon to be perceived as critical ideological symbols, rather than as convenient administrative procedures, in any analysis of the relationship between the state and the universities in Britain. The challenge, consequently, has had both ideological and administrative dimensions. On the administrative front, the special status of the universities was allegedly a major obstacle to the effective planning of a national system of education. On the ideological front, the universities' control of the reproduction of knowledge was arguably one of the critical reasons for the failure of Britain to match its societal needs – especially the needs of the economy – to the performance of its educational system. It is our contention that both these challenges were taken up and developed by the Ministry of Education and then subsequently by its successor the Department of Education and Science. Many pressures may have interacted to force change upon the British universities, but at their very centre has been the state itself.

This chapter represents our final reflections on these four key problems. They will be considered within the context of examining the first tentative steps of the UFC and of offering a prognosis of future developments. This will enable us to reflect in general terms on the changing character of higher education in Britain and the future place of the Universities of Oxford and Cambridge within the newly emerging model. In particular, has the creation of a new funding body made a fundamental difference to how we have interpreted the relationship between state, society and the universities? The situation, however, is in flux and it would be unwise to be too categorical! Finally, we wish to make a personal assessment of the universities' political performance in the past decade. Could they have adopted more meaningful strategies in response to the external demands?

The new model university system: State and society as contractors and the accountable university

For most of the twentieth century, the UGC constituted the critical bridge between the state and the universities. Although formally it may have been part of the state, it was not perceived as a blunt instrument of government policy. However, when the UGC assumed the responsibility in 1981 for managing the government-imposed cuts in its recurrent grant, its role in the eyes of many changed. None the less, the UGC continued to make most of its monies available in the form of a block grant, and the universities remained free to spend on the basis of their own planning. Thus, so the argument ran, the universities remained autonomous institutions and the UGC was still the honest broker between the state and the universities. But to cling to the continuity of the block grant as the litmus test of autonomy is to understand even the *financial* relationship between the state and the universities in narrow and simplistic terms (see Chapter 3). Moreover, the UGC moved towards a restructuring of the academic character of the universities in a manner that increasingly suggested that the system was planned from the centre rather than evolved from below. The key considerations were the UGC's ever more refined constraints on student numbers, the use of earmarked funds to pro- mote specific knowledge areas, the numerous attempts to reorganize the distribution of subjects among the universities (with important recommenda- tions on Physics and Chemistry waiting to be acted upon at the time of the UGC's demise), and the move (strongly supported by the ABRC) to separate teaching from research. In the past it had proven possible to reformulate the understanding of university autonomy, but in our judgement only the most perverse re-reading of history could claim that British universities remained autonomous institutions in the final days of the UGC. They may have retained the right, and perhaps still do, to mismanage their financial affairs (as the Public Accounts Committee has recently claimed) but within itself this merely constitutes irresponsibility not autonomy.

The question we need to consider is whether the replacement of the UGC by the UFC has placed the relationship between the state and the univer- sities on a new foundation. The UFC is a smaller body than the UGC (15 as opposed to 18 members) with a stronger representation of those who 'have shown capacity in industrial, commercial or financial matters or the practice of any profession' (Education Reform Act, 1988, 131 (3)). Undoubtedly, the most critical decisions are those that determine how the UFC is to distribute its annual grant to the universities. An early decision was to separate clearly research from teaching income, to increase relatively the amount allocated for research, and to introduce a stronger element of selectivity in the distribution of research income. In the 1990–91 allocations, Oxford and Cambridge received 45 and 44 per cent respectively of their UFC incomes for research, more than any other university (THES 1990a: 3). Like its predecessor, the UFC is, therefore, making it more difficult for universities to sustain the idea that every academic combines the roles of both teacher and researcher. The UFC is also committed to maintaining the research selectivity exercises which will form the basis of how it distributes the research component in its annual grant. Although there is some evidence that universities are resisting the funding implications that follow from such reviews, it is difficult to know how widespread the resistance is and how long it can be expected to last.

A more interesting decision was the intention to fund, from the academic year 1991–92, the universities' teaching activities on the basis of guide prices issued by the UFC (UFC 1989: Annex D (revised)). As the universities made only 7 per cent of their initial bids below the guide prices the UFC decided to abandon the system, throwing both the universities and probably itself into a state of at least temporary turmoil. Clearly, the guide price arrangements were devised with the intention of increasing student numbers without a commensurate increase in funding. The proposals also marked a significant turning away from the dirigisme that the UGC had exercised in its final years. Individual universities could decide their own student numbers and the income they required to teach them. The overall size of the UFC's budget limited the number of students it could finance at the guide prices and thus a large expansion of the system could be met only if universities were prepared to bid below guide prices, even to take students if they brought with them only their LEA fees. The UFC was attempting to create a managed market and the failure of the universities to cooperate provoked the then Secretary of State to issue the following warning to a meeting of the vice-chancellors:

> Can universities really have so little marginal capacity that all additional students need to be supported at the average cost? I find that difficult to believe. And I have to tell you that, unless the universities can achieve further economies of scale in responding to the increasing demand for places, I shall need to consider carefully the balance between the resources made available to the two sectors (i.e. the universities as opposed to the colleges and polytechnics) (as reported in *The Times*, 27 September 1990).

In the early 1980s, as the universities turned away students in an attempt to maintain their staff–student ratios (legitimated by the claim that this was the only way in the circumstances they could maintain their commitment to research), so the polytechnics increased their student numbers. For a second time, the universities were resisting the pressure to lower their unit costs. The UFC reacted by adjusting its funding strategy, so that those universities who were prepared to accept an above-average proportion of fees-only students could qualify for additional fully funded students. The expanding universities would be those prepared to accept what the Secretary of State referred to as 'further economies of scale' and which many – at least within the universities – see as expansion on the cheap.

Given that the funding arrangements would be manipulated to ensure that the government's will prevailed, perhaps a more sophisticated response by the CVCP to the bidding system would have been to ensure that enough bids were made below guide prices to have satisfied the Secretary of State. At least this would have enabled the vice-chancellors to maintain some control over this pseudo-market and the CVCP would have become the forum for deciding the overall pattern of the universities' bids. Whether individual vice-chancellors would want the CVCP to have such a function, or whether internal university pressures would have allowed them to hand over such authority, is another matter. The problem is that the CVCP could have been reduced to the role of the UGC in 1981, managing something of which it disapproved. Now, however, it seems that the universities will be required to operate a system over which they can exercise even less collective control unless they are prepared to accept static student numbers.

While the bidding system has gone, teaching is still financed on the basis of the guide prices, which continues to place stresses and strains upon the internal structures of individual universities. The variations in the guide prices may have had a sound historical basis, but none the less they raise the hackles of some academics who believe that their subjects have been undervalued. Although the UFC permits cross-subsidization, those who are subsidized must experience some vulnerability. There has already been considerable hostility in many quarters to the research selectivity exercises with several disciplines claiming they have been harshly treated, while the complaints from particular departments have been both numerous and fierce. The reason for the sensitivity is obvious: these are decisions that make judgements about professional reputations and carry significant resource implications. That cosy world of academe in which all were considered worthy, and in which financial matters were quietly pushed to one side, has disappeared forever. However, it would probably make sense for the UFC to operate with a more restricted range of guide prices. It would smooth a few ruffled academic feathers, it would enhance the UFC's attempt to distance itself further from the detailed planning image that came to encapsulate the UGC, and it would permit the universities more flexibility.

While pledging itself to another research selectivity exercise, the UFC has abandoned – at least for the present – subject reviews. The onus is upon the universities to make their own decisions about the academic maps they wish to develop; they will be driven by financial considerations and academic judgements rather than dictated to by the forces of so-called rationalization. But these decisions will not be made in circumstances of their own choosing. Authority is delegated within parameters designed to achieve certain policy objectives: the universities will admit more students at lower unit costs, the specialization of academic responsibilities within and between universities will be more sharply defined than ever before, and each university will have to engage in forward planning. The intention may be to avoid the academic planning associated with the UGC and the ABRC, but the goal of a university system clearly differentiated along well-pronounced lines is as firm as ever. It remains to be seen whether the managed market can achieve it.

In the build up to, and the passage of, the 1988 Education Reform Act, there was considerable discussion of how the new funding body should relate to the Secretary of State. For many academics, the key requirement was whether this body would have the right to give the Secretary of State its advice on policy matters including proposed funding levels. It was the omission of this role from the White Paper, coupled with what appeared to be the advocacy of a system of contract funding (DES 1987), that led Shattock to conclude that a significant break with the past was about to take place:

> The new Universities Funding Council seems likely to represent not an evolution from but a clear break with the model embodied in the University Grants Committee. We have moved not just from the days when the Committee was regarded as 'a collective Minister' for the universities, to the situation where it tendered advice to a secretary of state, accepting that it was for the government ultimately to determine policy, but to a new position where policy is entirely created in the Department of Education and Science and where the new council's functions are not to advise on policy matters, but simply to allocate those resources made available in accordance with the principles laid down by the government (Shattock 1987: 485).

As it turned out, the CVCP launched a powerful campaign against the higher education clauses of the 1988 Education Reform Bill including the limited role prescribed for the UFC and the concept of contract funding (Crequer 1989: 3–19). There is no explicit requirement in the Act for the UFC to make its funds available on the basis of contracts: 'The Council shall have power to make grants, subject to such terms and conditions as they think fit, to the governing body of any university in respect of expenditure incurred or to be incurred by them for the purposes of any activities eligible for funding under this section' (Education Reform Act, 1988, Clause 131 (6)). And the UFC can provide the Secretary of State 'with such information and advice relating to activities eligible for funding under this section as they think fit' (Education Reform Act, 1988, Clause 131, (8)(b)). By ruling out specific references to contract funding, the government may have made a major concession to its critics, but the then Secretary of State always maintained that he intended to work in close consultation with the two funding councils (that is the UFC and the PCFC), so the latter changes may have been essentially tactical.

The key issue is whether these changes will enable the UFC to pursue its functions more in line with the traditions established by the UGC or whether, along with Shattock (admittedly expressing a view before the concessions were made), we would still want to assert that there has been a clear break with the past. Moodie (1987: 342–3) has argued that it is in the interests of both the DES and the universities to ensure that UFC functions effectively. The problem is that the respective parties may understand the UFC's performance in different terms. Moodie has spoken of the need to preserve 'the essential virtue of higher education' (ibid.: 343) but is less than precise as to what that essential virtue may be. The Secretary of State's ire at the failure of the universities to make many bids below the guide prices demonstrates that the UFC and the universities are not going to be allowed to conduct their affairs free from the close attention of the DES. In other words, the Council and the universities can expect a free hand only as long as they act broadly in line with departmental expectations. It could be argued that this was always true, so we are back to the question of defining how much their freedom of action has to be eroded before the universities can no longer be described as autonomous institutions. The question will be answered on the basis of experience but the omens are threatening. It is hard to imagine that in the days of the UGC, the Secretary of State would have raised so explicitly the threat of financial penalties to coerce the universities into eroding their staff–student ratios.

There is a more general context to this debate which cannot be ignored. The DES may want to exercise its responsibilites for higher education indirectly, and the government may have conceded that the UFC could give advice to the Secretary of State, but it would be quite impossible to suggest that UFC was created with the intention of acting as a buffer between the state and the universities. While perceptions of the origins of the UGC have been embellished over time, the UGC was never seen as the creature of the state. But this is precisely – rightly or wrongly – how the UFC is widely perceived in university circles. Moreover, to assume that the UFC will – like the UGC before it – be able to control some middle territory between the state and the universities presupposes that this territory still exists. There is no reason why the UFC should see its future as a buffer between the state and the universities. There is another way of interpreting the UGC's actions in the crisis of 1981, an interpretation that has not been given the serious consideration it merits. While deploring the cut in its recurrent grant, the UGC may have relished the chance to act more directly and positively. In the long term perhaps, the UFC will be less inclined to give advice to Secretaries of State and more inclined to investigate whether there really is no slack in the university system. If the universities cannot find the slack to accommodate the extra student numbers without a commensurate increase in resources, then perhaps the UFC will find it for them. It does appear that to run with the state is an easier (there is no struggle to re-establish the middle ground), a more natural (there is no need to counter the widespread image of being part of the state apparatus) and a more potent (there are endless opportunities to reshape the affairs of the universities) future for the UFC than trying to re-establish the thankless role of the buffer between the state and the universities. To date, the emphasis has been upon the development of the appropriate mechanisms to achieve the desired goals rather than continuing with the direct interventionist strategy of the UGC. Evidently, there is more than one way to skin a cat.

The future of the UFC cannot be understood without taking into account the changing relationship of state, society and higher education in Britain. If the universities are to be more firmly integrated into the educational system, then inevitably one of the first stages in this process is to place the responsibility for higher education (i.e. the universities, the polytechnics and the colleges) in the hands of one body. During the passage of the 1988 Education Reform Act, and subsequently, there have been many calls, both inside and outside Parliament, for the amalgamation of the UFC and the Polytechnics and Colleges Funding Council (PCFC). Not only does it make sense in planning terms, but it also has almost universal political support. For example, the Labour Party is currently committed to setting up 'a Higher and Continuing Education Council, to advise government on policy in respect of the whole of post-eighteen education and to allocate resources to institutions' (Labour Party 1990: 50). Given the current diversification of higher education, it makes no sense to pretend that there is anything other than an increasingly artificial dividing line between universities and polytechnics and colleges. Moreover, if the dual funding system that has underwritten university research is about to collapse, then the distinction between the two sectors of higher education has little basis other than nomenclature and perceived status. Not all universities, or at least not all university departments, will have research responsibilities, which has been one of the traditional distinctions between the universities and the polytechnics. As far as higher education was concerned, the most important aspect of the 1988 Education Reform Act (and one that received scant attention – at least in Parliament – in comparison to the time devoted to the fears of the universities) was the wresting of the responsibility for the polytechnics and colleges away from the local authorities. On all fronts, therefore, the preconditions for the amalgamation of the UFC and the PCFC have been met.

While on the one hand we can expect an amalgamation of the higher education funding bodies, on the other hand higher education in Scotland may well be placed under the auspices of a separate body, responsible to the Scottish Education Department and through it to the Scottish Office. Such a move could be interpreted as both a concession to devolutionary pressures and a recognition of the continuing uniqueness of the Scottish tradition of higher education. What the substantive consequences would be, for example on funding levels, methods of funding and the academic character of higher education in Scotland, are more difficult to predict. However, if the general trend is towards the diversification of higher education, it makes less sense to influence the system from the centre.

Another potent threat to the UFC, and indeed any replacement body, is that its crucial financial functions could simply be reallocated. This has already started to take place and it is possible that the process could be speeded up. There is no reason why all the resources for research activities should not be transferred to the research councils. The British Academy, currently responsible for supporting postgraduate work in the humanities, could be given the same functions as the research councils. If the assumption that all university academics are engaged in research is removed, and some institutions (or at least some departments within them) are designated as teaching centres, then research costs could be met on the basis of bids by individuals and/or departments with corresponding selectivity in meeting the overhead costs of research. Currently, the pressure in favour of giving students vouchers to cover teaching costs is muted, but this is not to say that it has been excluded permanently from the political agenda. Although there would have to be an administrative mechanism for issuing vouchers, and more significantly policy decisions on how the overall sum was to be distributed, the student rather than the UFC would be the channel through which state monies reached the universities to cover their teaching costs. Since 1991–92, tuition fees have been set for three band levels and considerably increased (UFC 1989: Annex L). This could be extended so that in future tuition fees were set so they covered the full costs of a course, thus making the UFC as good as redundant. While this may not have the same alleged effect as a voucher system in which the student pays the fees directly, it would clarify and intensify the relationship between the input of student numbers and university incomes.

Despite considerable pressure in recent years for the abolition of the research councils, to be swallowed up in one super research council, their survival, at least in the near future, is assured. But survival has its price, for henceforth the councils will face more scrutiny and direction from a revamped ABRC. The reconstituted ABRC marks a further stage in the centralization of the state's control of its input into university research. Under its new terms of reference, the ABRC 'will act as a single unit throughout, to produce a corporate view of the overall interests of the research council system' (Sir David Phillips, chairman of the ABRC, as reported in the THES 1990b: 7). Undoubtedly, part of the stimulus for change was the alleged difficulty of generating resources for new, especially interdisciplinary, projects from research councils that tended to be dominated by established disciplinary interests. The biologists, especially those in biotechnology, seemed to have been particularly aggrieved. For individual universities, the key consideration is whether they can manage their research activites in a manner that is sensitive to shifts in the direction of research funding.

On both the teaching and research fronts, therefore, the universities will be required to undertake a considerable measure of forward planning in which they will need to be sensitive to changes in the demand for their varying services. The issue is whether universities can both predict and respond to the expansion and contraction of knowledge areas. Clearly, the corporate plans of the new model ABRC should be read intently by those pushing for major developments within a university's research profile. It is obvious, therefore, that the successful universities of the future will need a more pronounced and sophisticated administrative input into their decision-making processes. The universities have been placed in a more competitive and uncertain environment which, perhaps ironically, they can better cope with only by becoming more carefully managed institutions. This is not to say that decision making has either to be centralized or to be the formal responsibility of university officials, but it does mean that there is a need for the positive interaction of academic leadership and official expertise. Although the notion of corporate planning may suggest a centrally directed exercise, the final product could be constructed out of priorities formulated at the grass roots. The role of the centre would be to co-ordinate and establish an overall sense of direction rather than impose its will.

The increasing diversification within and between universities is comparatively easy to document: the differential ramifications of the separation of teaching from research, the variations between universities in lessening their dependence upon the Exchequer's recurrent grant, the evaluation of departmental research records, and greater variation in the academic profiles of universities thanks to the UGC's rationalization programmes and the willingness of some universities to sponsor new or previously excluded knowledge areas. However, even if universities have increasingly less in common, none the less it may be some time before the old ideology, which saw them as sharing common values and pursuing common ends, loses its force. Although there are other variables that have to be taken into consideration, this does explain in part the opposition of both the CVCP and the Association of University Teachers (AUT) to many of the recent changes in higher education. They – and more especially the AUT – have their constituent interests to defend and frequently do so with reference to the values of a university system that is rapidly disappearing. As the old binary line fades, so it will make sense for both the AUT and the CVCP to broaden their membership base. While this will enable them to provide some glue to a less tightly structured system of higher education, it will also mean they have to take on board values that recognize the increased internal differentiation. In policy terms, although national agreements may be negotiated, they will then be tailored to fit differing local circumstances.

At the level of the individual institution, the state has demonstrated that it possesses – for better or worse – the means to force universities to respond to many of its demands. Not surprisingly, the key resource is the state's control of the purse strings. The parliamentary attack upon how the universities handled academic redundancies in the early 1980s was to some extent unjustified. These were institutions responding to an unfamiliar crisis; the pressure was intense, time was short and the circumstances unparalleled. But act they did. To give a specific example, powerful elements in the University of Cambridge were opposed to making discretionary payments to professors but, as a report of the General Board noted, the university had no discretion in the matter if it expected to receive funds to finance the 1989 pay settlement (University of Cambridge 1989b: 756–8). Despite the principled professorial opposition (some expressed a wish not to be considered for

ntary payments), the university inevitably fell into line. In much
way we can expect that the expansion of student numbers will not
ed by a commensurate increase in financial support from the UFC.
There may be an additional resource input but teaching will not be funded
as generously as in the past and the universities will fall into line. But the
pressures are not only financial. There are now a whole range of performance
indicators in place, and although cross-institutional comparisons may be of
dubious value, there is no doubt that they will be made, and institutions will
either have to take measures to improve their performance or to justify their
apparent inefficiency. Already universities are required to take external ex-
aminers' reports more seriously than they did in the past and the monitoring
of the teaching process will intensify as the CVCP's brainchild, the Academic
Audit Unit, moves into action (CVCP 1989: VC/89/178a).

In many cases, it would be more accurate to describe the universities'
response to the pressures for change as recognition of the fact that further
resistance was impossible rather than as flexibility in the face of new circumstances. This was partly a consequence of the strength of the established
value system and partly because academic tenure made it difficult to restructure the universities rationally. Universities had to accommodate external
pressure in a piecemeal manner. Under the terms of the 1988 Education
Reform Act, statutory commissioners have been appointed to lay down
conditions that will permit the dismissal of academic staff on the grounds of
redundancy. Although the new terms of employment will not apply to faculty
appointed prior to 20 November 1987, unless they enter into a new contract
of employment after that date, the academic labour force is now more
malleable. The abolition of academic tenure may have offended one of the
central values of the traditional ideal of the university, but it has made
universities much more flexible institutions. However, if flexibility is to have
substantive meaning, then it has to be centred around the idea that universities think creatively about their futures, that they anticipate events and act
in advance of them. The most imaginative will develop a vision of their
future and shape events to that end rather than merely reacting to them. But
it would be wrong to dodge the fact that it is easier to engage in forward
planning which tries to predict new developments if academic faculty do not
have job tenure. There is no doubting that some universities have proved
more adept than others at responding positively to the various crises of the
recent past. Inevitably, in the future, the quality of university leadership will
continue to vary, but it will be impossible for any university to assume that it
is operating within a stable environment and has no need to plan ahead.

What is emerging, therefore, is a more diversified system of higher education in which the individual institutions are more dependent upon the quality
of their administrative expertise and academic leadership for their future
welfare. They have to accept the fact that they are going to be more closely
accountable for the resources they receive from the Exchequer and more
dependent upon inputs from the marketplace (fees, research monies, endowment appeals and sponsorship) to underwrite certain of their most valued

activities. They will be more managed institutions, but it will need to be a form of management that is not only administratively competent (for example, in calculating full-cost research overheads) but also capable of exercising academic leadership (for example, backing with internal resources new research ideas or even ideas which cannot obtain external funding). It is a system in which the individual parts create the whole, rather than – as in the recent past – each individual part seeks to be a replica of the whole.

Within this new model, what is to be the role of the Universities of Oxford and Cambridge? Within a more differentiated university system, it is likely that small institutional networks will develop. For example, frequent reference is made to an Oxbridge, Durham, Bristol, York and Exeter admissions network, while the rankings of the research selectivity exercises led the *Times Higher Education Supplement* to refer to the golden triangle of Oxford, Cambridge and London. If the British model of higher education is moving closer to its American counterpart, then it may be developing its own version of the Ivy League universities. Although their influence may be more restricted in the future, the prestige of Oxford and Cambridge will remain as high as ever. Within a system whose component parts perform different functions, the idea of a status hierarchy based on common criteria should be irrelevant, but the old values die slowly and if Oxford and Cambridge can retain their commitment to small-group teaching centred in the colleges, and maintain their first-rate research records, they will continue to be seen as Britain's premier universities. It may be politically and financially necessary to embrace the cause of low unit costs, 2-year degree programmes and high contract research incomes, but in the short run these will not present much of a threat to the established value system – at least not in the eyes of most academics.

Though the challenge to the Education Reform Bill in the Lords featured a number of prominent Oxbridge personalities, neither university will be in a position to – although some might wish to – reinforce the traditional value system and their pre-eminent positions within it. They can be expected to diversify further their income sources both by attracting more research grants from the state and the marketplace, and through the successful management of their respective appeals, Whether they will initiate the move towards top-up fees is another matter. Statements from both universities have strongly opposed such a possibility, but their prestige is such that it remains a potentially viable option. If they were given no choice in the matter, and soon Cambridge may be required to charge top-up fees for students in the veterinary sciences, then the floodgates could open. Again there is the possibility that the CVCP could manage a programme of top-up fees but for the present the vice-chancellors as a body remain implacably opposed.

Of more pressing concern to Oxbridge is whether the state will continue its commitment to pay college fees. Any sensible prognosis would have to reflect a combination of what has happened historically and the continuing ability of the two universities and their respective colleges to fight sophisticated political campaigns to maintain their advantage. There is no reason why, if an Oxbridge education is more expensive than higher education elsewhere, the additional costs should not be met by the recipients of that education (i.e. the students) or, if there is concern about the way in which this might affect the social composition of the student populations, by the two universities and their colleges through bursaries. If the input is needed to enable them to maintain their reputations as world-class universities, then this needs to be part of the public debate about the funding of higher education. Do we need two, or indeed more, world-class universities? If so, where should the resources be concentrated? Alternatively, are there better ways to spend the money? In concrete terms, what are the extra societal benefits of educating students at Oxford and Cambridge? In his 1988 Oration to the University of Oxford, the vice-chancellor fiercely defended the tutorial system of teaching as 'the best method ever devised for training minds and exposing fallacies', and followed this with the observation that 'Generations of Oxford graduates owe their subsequent success in life to their tutors' (University of Oxford 1988: 171). But the issue for the state is whether these alleged benefits are also worth the additional costs to the Exchequer, and therefore to the taxpayer, of financing Oxford's tutorial system?

To date, public debate on the issue of college fees has been conspicuous by its silence. But the situation may be about to change. The British Academy, in order to support more postgraduate students in the humanities, is currently discussing whether to distribute its awards to universities on the basis of a quota system (THES 1991: 8). Thanks to college fees, the cost to the British Academy of supporting a postgraduate student at Oxbridge is higher than at other British universities. Whereas the UFC adjusts its block grant to Oxford and Cambridge because of the fees that colleges receive from the LEAs for their undergraduates, the research councils and the British Academy receive no compensation for the extra cost of supporting Oxbridge postgraduates. Presumably only by setting quotas for Oxford·and Cambridge that are markedly lower than its traditional support for Oxbridge postgraduates is the British Academy likely to release sufficient funds to make a significant impact upon the total number of postgraduates it can support. Although matters may now be somewhat improved, excepting the science departments, neither university has done particularly well by its postgraduates in the past. As long as governments are determined to monitor closely the Exchequer's input into higher education, while at the same time supporting an expansion of student numbers, this is an issue that looks set to run and run (*The Guardian*, 29 January 1991).

Both the Universities of Oxford and Cambridge have produced plans which cover their academic developments until the turn of the century (University of Oxford 1990e; University of Cambridge, 1989c: 787–90). Neither university expects to expand at the same rate as in the recent past and, although there will be new developments, the general academic contours of the two universities will not be disturbed. While both universities will be committed to widen the social base of their student populations, they will not create part-time undergraduate degree programmes and are more likely to increase the time it takes to complete a first degree to 4 years rather than to shorten it to 2 years. In a world in which teaching and research are going to be more clearly differentiated from one another, Oxford and Cambridge can be expected to retain their traditional commitments to both. However, the external pressures in favour of such differentiation, as well as the shifting financial balance between the universities and the colleges, will require closer university–college liaison on academic matters. For some time there have been calls within Oxford for a revamping of its lectureship structure with particular reference to those who hold joint college–university posts, that is the CUF lecturers (Lucas 1987: 8; Shock 1990: 11–12). Maurice Shock believes that the time has passed for setting up a council of colleges on the lines proposed by the Franks Inquiry but refers – albeit in a not too encouraging tone – to the possibility of making more of the Conference of Colleges, 'despite its unhappy history' (ibid.)!

Should the Wass Report lead to more effective intercollegiate government and closer college–university liaison at Cambridge, then it could well succeed where the Franks Inquiry failed. While prepared to criticize college government (arguing the need for more delegation of authority to Heads of Houses and other senior college officers to facilitate the speed at which intercollegiate agreements were reached), the Report's recommendations were circumspect. As at Oxford, the central issue is whether the colleges are prepared to function under the auspices of a representative body which has a wide measure of delegated authority that it can use both to formulate the overall direction of intercollegiate policy and to co-ordinate the work of its subcommittees (University of Cambridge 1989a: 636–9). At present, Cambridge has the following intercollegiate committees: a Colleges Committee (comprised mainly of Heads of Houses), the Tutorial Representatives Committee, the Admissions Forum and the Bursars' Committee. Co-ordination with university policy is achieved by consultation, through joint committees (e.g. the recently established Joint Consultative Committee on Admissions), and the time-honoured practice of placing key university personnel on college committees and vice versa. While the Wass Report argued for the retention of the existing college committees, it was clearly arguing for structural change in the sense that these committees should interrelate with one another on a different basis. The initial reaction to this line of thought suggests, however, that the colleges are unlikely to concur, and the Tutorial Representatives Committee, in particular, has responded negatively to the proposed downgrading of their committee:

[The Representatives] . . . were convinced that the proper place for the integration of University and College Policy remained the Committee of the Tutorial Representatives. It was in this Committee, amongst those directly concerned with College teaching, the day-to-day detail of the lives of students, and the impact of University proposals upon them, that liaison with Faculties existed and should be extended. Comprised, as it is, mainly of Heads of Houses, the Colleges Committee did not seem to constitute a logical choice for the provision of 'closer liaison between Colleges and Faculties' (University of Cambridge 1989e: 174).

But could not the Tutorial Representatives Committee retain its remit within the framework of a committee structure headed by the Colleges Committee? The reaction of several of the colleges also suggests that such a development is unlikely. The prevailing arrangements were seen to work well and there was widespread antagonism at the Syndicate's perceived attempt to impose an unduly rigid structure upon matters that required flexible handling (consider, for example, the comments of Churchill College, Clare College and Corpus Christi College; ibid.: 175–7). However, some of the colleges held their fire and one, Magdalene College, even criticized the report for *not* going far enough and predicted that in due course this failure would make a visitation by a royal commission inevitable (ibid.: 183). The colleges have been invited by the Wass Syndicate to consider action on intercollegiate government and it will be interesting to see if they take up the offer and, if so, how they intend to proceed.

At both Oxford and Cambridge, the strength of feeling that formal college autonomy is integral to the idea of the collegiate university is still very strong. Although we concur with Magdalene's sentiment that university and college affairs are intimately interrelated, and we would add that neither university has formulated completely satisfactory arrangements for making this work in practice, it is difficult to imagine that anything other than the present arrangements will prevail in the near future. Radical change is impossible given the strength of the prevailing ideology. Of course, that does not mean that nothing will take place. The Regent House overwhelmingly approved the grace 'That the Colleges be invited to consider the proposals for the revision of the work of the inter-College bodies that are set out in section 14 [which considered intercollegiate and college–university relations] of the Report of the Syndicate on the Government of the University' (Placet 991; Non Placet 209). It is possible to imagine a wide range of refinements to the present arrangements – more administrative support for the committees, more frequent committee meetings, a broader exchange of the members of university and college committees dealing with overlapping business accompanied by a sharper awareness of their co-ordinating roles, members serving committees for longer periods of time, more joint committees and the delegation by colleges to their committee representatives of executive authority on *specific* matters. But general structural change – and this is as true of Oxford as of Cambridge – is unlikely. Perhaps Magdalene College is correct and inevitably this will mean a visitation by a royal commission, but this presupposes a level of chaos and concomitant concern that we feel is unlikely. It may be thought preferable that institutions should work tolerably well by building consensus from the grass roots upwards and not offend deep-seated and widely held sensibilities, than that they should work very efficiently through centralized executive authority but in the process generate deep and wide resentment.

Whatever happens to intercollegiate government and college–university relations, the University of Cambridge has gone too far down the road of reforming its own government and administration to turn back and the key graces approved by the Regent House in April 1990 are now being put into effect. We consider that the reforms instigated at Oxford by the Franks Inquiry were more substantive than subsequent blasé opinion has suggested, that there were successes as well as defeats, and that within itself it was an important achievement to marry the university's constitutional precepts with its actual mode of operation – especially so in view of the recent official strictures on such matters. Even if scepticism regarding the impact of the Franks Inquiry upon Oxford can be justified, statutory change at Cambridge based on the graces approved in April 1990 will usher in far-reaching formal changes. For the first time, there will be a coherent administrative structure, the relations between the university's chief officials and their offices will have been co-ordinated in a manner that leaves no doubts as to their respective duties and authority, and the Regent House will by statute have a clear legislative – and only a legislative – function.

Since the extensive revision of Oxford's formal machinery of government in the wake of the Franks Inquiry, there has been little internal pressure for further reform and Oxford has not faced the external pressure experienced of late by Cambridge. The kinds of minor adjustments to intercollegiate government and to college–university relations that we expect to take place at Cambridge will probably also occur at Oxford. With the possible exception of its failure to establish the Council of Colleges, the greatest snub Oxford gave to the Franks Inquiry was its refusal to revise its faculty structure. However, this was mitigated somewhat by the regeneration of the General Board, thanks in part to the appointment of a full-time vice-chairman. The status of the General Board was enhanced greatly by the effective manner in which it helped the University of Oxford to cope with the economic crisis of the 1980s. Furthermore, the General Board has gone a long way towards assuming the function of shaping the overall academic map of Oxford while delegating much of its previous authority to departments and faculties. None the less, the recent creation of a Department of Physics with its own management committee does suggest the need for the closer interrelationship of knowledge areas with overlapping interests, and these developments in physics may provide a model for future structural change. The key step would be the amalgamation of some of the smaller faculties along the lines of Cambridge's Schools, which can best be likened to super-faculties. The pressures of academic rationalization and the increasing appeal of inter-disciplinary research point to this as a likely conclusion. Of course, there is nothing sacrosanct about the management of knowledge and it is possible that the applied sciences at Cambridge – for academic, financial and internal political reasons – may decide to split off from the School of Physical Sciences.

If institutions need to respond flexibly to the changing environment, then it follows that they will have to establish structures that can be modified without causing internal trauma. It is clear, however, that whatever authority is delegated to the differing levels and individual units within the overall academic framework, they will be held accountable for how they use their authority. In concrete terms, this means that their performance will be monitored by the centre and evaluated according to agreed criteria. Thus Oxford's Department of Pharmacology was asked to account for its above-average laboratory costs and the School of Biological Sciences decided that it was time to put the final nail in the coffin of Cambridge's Department of Applied Biology. The General Boards of both universities are committed to undertaking regular reviews of the performance of the various academic units under their control and one can expect, therefore, more such decisions. The wider context is such that it is more difficult for universities to turn a blind eye to departments that incur persistently higher costs and/or underachieve academically.

Excepting perhaps the past decade, the state has used its legal, administrative and financial powers to reshape the character of British universities parsimoniously. While indirect controls, especially since the 1960s, became more pervasive, so the ideology of university autonomy and donnish domination remained substantially intact. What has occurred in recent years is the move from indirect to direct control. Whereas at one time the universities followed UGC guidelines in formulating their quinquennial plans, by the 1980s the UGC was forcing universities to rationalize – according to its perspective – their courses, so influencing profoundly the overall structure of the knowledge maps in Britain. This dirigisme of the UGC may have lessened somewhat since the creation of the UFC, but what has not changed is the attack on the traditional value system. Universities are more accountable for their state monies and required to be more sensitive to the demands of the marketplace in order to fulfil many of their academic goals. It is our contention, however, that as long as the universities remain overwhelmingly dependent upon public money to fund their activities (and it is hard to perceive that this will change substantially in the foreseeable future), then no matter what mechanisms are devised to make those resources available to them, the intention will be to ensure that they are put to publicly approved purposes. In other words, university autonomy as it was understood for much of the twentieth century is dead.

The central theme of this book is that the university system as a whole, including Oxford and Cambridge, has been increasingly sensitive to external pressure. The moves towards intercollegiate government were on several fronts strongly influenced by events occurring outside the two universities. Thus the creation of UCCA was crucial in forcing the colleges to co-ordinate their admissions procedures and establish their admissions offices, and the decision of the DES to control the increase in college fees led to the creation of fees committees. The next big step in college government is the rationalization of the system of intercollegiate government and the better co-ordination of that system with university government. The University of Oxford reformed its government at an earlier stage than Cambridge and, although Cambridge's present reform movement will lead to a Regent House which has the authority to submit graces, it marks a watershed in the history of the university's government. Cambridge's democratic traditions are not about to disappear, but they will be reformulated in a manner that will give more weight to the central authorities and to the university's officials. Indeed, at both Oxford and Cambridge, the idea of the don as intermittent, part-time university administrator with the consensus building committee as the main means of government is disappearing.

In certain respects, the special character that has defined Oxbridge in the past will continue to be part of its future. It seems likely, for example, that they will succeed in resisting Jarratt's call for a greater representation of laypersons on their governing bodies, and it is even possible that both the DES and research councils/British Academy can be persuaded to continue paying college fees. These are deviations that in part are dependent upon the ability to establish a special relationship to the state. Their exceptionalism has been due to the willingness of successive governments to treat them more generously than other universities. But it has also been due to their willingness to compete effectively for resources that, at least on the surface, are distributed solely on the basis of rational criteria. Thus their early and continuous success in securing funds from the reseach councils and their ability to obtain a disproportionate amount of the resources in the 1980s that were earmarked for special initiatives. They are likely, therefore, to remain the premier British universities, but whether they are 'world class' or not is an entirely different matter. Perhaps in the past we have judged their academic pre-eminence rather too easily, measuring it against a British standard of variable quality rather than the leading universities worldwide.

What in future Oxford and Cambridge cannot expect to be (and there is no evidence that they consciously sought this) are models for the rest of the British university system. Their exceptionalism will be there to be admired, envied or despised, but it will not be for replication. Although in the past British universities had different characteristics, they also shared a common idea of what it meant to be a university. We are moving rapidly towards an ever more differentiated system in which the universities – including Oxbridge – are not in control of their values and purposes. This is not to suggest the universities now find themselves in a straitjacket woven by state and society, but to make the point that the universities now work within parameters which are both more clearly defined and more all-encompassing than ever before. It is possible to be the best but increasingly less possible to determine what it means to be best, and how to manage and sustain it.

Reflections on a failing strategy

From the perspective of the universities, the history of their relationship to the state in the twentieth century has for the most part been highly beneficial. They would not have expanded at anywhere near the rate they did without the continuous infusion of large sums of money from the Exchequer.

Expansion has meant more jobs, improved teaching and research facilities, better conditions of employment and higher salaries. It is not too great an exaggeration to claim both that the state created the academic profession in Britain and did so on terms that were essentially advantageous to the academics. However, since the economic crisis of the mid-1970s, the relationship between the universities and the state has soured. In the past, the universities proved adept at responding to pressures for change in a manner that left their core characteristics intact and, although of late there has been a loud assertion of traditional academic values, this has done nothing to disguise the fact that the British universities are being reshaped radically. In key respects, the circumstances are different from the past: the pressures for change have been both more intense and more protracted, they are qualitatively different pressures inasmuch as that they have challenged the very purpose of the universities and their established relationship to state and society, and the universities have been forced to adjust while experiencing considerable financial difficulties so that the retrenchment decisions have been more keenly felt.

How have the universities responded to this crisis? The strategy has oscillated between resistance through the almost ritualistic reaffirmation of past values and practices, and accommodation which has attempted to demonstrate how the universities can adapt to the new circumstances in a manner that best serves their interests. Invariably, the two threads in the strategy are unified so that resistance occurs within an overall accommodationist perspective, and accommodation is designed to enable the universities to carry on with as few concessions to the new pressures as possible. Undoubtedly, the best example of resistance was the response of the universities to the 1988 Education Reform Bill. It was inevitable that the Bill would be enacted, and thus the universities had no option but to accept the fact that eventually they would have to adapt to its clauses. In the meantime, the friends of the universities, especially in the House of Lords, engaged in an effective campaign of resistance. It was resistance, however, that was centred upon the defence of various key components of the traditional model of the English university: that a clause guaranteeing the right to academic freedom should be built into the legislation, that academic tenure of employment should not be eroded, that the new funding body should be given a statutory right to offer its advice to the Secretary of State, and that there should be no element of contract (which had appeared in the preceding White Paper) in the way the new funding body would make the Exchequer's annual grant available to the universities. Although evaluations vary, it would be churlish to deny that these friends of the universities fought a sophisticated rearguard action and that the government was forced to make what it would regard as some unwelcome concessions.

Of course accommodation of the new and emerging circumstances occurs daily within the universities. As much as it may be regretted, the universities cannot function unless they are prepared to work within the new parameters. Thus, to repeat the story of a minor confrontation, some Cambridge dons may resist the idea that professors should be given discretionary pay awards but the university has no option but to impose in some form or other the requirement that such awards should be made. On a more general level, there are those, like Moodie (1987), who have argued that the new institutions and procedures may evolve in a manner that is supportive of university interests. In other words, the universities may change the order from within: there is no point in resistance if subversion can be more successful. Sizer (1987: 366–71), in perhaps more realistic vein, has offered a number of 'managerial guidelines for managing financial reductions' and proffered the advice that probably the key variable in accounting for the success of an institution is the effectiveness of its leadership. With Sizer, therefore, there is a clear shift from a strategy of accommodation that looks to the past for its value reference points to one in which the focus is upon how best to manage the present context. This is less a damage limitation exercise and more a blueprint on how to cope with adversity, and so great is the emphasis on the newly created opportunities for leadership and managerialism that the adversity is almost forgotten.

There is an air of resignation that surrounds the responses of the universities to the growing encroachment of state and society. Their financial dependence upon the Exchequer meant that any resistance would be little more than token, although this is perhaps to undervalue the sterling efforts of many individuals and institutions. The crux of the matter is that too much of the resistance has been directed at sustaining values that were not so much outworn as always indefensible in the context of a system of higher education that was overwhelmingly dependent upon the Exchequer for its survival. There are those, like Lord Beloff, who believe that the increased pressure upon the universities 'does not flow merely from the policies of individual governments or the ambitions of civil servants but reflects the indifference of the general public to university values' (Beloff 1990: 3). But at the very core of those values was the idea that universities should be trusted to spend taxpayers' money without being accountable for that expenditure. By his strident opposition to the opening of the accounts of the UGC and the universities to the Public Accounts Committee, Beloff rejected accountability in both technical and policy terms. To have held a chair of government and public administration may have assisted Beloff – as he implies (ibid.: 19) – to foresee that he who pays the piper eventually calls the tune, but apparently it was of little use in enabling him to judge what was politically feasible in this further matter. Autonomy at the taxpayers' expense is no longer a viable option. For Beloff, therefore, the only salvation from 'state-financed mediocrity' may be found in those institutions that can escape the financial clutches of the state. But no-one who has given the figures a mere cursory examination can imagine that there is much hope of this. Should their appeals succeed even beyond their wildest dreams, Oxford and Cambridge will continue to remain for the foreseeable future essentially state-financed institutions.

What has been lacking in the recent crisis has been any serious attempt to formulate a new model of the English university. It may now be too late for this and the best that the universities can hope to do is to travel down Sizer's route of competent leadership and managerial efficiency. Even so, one would have hoped for a concerted attempt to escape the confines of nostalgia and damage limitation. Surely the most profound criticism of the universities has been their failure to create their own vision of the future? One that, because it was based upon a political reality combining the best of the past with the recognition that universities were going to be very different kinds of institutions in the future, could be sold to the public at large. The age needed a Newman, or even a Moberly; it conjured up a more assertive CVCP.

Appendix

College accounts (Tables 4.1–4.5)

The gross endowment incomes of the Cambridge colleges were obtained by combining the income figures listed in Account 1A (External Revenue Account) and Account 1B (Trust and Other Funds Subject to University Contribution). To obtain the gross endowment incomes of the Oxford colleges in the pre-Franks accounts, we recorded the total income figures shown in Account A (i.e. External Income) of the Revenue Account, while for the post-Franks accounts we used the gross endowment income figures listed in Statement 111 (known as the Endowment Account). For the Cambridge colleges, the total income is taken to mean the gross endowment income plus the income recorded in the Internal Revenue Account and the Tuition Account (minus university composition fees). For the Oxford colleges, the total income in the pre-Franks accounts is the combined income totals for the External and Internal Accounts of the Revenue Accounts. While for the post-Franks accounts, total income is gross endowment income plus the income from 'fees, dues and charges' (less that collected on behalf of the university) in Statement 1 of the Consolidated Revenue Statement. The college accounts presented in the evidence to the Asquith Commission have been modified slightly to fit into this pattern (Royal Commission on Oxford and Cambridge Universities 1922b: 325–33).

Expenditure of academic areas met from research grants: University of Oxford (Tables 7.3 and 7.4)

The various departments and faculties are categorized as in the *Schedules to Income and Expenditure Accounts, 1966*. For example, although re-categorized over time, the Department of Experimental Psychology is placed consistently in the Biological Sciences. However, in the 1980s, a new Department of Plant Sciences (which incorporated elements of the old Departments of Botany, Agriculture and Forestry) was created. Research expenditure for the extinct

Faculty of Agriculture and Forestry is placed therefore in the Biological Sciences, which is where the Department of Plant Sciences is located. In the 1980s, Pre-clinical Medicine was replaced in the Schedules by the two categories of 'Anatomy, Physiology and Pharmacology' and 'Bio-Chemistry', but we have retained the original label. In the 1966 Schedules, Mathematics, the Mathematical Institute and the Computing Laboratory were included in the Physical Sciences and we have simply separated out their comparatively meagre research grants for that year. Computing now warrants a separate designation, although we have continued to combine it with Mathematics. The Applied Sciences category consists of two departments, Engineering Sciences and Metallurgy. Finally, Education does not include Adult Education which has been excluded from the calculations.

Expenditure of academic areas met from research grants: University of Cambridge (Tables 7.5 and 7.6)

We have used the subject labels found in the *Abstract of Accounts, 1988/89* (note we have not used the latest edition of the Abstract because, as explained in the text, the university changed the manner in which it presented its accounts for 1989–90). Earlier descriptions and defunct subjects are added when it aids clarification:

- *Arts*: All subjects listed under Faculty Group I except Architecture.
- *Social Studies*: All subjects listed under Faculty Group II except Education, Geography (in Faculty Group III), Archaeology and Anthropology, Archaeology, Biological Anthropology and Social Anthropology (all in Faculty Group IV), and all subjects listed under 'Other Institutions' except Biotechnology and Extra-Mural Studies which have been excluded from the table.
- *Education*: Education listed under Faculty Group II.
- *Physical Sciences*: Colloid Sciences (now defunct), Physical Sciences, Earth Sciences (formerly Geology, Mineralogy and Petrology, and Geodesy and Geophysics), Organic and Inorganic Chemistry, Physical Chemistry, Physics, the Scott Polar Institute, and Superconductivity, all listed under Faculty Group III.
- *Applied Sciences*: Engineering, Chemical Engineering, Material Sciences and Metallurgy, and Aerial Photography (all listed under Faculty Group III) and Architecture listed under Faculty Group I.
- *Astronomy*: Astronomy (previously the Observatories and the Institute of Theoretical Astronomy) listed under Faculty Group III.
- *Mathematics*: Pure Mathematics and Mathematical Statistics, Applied Mathematics and Theoretical Physics, and the Computer Laboratory listed under Faculty Group III.
- *Biological Sciences*: Applied Biology (formerly Agriculture), Botany, Botanic

Gardens, Genetics, and Zoology (all listed under Faculty Group IV) and Biotechnology listed under 'Other Institutions'.

- *Pre-clinical Medicine*: Anatomy, Biochemistry, Experimental Psychology, Pathology, Pharmacology, and Physiology listed under Faculty Group IV.
- *Clinical Medicine*: Previously listed separately as Experimental Medicine, Hospital Laboratory Service, Human Ecology, Investigative Medicine, Medicine, Parasitology, Radiotherapeutics, and Surgery, which were listed under Faculty Group IV.
- *Clinical Veterinary Medicine*: Previously listed separately as Animal Pathology, Veterinary Clinical Studies, and the School of Veterinary Medicine, which were listed under Faculty Group IV.

References

Advisory Board for the Research Councils (1976). *Second Report.* London, HMSO.

Advisory Board for the Research Councils (1987). *A Strategy for the Science Base.* London, HMSO.

Advisory Board for the Research Councils/Advisory Council on Applied Research and Development (1983). *Improving Links between Higher Education and Industry.* London, HMSO.

Advisory Council on Applied Research and Development (1986). *Exploitable Areas of Science.* London, HMSO.

Advisory Council on Scientific Policy (1962). *Annual Report 1961–62.* London, HMSO.

Advisory Council on Scientific Policy (1964). *Annual Report 1963–64.* London, HMSO.

Aitken, Sir Robert (1969). 'The Vice-Chancellors' Committee and the UGC'. *Universities Quarterly*, **23** (2), 165–71.

Armytage, W.H.G. (1955). *Civic Universities.* London, Ernest Benn.

Aspen, P. (1985). 'Oxford Blasts Cutbacks'. *The Times Higher Education Supplement*, 13 December.

Bantock, G.H. (1965). 'T.S. Eliot and Education'. *Universities Quarterly*, **19** (2), 109–14.

Baskerville, E.A. (1986). 'Oxford and the Schools', Nuffield College, Oxford, 17 October.

Beloff, Lord (1990). 'Universities and the Public Purse: An Update'. *Higher Education Quarterly*, **44** (1), 3–19.

Berdahl, R.O. (1959). *British Universities and the State.* Cambridge, Cambridge University Press.

Boys Smith, J.S. (1959). 'The College Accounts: An Explanatory Note', Cambridge, St John's College.

Bullock, Lord (1986). 'Reminiscences of a Former Vice-Chancellor', Nuffield College, Oxford, 24 October.

Cambridge Tutorial Representatives (1984). *Sixth Term Examination for Admission to Cambridge.* Cambridge, CTR.

Cambridge Tutorial Representatives (1985). *Final Report of the Working Party on Admission to Cambridge.* Cambridge, CTR.

Cambridge Tutorial Representatives (1990). *Cambridge: Admissions Prospectus, 1991–92.* Cambridge, CTR.

Carswell, J. (1985). *Government and the Universities in Britain.* Cambridge, Cambridge University Press.

Central Advisory Council for Education (England) (1959). *15 to 18*, Vol. 1 (The Crowther Report). London, HMSO.

Committee on Undergraduate Admissions (1983). *Report* (Dover). Oxford, Oxford Colleges Admissions Office.

Committee of Vice-Chancellors and Principals (1985). *Report of the Steering Committee for Efficiency Studies in Universities.* London, Committee of Vice-Chancellors and Principals.

Committee of Vice-Chancellors and Principals (1989). *The Teaching Function: Quality Assurance.* London, Committee of Vice-Chancellors and Principals

Committee on Higher Education (1963). *Report* (Robbins). London, HMSO.

Conservative Party (1979). *Manifesto.* London, Conservative Party.

Conservative Political Centre (1985). *No Turning Back.* London, Conservative Political Centre.

Council for Scientific Policy (1966). *Report on Science Policy.* London, HMSO.

Council for Scientific Policy (1967). *Report on Science Policy.* London, HMSO.

Council for Scientific Policy (1971). *The Future of the Research Council System.* London, HMSO.

Crequer, N. (1986). 'The Strengths and the Weaknesses'. *The Times Higher Education Supplement*, 30 May, pp. 4–6.

Crequer, N. (1989). 'The Passing of the Education Reform Act', *Higher Education Quarterly*, **43** (1), 3–19.

Curzon, Lord (1909). *Principles and Methods of University Reform.* Oxford, Clarendon Press.

Department of Education and Science (n.d.). *Tuition Fees and College Dues Claimed by Cambridge University Colleges for Sessions 1968–69, 1969–70 and 1970–71.* London, DES.

Department of Education and Science (n.d.). *Tuition Fees and College Dues Claimed by Oxford University Colleges for Sessions 1968–69, 1969–70 and 1970–71.* London, DES.

Department of Education and Science (1970a). *Education Planning Paper No. 1: Ouput Budgeting for the DES.* London, HMSO.

Department of Education and Science (1970b). *Education Planning Paper No. 2: Student Numbers in Higher Education in England and Wales.* London, HMSO.

Department of Education and Science (1972). *Education: A Framework for Expansion.* London, HMSO.

Department of Education and Science (1975–76). *The Education (Mandatory Awards) Regulations.* London, DES.

Department of Education and Science (1985). *The Development of Higher Education into the 1990s.* London, HMSO.

Department of Education and Science (1985–86). *The Education (Mandatory Awards) Regulations.* London, DES.

Department of Education and Science (1987). *Higher Education: Meeting the Challenge.* London, HMSO.

Dodds, H.W. *et al.* (1952). *Government Assistance to Universities in Great Britain.* New York: Columbia University Press.

Dorey, W. (1986). 'The University Administration', Nuffield College. Oxford, 21 November.

Education Reform Act, 1988.

Edwards, A.W.F. (1981). '1963: The Downfall of Cambridge's Constitution', *The Cambridge Review*, 23 October, pp. 4–10.

Engel, A.J. (1983). *From Clergyman to Don: The Rise of the Academic Profession in Nineteenth Century Oxford.* Oxford, Clarendon Press.

Ferns, H.S. (1969). *Towards an Independent University.* Occasional Paper No. 25. London, Institute of Economic Affairs.

Franks, Lord (1986). 'The Franks Report in Retrospect', Nuffield College, Oxford, 31 January.

Griffiths, S. (1991). 'UFC Quality Ratings Ignored', *The Times Higher Education Supplement,* 12 April, p. 1.

The Guardian (1986). 29 May.

The Guardian (1991). 29 January.

Halsey, A.H. (1961a). 'British Universities and Intellectual Life'. In Halsey, A.H., Floud, J. and Arnold, C. (eds), *Education, Economy and Society.* New York, Free Press.

Halsey, A.H. (1961b). 'The Changing Functions of Universities'. In Halsey, A.H., Floud, J. and Arnold, C. (eds), *Education, Economy and Society.* New York, Free Press.

Halsey, A.H. (1969). 'The Universities and the State'. *Universities Quarterly,* **23**, 128–48.

Halsey, A.H. (1979). 'Are the British Universities Capable of Change?'. *New Universities Quarterly,* **33** (4), 402–16.

Halsey, A.H. (1984). 'Oxford's Power Game', *The Times Higher Education Supplement,* 6 January, p. 14.

Halsey, A.H. and Trow, M.A. (1971). *The British Academics.* Cambridge, Mass., Harvard University Press.

Hamilton, Sir William (1852). *Discussions on Philosophy and Literature, Education and University Reform.* Edinburgh, MacLachlan and Stewart.

Hansard (Lords) (1923). Volume 53, Column 745, 19 April.

Hansard (Commons) (1981). Written Answers, Columns 449–50, 2 July.

Hansard (Commons) (1986a). Written Answers, Columns 443–4, 13 January.

Hansard (Commons) (1986b). Written Answers, Columns 15–16, 9 June.

Kedourie, E. (1988). *Diamonds into Glass.* London, Centre for Policy Studies.

Labour Party (1961). *Science and the Future of Britain.* London, Labour Party.

Labour Party (1963). *The Years of Crisis.* London, Labour Party.

Labour Party (1973). *Higher and Further Education.* London, Labour Party.

Labour Party (1990). *Meet the Challenge, Make the Change: A New Agenda for Britain* (Final Report of Labour's Policy Review for the 1990s). London, Labour Party.

Lee, D. (1972). *Entry and Performance at Oxford and Cambridge, 1966–71.* London, Schools Council Research Studies.

Letwin, O., Minford, P. and Sexton, S. (eds) (1988). *Higher Education: Freedom and Finance.* London, Institute of Economic Affairs.

Lockwood, G. (1986). 'Efficiency Measures', *The Times Higher Education Supplement,* 28 February, p. 15.

Lucas, J.R. (1987). 'In Place of the CUF', *Oxford Magazine,* No. 27, 8.

McCrum, M. (n.d.). 'Cambridge University: Past, Present and Future'.

Mason, D. (1986). *University Challenge.* London, Adam Smith Institute.

Maynard, A. (1975). *Experiment with Choice in Education.* London, Institute of Economic Affairs.

Ministry of Education (1956). *Technical Education.* London, HMSO.

Ministry of Education (1958). *Education in 1958.* London, HMSO.

Ministry of Reconstruction (1918). *Report of the Machinery of Government Committee* (The Haldane Report). London, HMSO.

Moberly, Sir Walter (1949). *Crisis in the University.* London, SCM Press.

Moodie, G. (1987). 'Le Roi est Mort: Vive le Quoi? Croham and the Death of the UGC'. *Higher Education Quarterly*, **41** (4), 329–43.

Moodie, G. and Eustace, R. (1974). *Power and Policy in British Universities*. London, Allen & Unwin.

Niblett, W.R. (1952). 'The Development of British Universities since 1945'. In *The Yearbook of Education*. London, Evans/Institute of Education.

Oxford Colleges Admissions Office (1969). 'Procedure for Reaching Final Decisions on Admissions Policy'. Oxford, Oxford Colleges Admissions Office.

Oxford University Commission (1852). *Report of the Commissioners*, British Sessional Papers, Vol. XXII.

Pattison, M. (1868). *Suggestions on Academical Organization*. Edinburgh, Edmonston and Douglas.

Peacock, A.T. and Wiseman, J. (1964). *Education for Democrats*. Hobart Paper No. 25. London, Institute for Economic Affairs.

Pearson, R. (1989). 'After Baskerville'. *Oxford Magazine*, No. 46, 10–12.

Phillips, D. (1989). 'Trends in University Research: A Challenge for Management', Conference of University Administrators, University of Sussex, 14 April.

Pratt, J. and Burgess, T. (1974). *Polytechnics: A Report*. London, Pitman.

Prest, A.R. (1966). *Financing University Education*. Occasional Paper No. 12. London, Institute for Economic Affairs.

Richards, H. (1989). 'Countdown to Excellence', *The Times Higher Education Supplement*, 1 September, pp. 2–4.

Rose, J. and Ziman, J. (1964). *Camford Observed*. London, Victor Gollancz.

Rothblatt, S. (1968). *The Revolution of the Dons*. London, Faber and Faber.

Rothschild, Lord (1971). *A Framework for Government Research and Development*. London, HMSO.

Royal Commission on Oxford and Cambridge Universities (1922a). *Report* (Asquith). London, HMSO.

Royal Commission on Oxford and Cambridge Universities (1922b). *Appendices to the Report of the Commission*. London, HMSO.

Salter, B. and Tapper, T. (1981). *Education, Politics and the State: The Theory and Practice of Educational Change*. London, Grant McIntyre.

Salter, B. and Tapper, T. (1985). *Power and Policy in Education: The Case of the Independent Sector*. Barcombe, Falmer Press.

Shattock, M. (1987). 'The Last Days of the University Grants Committee', *Minevra*, **25** (4), 471–85.

Shils, E. (1955). 'The Intellectuals, 1. Great Britain', *Encounter*, **4** (4), 5–16.

Shinn, C. (1986). *Paying the Piper: The Development of the University Grants Committee, 1919–1946*. Barcombe, Falmer Press.

Shock, M. (1990). 'Rethinking the Structures', *Oxford Magazine*, No. 1990, 11–12.

Sizer, J. (1987). 'Universities in Hard Times: Some Policy Implications and Managerial Guidelines', *Higher Education Quarterly*, **41** (4), 354–72.

The Sunday Correspondent (1989). 29 October.

Tapper, T. and Salter, B. (1978). *Education and the Political Order*. London, Macmillan.

The Times (1987). 11 March.

The Times (1988). 31 May.

The Times (1989). 16 November.

The Times (1990). 27 September.

The Times Higher Education Supplement (1975). 7 March.

The Times Higher Education Supplement (1976). 26 November.

The Times Higher Education Supplement (1985). 22 November.

The Times Higher Education Supplement (1986). 23 May.

The Times Higher Education Supplement (1987). 27 February.

The Times Higher Education Supplement (1988). 13 May.

The Times Higher Education Supplement (1990a, b). 30 March.

The Times Higher Education Supplement (1991). 12 April.

Truscot, B. (1943). *Redbrick University*. London, Faber.

Turney, J. (1989). 'UFC Confirms Triangle's Triumph', *The Times Higher Education Supplement*, 1 September, p. 1.

Universities Central Council for Admissions (1961–63). *First Report*.

Universities Funding Council (1989). *Circular Letter 39–89*, 12 December.

Universities Funding Council (1990a). *University Statistics: 1989–90*, Vol. 1, *Students and Staff*.

Universities Funding Council (1990b). *University Statistics: 1988–89*, Vol. 3, *Finance*.

Universities of Oxford and Cambridge Act (1923).

University Grants Committee (1921). *Report*. London, HMSO.

University Grants Committee (1922–23). *Annual Return*.

University Grants Committee (1925–26). *Annual Return*.

University Grants Committee (1929–30). *Annual Return*.

University Grants Committee (1936). *Report for the Period 1929–30 to 1934–35*. London, HMSO.

University Grants Committee (1938–39). *Annual Return*.

University Grants Committee (1939–40). *Annual Return*.

University Grants Committee (1948). *University Development from 1935 to 1947*. London, HMSO.

University Grants Committee (1949–50). *Annual Return*.

University Grants Committee (1950–51). *Annual Return*.

University Grants Committee (1956). *Methods Used by Universities of Contracting and of Recording and Controlling Expenditure*. London, HMSO.

University Grants Committee (1957). *Report of the Sub-Committee on Halls of Residence* (The Niblett Report). London, HMSO.

University Grants Committee (1958). *University Development from 1952 to 1957*. London, HMSO.

University Grants Committee (1959–60). *Annual Return*.

University Grants Committee (1960). *Methods Used by Universities of Contracting and of Recording and Controlling Expenditure*. London, HMSO.

University Grants Committee (1964). *University Development, 1957–62*. London, HMSO.

University Grants Committee (1968a). *University Development, 1962–67*. London, HMSO.

University Grants Committee (1968b). *Statistics of Education*, Vol. 6, Universities.

University Grants Committee (1970). *Statistics of Education*, Vol. 6, Universities.

University Grants Committee (1972–73). *Annual Survey*.

University Grants Committee (1973–74). *Annual Survey*.

University Grants Committee (1975–76). *Annual Survey*.

University Grants Committee (1980a). *University Statistics*, Vol. 1, Students and Staff.

University Grants Committee (1980b). *University Statistics*, Vol. 3, Finance.

University Grants Committee (1980–81). *Annual Survey*.

University Grants Committee (1981–82). *Annual Survey*.

University Grants Committee (1982–83). *Annual Survey*.

University Grants Committee (1984–85). *Annual Survey.*

University Grants Committee (1984). *A Strategy for Higher Education into the 1990s: The UGC's Advice.* London, HMSO.

University Grants Committee (1985). *Planning for the Late 1980s: The Resource Allocation Process.* Circular Letter 22/85, November.

University Grants Committee (1986). *Planning for the Late 1980s: Recurrent Grant for 1986–87.* Circular Letter 4/86, May.

University of Cambridge (1931). *Reporter*, 14 February.

University of Cambridge (1941). *Reporter*, 7 February.

University of Cambridge (1951). *Reporter*, 30 March.

University of Cambridge (1957). *Reporter*, 5 June.

University of Cambridge (1961). *Reporter*, 2 February.

University of Cambridge (1962). *Reporter*, 13 March.

University of Cambridge (1964). *Reporter*, 1 May.

University of Cambridge (1965). *Reporter*, 8 December.

University of Cambridge (1966). *Reporter*, 15 December.

University of Cambridge (1967a). *Reporter*, 16 August.

University of Cambridge (1967b). *Reporter*, 13 October.

University of Cambridge (1971a). *Reporter*, 2 February.

University of Cambridge (1971b). *Reporter*, 14 May.

University of Cambridge (1971c). *Reporter*, 11 August.

University of Cambridge (1971d). *Reporter*, 21 July.

University of Cambridge (1976). *Reporter*, 25 August.

University of Cambridge (1980a). *Reporter*, 13 August.

University of Cambridge (1980b). *Reporter*, 17 December.

University of Cambridge (1981). *Reporter*, 3 April.

University of Cambridge (1980c). *Reporter*, 16 December.

University of Cambridge (1985). *Reporter*, 27 November.

University of Cambridge (1986). *Reporter*, 3 June.

University of Cambridge (1987). *Reporter*, 25 November.

University of Cambridge (1988a). *Reporter*, 20 January.

University of Cambridge (1988b). *Reporter*, 9 March.

University of Cambridge (1988c). *Reporter*, 17 August.

University of Cambridge (1988d). *Statutes and Ordinances.* Cambridge, Cambridge University Press.

University of Cambridge (1989a). *Reporter*, 19 May.

University of Cambridge (1989b). *Reporter*, 21 June.

University of Cambridge (1989c). *Reporter*, 29 June.

University of Cambridge (1989d). *Reporter*, 16 August.

University of Cambridge (1989e). *Reporter*, 10 November.

University of Cambridge (1990). *Reporter*, 19 December.

University of Cambridge (1991a). *Reporter*, 16 January.

University of Cambridge (1991b). *Reporter*, 19 March.

University of Cambridge (1991c). *Reporter*, 18 April.

University of Cambridge (1991d). *Reporter*, 9 May.

University of Oxford (1930). *The Abstracts of the Accounts of the Colleges.* Oxford, Clarendon Press.

University of Oxford (1940). *The Abstracts of the Accounts of the Colleges.* Oxford, Clarendon Press.

University of Oxford (1950). *The Abstracts of the Accounts of the Colleges.* Oxford, Clarendon Press.

University of Oxford (1960). *The Abstracts of the Accounts of the Colleges.* Oxford, Clarendon Press.

University of Oxford (1962). *Admissions to College* (Report of a Working Party). Oxford, Oxford University Press.

University of Oxford (1965). *Commission of Inquiry: Evidence.* Oxford, Oxford University Press.

University of Oxford (1966a). *Report of Commission of Inquiry*, Vol. I. Oxford, Oxford University Press.

University of Oxford (1966b). *Report of Commission of Inquiry*, Vol. II. Oxford, Oxford University Press.

University of Oxford (1966c). *Schedules to Income and Expenditure Accounts.*

University of Oxford (1970a). *Gazette*, 5 August.

University of Oxford (1970b). *Schedules to Income and Expenditure Accounts.*

University of Oxford (1970c). *The Abstracts of the Accounts of the Colleges.* Oxford, Clarendon Press.

University of Oxford (1971). *Gazette*, 5 May.

University of Oxford (1980a). *Gazette*, 25 September.

University of Oxford (1980b). *Schedules to Income and Expenditure Accounts.*

University of Oxford (1980c). *The Abstracts of the Accounts of the Colleges.* Oxford, Clarendon Press.

University of Oxford (1981). *Gazette*, 13 July.

University of Oxford (1985). *Gazette*, 26 September.

University of Oxford (1987). *Gazette*, 20 July.

University of Oxford (1988). *Gazette*, 17 October.

University of Oxford (1989a). *Statutes, Decrees and Regulations.* Oxford, Oxford University Press.

University of Oxford (1989b). *Gazette*, 20 November.

University of Oxford (1990a). *Financial Statements.*

University of Oxford (1990b). *The Abstracts of the Accounts of the Colleges.* Oxford, Clarendon Press.

University of Oxford (1990c). *Undergraduate Prospectus, 1991–92.*

University of Oxford (1990d). *Gazette*, 22 March.

University of Oxford (1990e). *Gazette*, 25 June.

University of Oxford (1990f). 'Indirect Costs of Research: Overheads', Research Support and Industrial Liaison Office, 19 October.

University of Sussex (1983). *Bulletin*, 19 April.

Wilkinson, Sir Denys (1986). 'Academic Breakthroughs', Nuffield College, Oxford, 5 December.

Winstanley, D.A. (1940). *Early Victorian Cambridge.* Cambridge, Cambridge University Press.

Yarde, R. (1990). 'Cambridge holds back on big student growth'. *The Times Higher Education Supplement*, 22 June.

Interviews

Allen, G.P. (1989). *Interview*, 11 July.

Annan, Lord (1986). *Interview*, 2 April.

Bowkett, K. (1989). *Interview*, 15 June.

Butler, R. (1989). *Interview*, 20 July.

Franks, D. (1989). *Interview*, 13 June.

Gardner, T. (1988). *Interview*, 9 April.
Horne, M. (1989). *Interview*, 11 July.
Howatson, A. (1989). *Interview*, 20 July.
Mitchell, R. (1989). *Interview*, 15 June.
Payne, J.R. (1989). *Interview*, 13 June.
Pippard, A.B. (1989). *Interview*, 15 May.
Shone, B. (1988). *Interview*, 9 April.
Smith, A.D. (1989). *Interview*, 6 July.
Smith, E.B. (1989). *Interview*, 15 September.

Personal communications

Unattributed personal communications: 14 April 1987; 16 April 1987; 7 July 1987 and 16 April 1988.

Index

The Society for Research into Higher Education

The Society for Research into Higher Education exists to stimulate and co-ordinate research into all aspects of higher education. It aims to improve the quality of higher education through the encouragement of debate and publication on issues of policy, on the organization and management of higher education institutions, and on the curriculum and teaching methods.

The Society's income is derived from subscriptions, sales of its books and journals, conference fees and grants. It receives no subsidies, and is wholly independent. Its individual members include teachers, researchers, managers and students. Its corporate members are institutions of higher education, research institutes, professional, industrial and governmental bodies. Members are not only from the UK, but from elsewhere in Europe, from America, Canada and Australasia, and it regards its international work as amongst its most important activities.

Under the imprint SRHE & Open University Press, the Society is a specialist publisher of research, having some 30 titles in print. The Editorial Board of the Society's Imprint seeks authoritative research or study in the field. It offers competitive royalties, a highly recognizable format in both hard- and paper-back and the world-wide reputation of the Open University Press.

The Society also publishes *Studies in Higher Education* (three times a year), which is mainly concerned with academic issues, *Higher Education Quarterly* (formerly *Universities Quarterly*), mainly concerned with policy issues, *Abstracts* (three times a year), and SRHE NEWS (four times a year).

The Society holds a major annual conference in December, jointly with an institution of higher education. In 1990, the topic was 'Industry and Higher Education', at and with the University of Surrey. Future conferences include in 1991, 'Research and Higher Education in Europe', with the University of Leicester, in 1992, 'Learning to Effect', with Nottingham Polytechnic, and in 1993, 'Governments and the Higher Education Curriculum' with the University of Sussex. In addition it holds regular seminars and consultations on topics of current interest.

The Society's committees, study groups and branches are run by members. The groups at present include:

Teacher Education Study Group
Continuing Education Group
Staff Development Group
Excellence in Teaching & Learning
Women in Higher Education Group.

Benefits to members

Individual

Individual members receive:

- The NEWS, the Society's publications list, conference details and other material included in mailings.
- Reduced rates for *Studies in Higher Education* (£9.75 per year – full price £72) and *Higher Education Quarterly* (£12.35 per year – full price £43).
- A 35% discount on all Open University Press & SRHE publications.
- Free copies of the Proceedings (or Precedings) – commissioned papers on the theme of the Annual Conference.
- Free copies of *Higher Education Abstracts*.
- Reduced rates for conferences.
- Extensive contacts and scope for facilitating initiatives.
- Reduced reciprocal memberships.

Corporate

Corporate members receive:

- All benefits of individual members, plus
- Free copies of *Studies in Higher Education*.
- Unlimited copies of the Society's publications at reduced rates.
- Special rates for its members, e.g. to the Annual Conference.

Subscriptions August 1991–July 1992

Individual members

standard fee	£47
hardship (e.g. unwaged)	£22
students and retired	£14

Corporate members

(a) teaching institutions	
under 1000 students	£170
up to 3000 students	£215
over 3000 students	£320
(b) non-teaching institutions	up to £325
(c) industrial/professional bodies	up to £325

Further information: SRHE, 344–354 Gray's Inn Road, London, wcIX 8BP, UK. Tel: 071 837 7880
Catalogue: SRHE & Open University Press, Celtic Court, 22 Ballmoor, Buckingham MK18 1xw. Tel: (0280) 823388